DEGREES OF INEQUALITY

ALSO BY SUZANNE METTLER

The Submerged State

Remaking America

Soldiers to Citizens

Dividing Citizens

DEGREES OF INEQUALITY

HOW THE POLITICS OF HIGHER EDUCATION SABOTAGED THE AMERICAN DREAM

SUZANNE METTLER

BASIC BOOKS
A MEMBER OF THE PERSEUS BOOKS GROUP
New York

Published by Basic Books,
A Member of the Perseus Books Group

Books published by Basic Books are available at special discounts for bulk purchases in the United States by corporations, institutions, and other organizations. For more information, please contact the Special Markets Department at the Perseus Books Group, 2300 Chestnut Street, Suite 200, Philadelphia, PA 19103, or call (800) 810-4145, ext. 5000, or e-mail special.markets@perseusbooks.com.

Some material in chapter 2 was adapted from Suzanne Mettler "Promoting Inequality: The Politics of Higher Education Policy in an Era of Conservative Governance," in *The Unsustainable American State*, edited by Lawrence Jacobs and Desmond King (New York: Oxford University Press, 2009), pp. 197–222; some material in chapter 5 adapted from Suzanne Mettler, *The Submerged State: How Invisible Government Policies Undermine American Democracy* (Chicago: University of Chicago Press, 2011) and some from Suzanne Mettler, "Eliminating the Market Middle-Man: Redirecting and Expanding Support for College Students," in *Reaching for a New Deal: Ambitious Governance, Economic Meltdown, and Polarized Politics in Obama's First Two Years*, edited by Theda Skocpol and Lawrence R. Jacobs © 2011 Russell Sage Foundation, 112 East 64 Street, New York, NY 20065. Reprinted with permission.

Designed by Trish Wilkinson
Set in 11.5 point Minion Pro

Library of Congress Cataloging-in-Publication Data

Mettler, Suzanne.
    Degrees of inequality : how the politics of higher education sabotaged the American dream / Suzanne Mettler.
        pages   cm
    ISBN 978-0-465-04496-2 (hardcover)—ISBN 978-0-465-07200-2 (e-book)
1. Education, Higher—Political aspects—United States. 2. Education, Higher—Social aspects—United States. 3. Education, Higher—Economic aspects—United States. 4. Educational change—United States. I. Title.
LC173.M48 2014
378.73—dc23

                                                                        2013043678

10 9 8 7 6 5 4 3 2 1

For Jeanne

CONTENTS

CHAPTER SEVEN

INTRODUCTION

ON FEBRUARY 18, 2011, SOMETHING UNUSUAL HAPPENED IN THE HOUSE of Representatives. It was in the midst of the 112th Congress, which earned the distinction of being the most polarized along party lines of any in modern history.[1] Yet on that day, the members of that divided institution gathered and managed to achieve an astonishing degree of bipartisan consensus. On one particular vote, 58 of the 193 Democrats gathered with all but 4 of the 240 Republicans on the same side of an issue.[2] What's more, minority leader Nancy Pelosi, House Democratic National Committee chair Debbie Wasserman Schultz, and members of the Black Caucus joined together with the entire Tea Party contingent. What brought this unlikely crew together?

The issue in question involved the so-called for-profit colleges, previously known as trade schools, proprietary schools, or career colleges. Enrollment in these institutions had exploded nearly tenfold in less than two decades, from 226,818 in 1993 to over 2 million in 2010.[3] During that time period, a new business model emerged and fourteen for-profits grew into vast multistate enterprises that in combination enroll three out of four of the sector's students. These companies, such as Corinthian Colleges, Kaplan, and the University of Phoenix, market themselves heavily, advertising regularly on public transportation, the Internet, television, and highway billboards. Some consumer groups worried that the schools preyed on vulnerable low income students and left them with staggering student loan debt. Consequently the US

1

Department of Education under the Obama administration proposed restricting their use of student aid funds under the Higher Education Act of 1965, America's landmark law that provides financial aid to college students.

In some respects, for-profit schools have distinguished themselves as inclusive innovators that dared to deviate from the established routines of traditional universities. They led the way in offering online education—a move that other institutions are racing to catch up with and emulate. They introduced flexible course scheduling to accommodate the needs of nontraditional students, whose lives are often packed with work and family responsibilities. As a result, these schools have attracted many students from less advantaged backgrounds, who might not otherwise have enrolled in college.

But the for-profits also charge substantial tuition—$15,172 per year on average for full-time undergraduates in 2012–2013. Although this amount is lower than private nonprofits' cost of $29,056, it is nonetheless substantial compared to $8,655 at four-year public universities and $3,131 at community colleges.[4] As a result, nearly all of their students—94 percent among those who gain bachelor's degrees—take out loans in order to attend, and the average debt per borrower—$32,700—dwarfs that accrued by students at other types of colleges and universities.[5] All this for an educational experience that often pales by comparison, as judged by differences in the investment in student instruction and graduation rates.[6] If students at the for-profits do graduate, their job prospects often fail to measure up to the high levels of student debt they shoulder.[7] As a result, they have by far the highest default rates on student loans—within three years, 23 percent have failed to maintain payments, and on net the sector accounts for nearly half of all defaults.[8] This combination of higher tuition, questionable job prospects, and burdensome debt means that many for-profit schools leave a large number of their students worse off than if they had never attempted to pursue advanced education in the first place.

Ironically, despite being regarded as part of the private sector, the for-profits are financed almost entirely by American taxpayers. They enroll about one in ten college students today, but utilize one in four dollars allocated through Title IV of the Higher Education Act of 1965, the predominant source of federal student aid.[9] A 1998 law permits the for-profits to gain up to 90 percent of their total revenues from this single source. Other government funds do not count against this threshold, so the for-profits also receive 37 percent of all Post-9/11 GI Bill benefits and 50 percent of Department of Defense tuition assistance benefits.[10] In recent years, this combination of public funds has provided the for-profit schools with 86 percent of their total revenue, to the tune of roughly $32 billion annually.[11]

So, we have substandard educational institutions producing many students who can't get good jobs, costing taxpayers billions. Question: who is actually benefiting from this arrangement? Answer: the businesspersons who own them and their corporate shareholders. The largest for-profits, though subsidized almost entirely by government, are now publicly traded on Wall Street, and during the 1990s and early 2010s they reaped enormous profits. Even in the midst of the financial downturn in 2008, the top nine companies enjoyed 4 percent growth in their stocks, while the S&P 500 declined by 39 percent.

Which brings us back to the surprising moment of bipartisanship in February 2011. A significant number of Democrats united with Republicans to oppose new regulations being developed by the Department of Education, rules that would make student aid to the for-profits contingent on their performance. A mere seventeen months earlier, when the House had voted on a major overhaul of federal student aid that terminated bank-based lending and strengthened Pell grants, partisan politics prevailed: only six Republicans supported it and only four Democrats opposed it.[12] Since 1995, House votes on higher education policy—an issue area that previously involved a fair degree of bipartisanship—had become starkly polarized along party lines.[13] Now the GOP and its Tea Party–supported members, generally zealous defenders of austerity, voted with Democrats who professed to cherish their party's role in creating the Higher Education Act, a law long associated with educational opportunity. Together, this bipartisan group implicitly voiced its support for continuing massive government spending on a sector of colleges and universities that has little to show for itself—aside from its ability to channel profits to business leaders and investors.

This vote could easily be passed off as small and insignificant. It involved only an amendment to a large budget bill, and it was dropped in the Senate version, never coming to a vote. Yet it showcases in microcosm a tragedy that has befallen the United States. To begin with, while the for-profits appear to give struggling Americans a shot at improving their life circumstances, in reality, these schools leave many worse off, to the point of financial ruin. Simultaneously, they lavish abundant profits on owners and corporate shareholders—at taxpayer expense— effectively benefiting the affluent even as they destroy the lives of the less advantaged. Most egregiously, the US government not only condones these circumstances but actively facilitates and sponsors them through nearly full subsidization of such schools—paired with, at present, only minimal regulation of how they conduct themselves. But the nation's support of the for-profits is not an isolated instance of public policy that has gone off course; instead, it is one of several developments that, in combination, amount to an abdication of one of the nation's proudest legacies: the promotion of higher education and, through it, the promise of the American dream.

The United States from its beginnings distinguished itself as a pioneer in fostering the development of a large and diverse array of colleges and universities. Then in the mid-twentieth century, landmark public policies ushered in a golden age of educational opportunity. Through federal policies ranging from the GI Bill through Pell grants, and extensive state-level support for public institutions of higher education, the nation expanded access to college to growing numbers of Americans from across the income spectrum. People from humble backgrounds became the first in their families to attain college diplomas, enabling them to enjoy occupational choices and a standard of living their parents could only have dreamed of, and to pass those advantages on to their own children.

Over the past thirty years, however, our system of higher education has gone from facilitating upward mobility to exacerbating social inequality. College-going, once associated with opportunity, now engenders the creation of a something that increasingly resembles a caste system: it takes Americans who grew up in different social strata and it widens the divisions between them and makes them more rigid. The consequences are vast, ranging from differences in employment rates and lifetime earnings to health and civic engagement. Besides the rise of the for-profits, several changes in federal student aid and the demise of state funding for public universities and colleges have also helped produce these circumstances. All told, the tragedy is that while public policies in the past helped mitigate inequality and open the doors to college to more Americans, today they themselves play a crucial role in segmenting our society.

At its core, this transformation represents a political failure, a breaking down of representative government so that it no longer provides effective mechanisms by which Americans can pursue a better life. Higher education policies that worked well in the past are still in place, but they have deteriorated or gone off course. Policymakers need to engage in policy maintenance, upkeep, and renovation if these policies are to function effectively for succeeding generations. But with rare exceptions, they do not carry out these basic tasks. Today the US political system has been besieged by two forces that undermine efforts to keep policy functioning effectively: political polarization, as the parties in Congress have grown more ideological and less willing to work together than at any point in at least a century, and plutocracy, the responsiveness of the political system primarily to the concerns of wealthy and powerful interests. These politics, in combination, have sabotaged the American dream.

―――――――

The promotion of education at all levels emerged as a distinctive component of American political development from the very start. As a young nation in the eighteenth and nineteenth centuries, the United States used land grants to the states to spur the creation of a vast network of colleges and universities. By the eve of the Civil War, the nation boasted 250 institutions of higher education.[14] The Morrill Act of 1862, also known as the Land-Grant College Act, signed into law by President Abraham Lincoln, ushered in a new educational model that combined traditional liberal arts education with training in agriculture, the natural sciences, and teaching. Kansas State University became the first institution established under the new law, and other fully public universities followed. By their very mission and through their expansive offerings in practical fields of study, the land-grant colleges reached out to a broader segment of the public than the institutions that preceded them. Congress enacted a second Morrill Act in 1890, leading to yet more new institutions, including seventeen historically black colleges and universities.[15]

The next great phase of the nation's leadership in higher education occurred after World War II, when the US Congress enacted a series of landmark laws that expanded access to colleges and universities, making them affordable to a wide swath of the population. This transformation began when policymakers created the first of several GI Bills, laws that enabled veterans to seek additional education at government expense. Fifty-one percent of the 15 million returning veterans of World War II used the benefits, one-quarter of them to attend college. As a result, college graduation rates among males, which had been slowly creeping upward, shot up from just over 100,000 annually in 1940 to well over 300,000 annually by 1950.[16] Soon after, lawmakers extended student aid to civilian students, first in the National Defense Education Act of 1958, which extended the first student loans. Then in 1965, as part of the constellation of programs that made up the Great Society, President Johnson promoted the comprehensive Higher Education Act, which included student loans, grants, and work-study.[17] Pell grants, created in 1972, marked the crowning touch of federal policy, with funds channeled explicitly to low income students. Unlike the GI Bill, these policies were fully available to women, who quickly began to use them at comparable rates to men, particularly once the passage of Title IX, in 1972, mandated an end to discrimination in college admissions.[18] Meanwhile, states expanded the range of educational options available to their citizens and provided ample support. By 1980, nearly 80 percent of all college students were enrolled in public two- and four-year colleges and universities, where they benefited from low tuition.[19]

This stream of landmark policy developments, in combination with rising high school graduation rates, yielded powerful effects on American society. In 1940, before it began, only one in twenty Americans held a four-year college degree; by 1977, that number had soared to one in four.[20] Advanced education, in turn, stimulated upward social mobility. Male veterans who utilized the GI Bill to go to college in many cases experienced leaps in occupational status compared to their fathers: a longshoreman's son became an attorney, a cobbler's son became an engineer, a coal miner's son became a geologist, and on and on.[21] It is well-known that those with greater education and income participate more in civic life.[22] In the case of the GI Bill, the experience of policy usage itself generated active engagement: comparing nonblack male veterans who used the education and training provisions with those who did not, GI Bill beneficiaries took part in twice as many civic organizations and one-third more political activities during the postwar era. Black veterans who utilized the benefits became a leadership cadre for the civil rights movement, and after marching and protesting to end discrimination in the 1950s and early 1960s, by the next period in time they took part in formal politics at high levels.[23] And the GI Bill had second-generation effects: one beneficiary commented that it "gave our family at 'boost' that has allowed us to help our children go to college more than I had expected, i.e., GI Bill benefits have been passed to a second generation!"[24] Women who utilized student loans and Pell grants attained more advanced education than those who did not, and subsequently they took part in politics at higher rates, helping close the gender gap in political involvement.[25] In these and myriad other ways, aid policies mitigated economic and political inequality.

But something happened beginning in the 1980s, with disastrous effects for the American dream—the belief that those who work hard can improve their circumstances—that is so central to the nation's values. Those born in the quarter century following World War II possess higher rates of college education than members of their generation elsewhere in the world, but that is no longer the case for younger generations. Eleven other nations—not only in western Europe but also Poland and Korea—have leapfrogged over the United States in the percentage of their young obtaining four-year college degrees.[26]

More importantly, the stalled progress in the United States occurred primarily among those from low to moderate incomes; indeed, people from those groups are barely more likely to graduate from college than were those of their parents' generation.[27] Making matters worse, this trend has developed during the same decades as economic inequality has widened and a college degree has become more critical than ever in determining Americans' chances of employment and income.[28] And this doesn't even take into account the *kind* of degree attained. Today, it matters increasingly not only whether you go to college, but also what type of college you attend. Many needy students are sequestered into separate and inferior institutions, including the for-profits, from which they are likely to emerge without degrees and too often with crushing levels of debt. In short, our system of higher education contributes, increasingly, to rising inequality, as it stratifies Americans by income group rather than providing them with ladders of opportunity.

What can explain why the United States has gotten off track from its historic legacy? My research indicates that problems in higher education policy today are not attributable solely to the usual suspects. Many would put the blame squarely on the shoulders of universities and colleges, pointing to the high tuition they charge. Indeed, tuition has skyrocketed since the 1980s, far outpacing inflation. The average published tuition at private nonprofit four-year institutions amounts to 36 percent of average family income, up from 16 percent in 1973. The tuition at four-year public institutions, though considerably less, has actually increased at a faster rate over the same time period, growing from 4 percent of average family income to 11 percent. Two-year community colleges typically charge a rate that approaches 4 percent of the average family income, up from 2 percent.[29] So whether you're a student at Harvard University, Grand Valley State in Michigan, or Hinds Community

College in Mississippi, you're feeling the strain of steep annual increases in tuition.

Tuition has soared for several reasons. Some colleges—particularly elite privates and flagship publics—serve large numbers of affluent students who are eager to benefit from their brand name and from the latest and best facilities and services they can offer. These students come from families who are willing and able to pay higher rates. Colleges in this tier compete with each other, aiming to outdo one another in pursuit of such students—by installing desirable features such as recreation centers with climbing walls, spa amenities, and luxurious dining and dormitory facilities. Colleges of all types have sought to elevate graduation rates by offering supportive services to students—such as mental health counseling and writing tutors—which increase costs.[30] Economists who study tuition increases in depth point out that higher education—like health care but unlike many other industries—relies primarily on a number of human services that cannot be as easily replaced or sped up by technological advances as other sectors of the economy.[31] Amazon.com can reduce what students pay for textbooks by automating the costs of shipping them, but student learning—even in an age of online education—still requires instructors. Moreover, in order to provide state-of-the-art education, it is necessary to rely on skilled professionals and up-to-date equipment and facilities. Therefore, even apart from the cost drivers noted above, college education tends to grow more expensive over time.

But tuition increases do not occur in a vacuum, with colleges and universities single-handedly determining the price that students pay for their education. The long history of federal and state support for higher education demonstrates powerfully that students have never been charged the full balance of the costs involved: government has always played a supportive role, in effect subsidizing the cost of tuition through a wide array of public policies. Even in the colonial period, public authorities contributed to the development of what became private colleges, beginning with Harvard in 1636. As recently as the 1980s, individual states contributed the lion's share of funds needed by public universities and colleges, and thereby managed to keep tuition low for state residents. And so rather than using tuition increases alone to explain the crisis in higher education, we need to consider what has become of government's role in supporting students and institutions.

Lackluster college graduation rates are also often blamed on students themselves, or on inadequacies in the K-12 educational system from which they come. Countless reports suggest that low and moderate income people may be insufficiently prepared for college, and therefore less likely to matriculate or to complete their degrees. They may find it difficult even to navigate the admissions and the financial aid processes, and to discern between credible institutions and those that are more likely to take advantage of the vulnerable. Each of these claims has some merit. Yet there is nothing new in the greater advantages the wealthy have in finding their way to college and succeeding once they get there. Here again, we need to consider what has *changed* over the past forty years—namely, government's capacity to enable growing numbers of ordinary Americans to graduate from college.

In recent decades public policies have functioned far less effectively than they did in the mid-twentieth century to ameliorate inequality in college-going. This policy failure is manifest in three areas. First, federal student aid—though more costly than ever—no longer promotes opportunity as effectively as it did in the past. This is in part because policymakers permitted Pell grants to fall behind in value as tuition escalated, leaving students with no option apart from borrowing more in student loans—and growing more indebted. Despite increases in Pell grants since 2007, the benefits still fail to keep pace with rising college costs. The value of the maximum grant award in covering the cost of tuition, fees, room and board at the average four year public university has fallen from nearly 80 percent in the 1970s to only 31 percent in 2012–2013.[32] Also, beginning in the late 1990s, lawmakers fashioned costly new tuition tax policies that provide a bonus to many fairly well-off Americans who would attend college regardless of whether or not they received aid. Expansions of these policies in 2009 deliver their largest benefits to households with incomes between $100,000 and $180,000.[33]

Second, state governments have diminished their commitment to public higher education, no longer treating it as the priority that it once was. The vast network of state universities and community colleges has long served as the access point for most Americans who pursue higher education by offering quality education at an affordable price. These institutions continue to enroll 73 percent of all college students.[34] But between 1990–1991 and 2009–2010, state governments decreased funding for them by an average of 26 percent in real terms—even as operating costs increased.[35] Unlike the elite private nonprofit universities that rely on private donations to close the budget gap, public institutions—outside of the flagship universities—lack such capacity.[36] They have instead raised tuition: at the average public four-year institution, it skyrocketed by 244 percent in real terms between 1980–1981 and 2010–2011.[37] In effect, public higher education has become increasingly privatized as students and their families have been left to shoulder the increased costs.

This means that public universities and colleges no longer offer the same degree of opportunity they provided to low and moderate income Americans as recently as a generation ago. In Minnesota, for example, the cost of tuition—adjusted for inflation—increased threefold. Nils Badrul, a student at St. Cloud University, was amazed to learn that his grandparents paid all expenses for his father, Badrul Bakar, when he was a student there. Bakar explains that back then, attending cost only "a few hundred dollars a quarter. Wow!" By contrast, his son's expenses are upward of $11,000 per year, and Bakar can do little aside from giving him small amounts every few weeks to help defray expenses. Nils received $5,000 per year in grants and borrows the rest through student loans. "At this time we have no choice because we can't afford it," explains Bakar.[38] For low to moderate income students, these escalating rates of tuition can make the difference between enrolling or not, and completing a degree or dropping out.[39] The shortfall in funding also leads to a widening of the resource gap between the public and private nonprofit sectors, with implications for the professor-student ratio and other key dimensions of the quality of the college experience.

Third, as noted earlier, lawmakers have permitted the for-profit education industry to capture a huge portion of federal student aid funds, despite their poor record in serving students. In fact, for a decade beginning in the late 1990s, lawmakers relaxed restrictions on the sector, making it even easier for it to take advantage of federal largesse. They did this even though these schools generally lack the established forms of self-regulation and quality control that have long been in place at most of the public and private nonprofit universities and colleges. The for-profits lack the intensive review procedures that traditional colleges use to evaluate faculty for tenure and promotion and the rigorous ethical guidelines they abide by for the admissions and financial aid process. And yet even in the absence of such self-governance by the for-profits, advocates of more extensive public regulation for the sector have faced an uphill battle in recent decades. The efforts by the US Department to Education to regulate the sector—to which the House objected in the 2011 vote described above—produced a watered-down set of rules that year, and most of them were discarded by a judge one year later.

These three sets of policy developments, in combination, have transformed the US system of education from one that provides access and opportunity to one that widens economic inequality and fosters social division. Young people's experiences of college itself and of government support in attending it both vary with their position on the income spectrum. At the upper end are those born into affluent families who would go to college whether or not government assisted them. They typically attend elite private or flagship public universities. These institutions do benefit from government largesse that reduces their operating costs, but through channels that are less than obvious. For instance, they enjoy tax-free status, meaning that they owe nothing to government on capital gains in their endowment. The tax system also incentivizes private donors to give to them by making contributions tax-free. Government-sponsored research grants, complete with allotments for indirect costs, fill out this portfolio. Such subsidies not only support faculty research but also enable such institutions to provide a very high-quality education to students at a cost considerably less than its actual value. Other colleges lack comparable support.[40] Upper middle class income families benefit directly from tuition tax breaks if they have household income under $180,000 per year. Students in these families are also often well positioned to win merit scholarships awarded by a growing number of states that permit them to attend flagship public universities at sharply reduced tuition.[41] They are also likely to be awarded merit aid at private nonprofit colleges, which use such funds as inducements to attract students who will pay nearly full tuition, rather than to provide more need-based aid to low income students, to supplement what they receive from Pell grants.[42] Students in solidly middle income families, by contrast, enroll especially in public universities and colleges where they face steeply rising tuition costs—and must borrow more and work more than those in the past to make ends meet. Being employed lengthens the time it takes them to get their degree and imperils their chances of finishing. They are also increasingly likely to be in large classes and to be deprived of the special services that assist students at better-funded universities. Worst of all are the circumstances of low income people—who must borrow heavily and work the most hours in order to attend. They are the most likely either to attend community colleges, where the investment per student—hovering around $12,000 annually—is far lower than that of the institutions noted above, or to be recruited by for-profit schools that invest far less in students and typically leave them heavily indebted.

The question yet to be answered is this: Why has the US political system permitted policies to veer so far off track, abandoning the tradition of expanding the ranks of the college educated? Why has it advanced policy changes that destroy the nation's legacy in higher education—particularly at a point in time when acquiring a college degree is more important than ever? In mountains of reports, economists and education experts have documented the US lag in college-going as well as the commensurate rise in inequality in college attainment.[43] Several notable books delve deeper still.[44] To name just a few, in *The Race Between Education and Technology* Claudia Goldin and Richard Katz show how inequality lessened as college degrees and technology grew in tandem in the early twentieth century, but rose again as education fell behind more recently.[45] Greg J. Duncan's collection, *Whither Opportunity?* and Richard Kahlenberg's *Rewarding Strivers* elaborate on the features of educational inequality, its socioeconomic consequences, and how it might be addressed.[46] However, scholars have yet to explain how and why the United States permitted these developments to occur. Unraveling that story requires us to put the American political system front and center, examining what happened to higher education policy over this time period and the forces that shaped it.

I have discovered that Americans have not become less supportive of college students than they were in the past; public opinion trends reveal at least steady support and by some indicators a growing commitment to promoting college degree attainment. Neither is the problem attributable simply to the textbook features of the American political system—such as the complexities of the separation of powers and federalism, and the power of interest groups—that routinely complicate the enactment of policy reform. Rather, the profound political dysfunction underlying trends in this issue area—as in many others—owes to particular features of contemporary American politics that are every bit as routine and established as those institutional features, but observers have not yet recognized their existence.

Today we dwell in what I call a *policyscape*, a political landscape densely cluttered with a vast array of policies of all varieties that were established at earlier points in time. These policies, in higher education and in other areas as well, do not function as effectively as they once did. In some measure, that's because circumstances in the environment have changed, and policymakers have failed to update the policies accordingly—a phenomenon that has been called "drift."[47] For example, tuition has grown for some reasons unrelated to government's role, as noted above, and student aid has failed to keep pace. But these external changes are only part of the problem.

It's also the case that existing policies themselves generate effects that, over time, can reshape their development—and in some cases, take them off the rails from their intended purposes. This may be caused by any of three dynamics: policy design effects, unintended consequences, or lateral effects. Policy design effects occur as inherent characteristics of policies act to foster their growth and expansion or, conversely, to make them vulnerable to deterioration or contraction. These tendencies, over the years, can transform policies and affect their capacity to achieve their original goals. Pell grants, for example, lack automatic cost-of-living adjustments; this means that their value necessarily diminishes as inflation occurs, unless lawmakers manage to raise rates through the cumbersome and contentious annual budget appropriations process in Congress. Student loans, by contrast, grow easily: lawmakers only need to agree to allow more students to borrow more money. This imbalance between grants and loans, paired with rising tuition, has led to increasing student indebtedness.

Unintended consequences happen when policies yield side effects that their creators did not anticipate, for example, by influencing the activity of individuals or organizations beyond those they aimed to affect. In some instances, such policy consequences may reshape the political system itself through "feedback effects" that can be salutary or perverse. Scholars find some evidence that universities and colleges—for-profit colleges in particular—may respond to the availability of federal aid by simply increasing the tuition they charge.[48] Federal student aid policies may also prompt industries to engage in behavior that economists call "rent-seeking," meaning attempts to influence the political system in order to extract profits from it, for example, by gaining new customers or commanding a higher price for their goods and services than they would otherwise. Student aid policies have created a windfall for for-profit schools, and those companies have, in turn, invested some of their earnings in enhancing their political capacity—through campaign contributions and lobbying—as a means of maintaining and extending the policies that benefit them so lucratively.

Lateral effects happen when policies are changed due to the impact of other, unrelated policies. Higher education spending in the states, for instance, has been effectively displaced as lawmakers have left it to dwindle while permitting spending areas such as K-12 education and health care to consume larger portions of state budget resources. In part this owes to the "mandatory" features of the latter policies, as governments are compelled by law to provide such services to those who are eligible, while aid for colleges and universities is instead "discretionary" and therefore more vulnerable to budget cutting.

What becomes clear is that when left to their own devices, policies can develop over time in ways that undermine their ability to achieve the societal goals they were created to address. But the existence of the policyscape doesn't mean that we are doomed to forces beyond our control; it is not inevitable that policies will go off track or that if they do, they will remain derailed. Rather, a fundamental task of contemporary governance is that of policy maintenance: lawmakers need to monitor policies, assess what sorts of repairs or renovation may be required, and conduct reforms as needed. As former senator Nancy Kassebaum, a Republican of Kansas, explains, "Public programs—just like any other programs—need to be managed."[49]

But the extent to which lawmakers engage in policy maintenance depends on the political context in which they dwell. Maintaining existing policies effectively requires that political leaders recognize and value the basic purposes of public policy—and identify when existing policies need updating. It demands public officials who are creative thinkers and flexible negotiators, willing to work across differences to repair and alter policies so that they continue to function well for future generations. Landmark higher education laws were created in the mid-twentieth century typically at the initiative of Democrats who controlled Congress at that time, but they enjoyed a fair amount of bipartisan support. Two of the most prominent ones were signed into law by Republican presidents Dwight Eisenhower and Richard Nixon. Following the 1980 election of President Ronald Reagan, a new conservative approach to governance emerged and Republicans gained control of the Senate. For a time higher education policies grew untended, as lawmakers couldn't agree on how to maintain them. Yet by the late 1980s and early 1990s, reform initiatives began to appear, emanating from both sides of the aisle and gaining bipartisan support.

Since the 1994 elections, however, constructive bipartisanship has all but vanished from the political landscape. Both chambers of Congress have grown more polarized than at any time since at least the early twentieth century, if not the Civil War. Both parties have become more internally homogeneous and unified, and moderates have become scarce.[50] This partisan environment has not only hindered chances that public officials will enact bold new landmark laws; it has also proven detrimental to their performance of even the basic tasks necessary to maintain existing ones. Polarization undermines lawmakers' willingness and ability to update policies and to make necessary adjustments when they veer off course. But that's only part of the problem.

Making matters worse, when factions within Congress *have* managed to unite in the past two decades, the interests they have responded to most reliably have been those with the deepest pockets; money lubricates political machinery that is otherwise stuck in gridlock. As demonstrated by the February 2011 House vote on the for-profits (described above), many public officials come together readily across the aisle when the interests of the affluent and powerful are at stake. These bipartisan "exceptions to the rule" endow the political system with features of a plutocracy, as if a wealthy class effectively controls the government. In the case of higher education issues, they ensure that shareholders and top management of businesses that benefit from student aid are represented, but the needs of ordinary Americans fail to gain attention. In sum, this polarized and plutocratic politics is a disastrous combination with the policyscape: it lacks the characteristics necessary for successful negotiation of the complex array of organizations, industries, and other policy effects that have emerged with long established policies.

The pairing of the dense policyscape that exists today with the politics of polarization and plutocracy has amounted to a tragic mismatch for effective governance. The unfortunate results are apparent not only in policies related to college-going, but also in many other seemingly intractable issue areas. If we continue along this path of dysfunctional governance, we will fail to address problems ranging from retirement security to immigration—areas in which we have existing policies, but ones that need updating. As a nation we will continue to slide away from the greater equality and more widespread upward mobility that characterized the mid-twentieth century, and become increasingly beleaguered by problems that could be mitigated through a reasoned public policy response.

Citizenship in the United States has never come with a guaranteed standard of living or political influence. Historically, however, it has offered the possibility of upward mobility. And it has provided means for citizens to improve their understanding of public life and their capacity to participate in it, thereby enhancing democracy. Not many decades ago, higher education was an important key to this dynamic.[51]

When the US House of Representative discussed federal aid for the for-profits in February 2011, to those listening in the gallery it might have sounded like this American tradition was being revived. The inclusive spirit of earlier higher education policies was echoed, for example, when Edolphus Towns of New York implored his colleagues to vote against federal restrictions on the for-profits: "Supporting this amendment is supporting educational opportunities for minorities. A 'yes' vote is a vote for economically disadvantaged students. Many of them are the first in their families to attend college. These students wish to have the opportunity to attend a flexible program that trains them to be the best they can be."[52] This view united him and other members of the Black Caucus together with Tea Party Republicans, who praised the schools as exemplars of the free market. The more telling indication of what was actually at stake, however, may have been provided in the midst of the economic downturn in 2008, when the top for-profit companies experienced growth in their stocks while other major companies posted huge losses. A for-profit analyst at the time noted with satisfaction, "We've been trouncing the S&P."[53] When elected officials coalesced in the House vote in 2011, they clearly endorsed opportunity for industry elites, but their actions provided little hope for Americans struggling for a better life.

CHAPTER ONE

CREATING DEGREES
OF INEQUALITY

As the Occupy Wall Street protests spread across the United States in the midst of the Great Recession, it did not take participants long to change their focus from the financial system to issues that struck closer to home for many: student debt and the value of a college degree. Their handwritten signs told their stories, with messages such as: "I have $50,000 in student loan debt and my B.A. is useless," and "Graduated college: May 2010. Debt: $35,000. Jobs in US: None."[1] In the nation's capital, demonstrators blocked the entrances to Sallie Mae, the student loan servicing company. In Boston, they rallied outside the Bank of America and the Harvard Club, chanting, "Not just for the rich and white, education is a right."[2] Suddenly, with so many young college graduates struggling to find employment, America's system of higher education—which had long managed to stay above the fray of popular discontent—became subject to a maelstrom of criticism.

The general public's concerns centered on rising tuition and student indebtedness, but politicians and journalists began questioning the widespread faith in the value of a college degree and criticizing the Obama administration's ambition to raise college graduation rates. Candidate Rick Santorum started the onslaught during the 2012 Republican presidential primary, asserting, "President Obama once said he wants everybody in America to go to college. What a snob. There are good, decent men and women who go out and work hard every day and put their skills to tests that aren't taught by some liberal college professor."[3] *Washington Post* columnist Robert Samuelson criticized what he termed the "college-for-all crusade" that had captivated US policymakers ever since the creation of the GI Bill in 1944. He pointed to the rise of debt-laden college graduates and to recent findings that students in a selected group of colleges showed little evidence of learning—or studying, for that matter—implying that universities had dumbed down academic standards in order to accommodate an increasingly unprepared student body. He lamented, "We overdid it. The obsessive faith in college has backfired."[4] In the *Atlantic Monthly,* reporter Clive Crook argued that the economic gains to a college degree had "flattened out" in recent years, showing that "college is not an economic cure-all."[5] One report noted that dropping out of college worked just fine for some of the nation's most successful contemporary entrepreneurs such as Mark Zuckerberg, Bill Gates, and Steve Jobs, and the founders of Twitter and Tumblr.[6] Peter Thiel, who left Harvard partway through his freshman year and later founded PayPal, started an organization that awarded $100,000 each to promising visionaries under age twenty on the condition that they would drop out of college and pursue their ideas.[7]

The common theme of these varied complaints is that there is a crisis in higher education and that colleges aren't worth the debt they impose on students. The critics are correct that the United States faces a higher education crisis today, but they miss the mark in identifying what it is. Contrary to claims that we have a glut of college graduates, in fact we are not producing enough. Even more troubling, our system of higher education is exacerbating inequality in the United States in multiple ways.

Understanding why higher ed has gone off course requires us to put American politics front and center. The higher education policies created by earlier generations still endure but require maintenance, updating, and rerouting if they are to function effectively. Yet the rise of partisan polarization has undermined the capacity of policymakers to engage in these fundamental tasks. And when lawmakers do legislate, they often cater primarily to powerful monied interests and wealthy households. As a result, the nation has failed to maintain its historic legacy of expanding opportunity through higher education.

Too Few College Graduates

In the middle decades of the twentieth century, the United States experienced a meteoric rise in the rate of people earning four-year college degrees, as it soared from 6 percent of twenty-five- to twenty-nine-year-olds in 1947 to 24 percent in 1977. During the next two decades, the percentage remained flat. In the mid-1990s, progress resumed but at a more modest rate; as of 2011, 32 percent of young adults had obtained bachelor's degrees.[8]

As recently as the 1980s, the nation was the undisputed international leader in the percentage of citizens graduating from college.[9] The baby boomers, born in the decades immediately following World War II, pursued higher education in large numbers. Entering college during the late 1960s and 1970s, they swelled the ranks of college students and became the most educated members of their generation worldwide. As shown in Figure 1.1, in 2010, 32 percent of Americans between fifty-five and sixty-four held four-year college degrees, a higher percentage than citizens in the same age group in any other nation. (Norway claims a distant second place, with 25 percent of its citizens in that age group as college graduates.)

But among younger groups, the US lead has disappeared. In 2010 Americans between twenty-five and thirty-four had a college graduation rate of 33 percent—a mere one percentage point increase over the older generation. By contrast, young people in the ten nations shown in Figure 1.1 have catapulted over their American counterparts.

Those who claim that the United States is sending too many people to college discount these global historical trends, focusing instead on data points such as how recent college graduates have fared since the financial crisis in 2008. Yet in fact, while 6.8 percent of them suffered unemployment during this period, that figure pales in comparison to the 24 percent of recent high school graduates who were jobless.[10] The

FIGURE 1.1.   OTHER NATIONS LEAP PAST THE UNITED STATES: PERCENTAGE
OF OLDER AND YOUNGER GROUPS WITH BACHELOR'S DEGREES
OR HIGHER, BY NATION (2010)

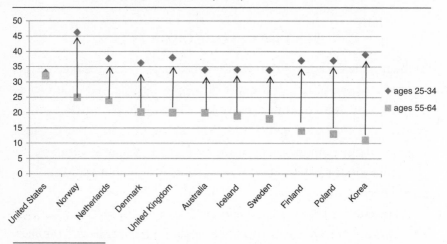

SOURCE: *OECD Education at a Glance 2012,* Table A1.3a.

recession accentuated a trend that has been under way for decades in the
United States: the loss of good paying jobs for low-skilled workers and
the increasing demand for highly skilled, well-educated workers. Since
the early 1980s, this development has led to the so-called wage premium for those with college degrees. In 2010, among young adults between twenty-five and forty, those with four-year college degrees earned
$40,000 on average compared to $25,000 for high school graduates.[11]

Moreover, the return from a college degree increases over an individual's lifetime, with the gains in employment prospects and income
being only the most obvious and easily measured benefits. One recent
study focusing on income estimated that a four-year college degree
pays an average return of 15.2 percent annually—far more than average returns in the stock market, at 6.8 percent since the 1950s; or corporate bonds, at 2.9 percent; or housing, at 0.4 percent.[12] Those with
higher rates of education enjoy better health and longevity.[13] They participate in larger numbers in politics and civic life, making their voices
heard in the public sphere and providing innumerable services to their

communities.[14] As economist Susan Dynarski testified to the US Senate Finance Committee in 2011, "A college education is one of the best investments a young person can make. Even with record high tuition prices, a bachelor's degree pays for itself several times over, in the form of higher income, lower unemployment, better health and enhanced civic engagement. Within ten years of college graduation, the typical BA will already have recouped the cost of her investment."[15]

However, not all college degrees offer these benefits. As we will see shortly, some institutions produce poor results for their students and interfere with what is otherwise a clear pattern of success. In the main, however, the evidence is quite unequivocal: the United States needs to increase the percentage of its citizens who attain college degrees.

Graduating Inequality

If we look more closely to see *who* completes college today, we find that the ranks of college graduates reinforce income inequality. Figure 1.2 shows the rates of four-year college degree attainment by age twenty-four among individuals who grew up in families in each quartile of the income distribution in 1970 and in 2011. While we would expect that those from more affluent backgrounds are likely to attain more education than those who grow up poor, the extent of their advantage over the bottom three-quarters of the income distribution is striking. For those who grow up in high income families today, going to college is a routine part of life—like getting childhood immunizations—and the vast majority of such individuals, 71 percent, complete their bachelor's degree in early adulthood. Among those in the upper middle income quartile, this same achievement, though more than twice as common as it was forty years ago, is still relatively unusual, reaching just 30 percent. Among Americans who have grown up in households below median income, the gains since 1970 have been meager: those in the lower middle quartile have increased their graduation rates from just 11 to 15 percent, and among those in the poorest group, from 6 to 10 percent. All told, degree attainment among upper income households so dramatically outpaces that of low- and

FIGURE 1.2. INEQUALITY IN COLLEGE DEGREE ATTAINMENT: PERCENTAGE OF
            AMERICANS WITH A FOUR-YEAR DEGREE BY AGE 24, BY FAMILY
            INCOME QUARTILE, 1970 AND 2011 COMPARED

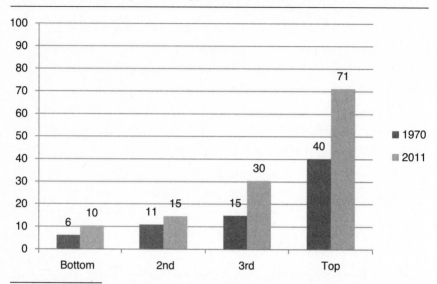

SOURCE: Thomas G. Mortenson, "Family Income and Unequal Education Opportunity, 1970–2011,"
Postsecondary Education Opportunity, November 2012, www.postsecondary.org.

middle income people that the percentage who obtain diplomas among
the top income quartile is greater than that of the other three quartiles
combined.[16] Our system of higher education not only fails to mitigate inequality but it exacerbates it, creating a deeply stratified society.

The unimpressive gains in graduation rates for most Americans have
occurred despite the fact that access to college—being admitted and then
enrolling—has improved dramatically over time, including among the
least advantaged. Increasing enrollment is in part attributable to sharp
increases in high school graduation rates, particularly among lower income groups, as many more now possess the necessary qualifications
for higher education. In 2010, 83 percent of all eighteen- to twenty-four-
year-olds had earned a high school diploma or equivalent certification,
and this included 73 percent of those in the bottom quartile—a nearly
20 percent improvement since 1970. Once individuals graduate from
high school, most of them now continue on to college—75 percent of

eighteen- to twenty-four-year-olds as of 2010. Here again, the biggest recent gains have been made in low income groups. Among students who enroll, however, completion rates by age twenty-four hover at only 47 percent. In effect, more students are starting college but they not graduating. Here economic inequality becomes apparent: nearly all of those from the highest income group who start college—97 percent— gain diplomas by age twenty-four, a stunning improvement of forty-two percentage points since 1970, compared to just 23 percent of those in the bottom quartile, a mere one percentage point improvement over the same period. Those in the second quartile fared little better, with only 26 percent reaching graduation by age twenty-four; and even in the third quartile, just over half (51 percent) completed degrees in a timely fashion.[17] In short, completing college, or at least doing so promptly, eludes most young people from low and moderate income backgrounds.[18]

Such outcomes may appear, at first blush, to indicate that our societal emphasis on the importance of college is misplaced. Certainly college is not for everyone and it should not be viewed as the only acceptable path following high school. The United States could do a far better job of linking those who are not college bound with jobs, a point made by James E. Rosenbaum in his insightful book, *Beyond College for All*.[19] But others who criticize calls for increased college attainment insinuate that those who fail to enroll or fail to complete college are simply not motivated. "School bores and bothers them," writes Robert Samuelson.[20] Richard Vedder claims that "college graduates, on average, are smarter and more disciplined and dependable than high school graduates."[21]

Without a doubt, the nation could do better by those who do not have an interest in or aptitude for college. However, the implication that less advantaged students fail to graduate owing to a lack of motivation or incompetence misses the mark. When we look closely at the link between income and college graduation, we find that more is at play. Certainly young people from higher socioeconomic backgrounds are typically better positioned to excel in the prerequisites for college admission and success.[22] They are more likely to attend better primary and secondary schools. Their parents invest heavily in providing enriching extracurricular opportunities, including music lessons, travel, summer camps, and so forth.[23] Not surprisingly, they earn higher grades and do better on standardized tests than those who grow up without such privileges. Yet scholars have found that even among individuals with the *same* academic credentials, those from less advantaged families are less likely to gain college degrees.[24] As Figure 1.3 shows, of students with high test scores, the vast majority from the highest income group graduate, while just over half of those in the middle income group and just a small majority of the rest manage to complete college. In fact, the college graduation rates of high-scoring low income individuals, at 30 percent, barely surpass those of low-scoring high income individuals, at 29 percent. Among students who enroll, attrition occurs most dramatically among those from families below median income.[25] Clearly there must be something else going on here other than the weeding out of the unqualified and unmotivated.

FIGURE 1.3. It's Not All About Aptitude: Percentage of Students Who Received A Four-Year College Degree or More, by Test Scores and Income, 2000

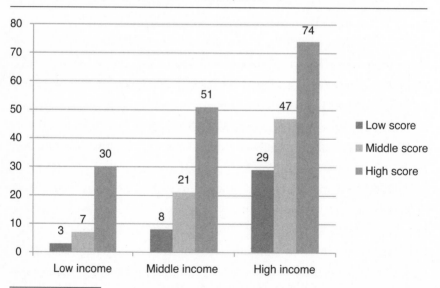

Source: US Department of Education, National Center for Education Statistics, National Education Longitudinal Study of 1988 (NELS: 88/2000), "Fourth Follow-up," unpublished data.

In fact, ample evidence reveals that neither changes in college readiness nor shifts in the demographic characteristics of college students go very far to explain the unimpressive college graduation rates.[26] A rigorous study by a group of economists, for example, found that rising tuition in public sector colleges bears most of the blame for this development. In addition, it shows that rising costs compel more students to work longer hours to finance their education, which makes it difficult for them to carry enough credits to graduate in a timely manner, if at all.[27] Illustrating these trends, in 2013 students at Central Connecticut State University braced themselves for a 4.1 percent increase in tuition and fees—$19,897 per year for those who live on campus. Amber Pietrycha, a junior, already works two jobs per semester on average in order to make ends meet. "Eight hundred bucks for me will bring it close to the line where I'm not entirely sure I could do it," she said. Sophomore Salam Measho agreed, explaining that the increase "means I'm going to have to work more hours on weekends back home. That means less time studying. That's too much of a strain on myself."[28] These developments are not inevitable, as demonstrated by a special program at the University of North Carolina–Chapel Hill that provided extra financial support to low income students, and significantly boosted their graduation rates.[29]

Not long ago, the United States led the world in promoting higher education for its citizens, spurring social mobility in the process. Many who grew up during the middle decades of the twentieth century became the first in their families to go to college. Many were assisted by generous GI Bill benefits or Pell grants, and all had access to public universities and colleges with affordable tuition.[30] Their lives were often transformed as they gained jobs, income, and opportunities to participate in public life that had been beyond the reach of their parents.[31]

Today, however, the United States has evolved into an international outlier for its lack of such mobility. A group of researchers compared ten countries in terms of the quality of children's lives on multiple dimensions—economic status, educational attainment, socioemotional well-being, and so forth—and found that in the United States quality of life was more determined by parents' level of education than in any of the

other countries investigated.[32] In fact, the single most powerful relationship they detected was between the educational level of American parents
and the subsequent level of education attained by their children: more
than anywhere else, the vast majority of children fortunate to be born to
highly educated parents acquired high levels of education, and conversely,
the children of those with little education were penalized by receiving little education. They concluded that the United States is "the country with
the least intergenerational mobility and the least equal opportunity for
children to advance."[33] For those who are left behind, the consequences
are severe. As recently as 1980, a male with a college degree earned about
20 percent more on average than one with a high school degree; by 2011,
the difference had grown to 45 percent.[34]

Citizens of the United States cherish the ideals of social mobility
and opportunity that are widely associated with the "American dream."
Many consider the chance to attend and graduate from college as both
an end in itself—a manifestation of that ideal—and a crucial means toward its fuller realization over the course of a lifetime. In the middle of
the twentieth century, federal student aid policies and public support of
state-run colleges and universities helped make a college education possible for growing numbers of individuals across the income spectrum.
Now, more individuals than ever from every income group pursue a
college education. But for most of those who do from the bottom half
of the income spectrum, the effort proves futile. Their greatest obstacle
to completing a four-year degree is not lack of ability or motivation, but
insufficient financial support. As nearly all of those in the most affluent
quarter of the population earn their diplomas in short order and reap
the benefits of doing so, social stratification becomes more deeply entrenched. For those who born into modest means, the gaps that separate
them from the upper echelon grow increasingly insurmountable.

NOT ALL COLLEGE DEGREES ARE CREATED EQUAL

If poor and middle income Americans are now finding it difficult to
graduate from college, it's also true that those who do manage this feat

often have a very different experience than their wealthier peers, depending on the institution they attend. In recent years, the gap has widened between what different types of institutions offer their students. In terms of faculty-to-student ratio, money allocated per student, class size, and general approach to learning, colleges are growing increasingly disparate. In addition, as seen in Table 1.1, institutions vary dramatically by sector in terms of the published "sticker price" for tuition and fees; the percentage of students who graduate within 6 years; and the extent of their reliance on student loans and indebtedness. Differences among colleges, therefore, are also exacerbating inequality.

TABLE 1.1. DISPARITIES IN THE COLLEGE EXPERIENCE, BY SECTOR

	Published Tuition and Fees, 2012–2013	Percentage of First-Time Full-Time BA Students Who Earned Degree Within Six Years	Percentage of Degree Recipients with Federal Loans, 2007–2008	Median Student Loan Debt Among Borrowers, 2007–2008 Graduates	Default Rates Among Borrowers, After Three Years, 2009
Private Nonprofits					
Bachelors	$29,056	65	69	$17,700	7
Publics					
Bachelors	$8,655	55	58	$22,400	8
Associate	$3,131	N/A	33	$7,100	18
For-Profits	$15,172				23
Bachelors		22	94	$32,700	
Associate		N/A	97	$18,800	

SOURCES: College Board, "Average Published Undergraduate Charges By Sector, 2012-2013," Annual Survey of Colleges, http://trends.collegeboard.org/college-pricing/figures-tables/average -published-undergraduate-charges-sector-2012-13; Sandy Baum and Kathleen Payea, "Trends in For-Profit Postsecondary Education: Enrollment, Prices, Student Aid, and Outcomes," College Board, Trends in Higher Education Series, 2011, http://advocacy.collegeboard.org/sites/default/files /11b_3376_Trends_Brief_4Pass_110414.pdf, p. 5; Patricia Steele and Sandy Baum, "How Much Are College Students Borrowing?" College Board, Policy Brief (August 2009), http://professionals .collegeboard.com/profdownload/cb-policy-brief-college-stu-borrowing-aug-2009.pdf; College Board, Trends in Higher Education, "Two-Year and Three-Year Cohort Default Rate by Sector," Fig. 9.b, http://trends.collegeboard.org/student-aid/figures-tables/federal-student-loan-default -rates-sector.

The Upper Tier

Students from high income backgrounds increasingly attend elite private universities and colleges and the flagship public universities—those with national and international reputations. This trend has accelerated in recent decades, driven by these colleges' use of sorting mechanisms such as SAT scores that identify a select student body from across the nation, by their selective reputations, as confirmed in *U.S. News & World Report* rankings, as well as by the availability of abundant resources to attract affluent students. At the most prestigious institutions, 70 percent of students come from the top income quartile and although the percentage from the bottom income quartile increased between 1994 and 2006, it changed only from 3 percent to 5 percent.[35] Overall, both highly selective and very selective colleges enrolled a slightly higher percentage of students from the top quartile in 2006 than they did in 1994, while the percentage of students from households below median income at these colleges remained unchanged.[36] Meanwhile, the percentage of white students at less selective and noncompetitive institutions declined from 79 to 58 percent between 1994 and 2006 as they flocked to more elite ones.[37]

The costs of tuition, room, and board at private, nonprofit institutions now run as high as $62,000 per year, and yet this "sticker price" can be misleading.[38] In fact, only some of the most affluent students pay full freight, whereas most students pay considerably less because they receive a financial aid package based on either merit or need, or both. In 2012–2013, the average private nonprofit college had published tuition and fee charges of $29,060, but in fact the average student—after receiving grant aid and tax benefits—received a bill of only $13,380.[39] Nationwide, the average "discount rate," as this reduction in charges is called, reached an all-time high of 45 percent in 2013.[40] As a result, the list price of the nonprofit colleges in particular overstates what most students actually pay.

The advertised prices of attending these universities may actually understate the value of what many of them offer their students. Some devote far greater resources to students than even their full-paying students contribute: the most selective colleges spend up to $92,000 per student while the least selective colleges spend approximately $12,000 per student.[41] Students attending the wealthiest 10 percent of institutions pay just twenty cents for every dollar spent on them, whereas at the other end of the spectrum, students contribute seventy-eight cents for each dollar. Private nonprofit institutions have been able to increase their spending per student by as much as 11 percent on average in recent years at research universities.[42] Although slowed somewhat by the economic downturn, they have also invested considerably in improving their buildings and facilities, hiring new faculty, funding programs, and in other ways enhancing the experience of the mostly affluent student body.

Degrees from elite institutions generally yield the most impressive returns for their graduates: their earnings are 45 percent higher than those who receive college degrees elsewhere, and they produce a disproportionate share of the nation's top corporate and government leaders.[43] The impact of these institutions for the few low income students who attend them, relative to those who attend elsewhere, are particularly impressive. These colleges and universities bear the hallmark of excellence, and those fortunate to attend them typically reap considerable value from doing so.

Certainly the sector classified as "private nonprofits" in Table 1.1 includes a wide array of colleges beyond the elites, and some of these admit more students of modest means but serve them poorly. They may do little to supplement low income students' Pell grants, charging them tuition that is very high relative to their family income, such that they take on excessive debt to attend. Some of these colleges could afford to help them but instead use their own resources to offer financial inducements to students with high SAT scores—a strategy that helps them to move up in the *U.S. News & World Report* rankings—and they also provide incentives to those who will pay nearly full tuition. Other nonprofit schools are cash starved and simply cannot offer extra assistance to students in need.[44] The most problematic among this latter group have earned the reputation of being "drop-out factories" because while they enroll many low income students, so few graduate; approximately thirty nonprofits have abysmal graduation rates of 20 percent or lower.[45]

Generally, however, nonprofit privates colleges serve most of their students well. Although the vast majority of their students—69 percent—must borrow student loans to attend, in fact they borrow far less than students pursuing the same degree at public and for-profit colleges. Moreover, these schools feature the highest graduation rates—65 percent on average complete their degrees in six years—and they have the lowest default rates, only 7 percent. Certainly the higher income status of many of their students contributes to these outcomes, but so does their comparative advantage in offering financial aid and substantial resources to students.

Gutting Public Sector Colleges and Universities

The nation's vast network of public universities and colleges, by contrast, have faced scarce resources over the past two decades as states have balanced their budgets by reducing their commitment to these institutions. Throughout the mid-twentieth century, these schools paired low costs with high quality for the vast majority of those attending college, particularly those from low and middle incomes. The flagships among them—especially renowned institutions such as the University of Michigan and University of Virginia—emulate private nonprofit universities, raising private donations from their alumni to make ends meet. But most public institutions lack such capacity. As a result, the gap between what the average public university and the average private nonprofit university can offer their students has widened considerably. In 2010, private nonprofit four-year universities spent $46,700 on average per student compared to $36,400 at public four-year universities and $12,400 at community colleges.[46] These differences manifest themselves in myriad ways, perhaps most obviously in the student-faculty ratio, which varies from 18 to 1 in highly selective private colleges to 22 to 1 in public flagship colleges, 28 to 1 in other public four-year colleges, and 57 to 1 in community colleges.[47]

As a means of dealing with budget shortages, public universities have turned increasingly to online teaching, which enables them to offer courses to many more students and at dramatically reduced costs.[48] As of 2011, 89 percent of four-year public universities had already provided online classes compared to only 60 percent of four-year private nonprofits.[49] Proponents believe this approach is nothing short of revolutionary; writes Thomas Friedman in the *New York Times,* "Nothing has more potential to lift more people out of poverty—by providing them an affordable education to get a job or improve in the job they have. Nothing has more potential to unlock a billion more brains to solve the world's biggest problems. And nothing has more potential to enable us to reimagine higher education."[50] The actual value of distance education compared to traditional methods, however, remains in question. Scholars who evaluated the performance of 40,000 students in 500,000 online courses found that those who enrolled in online courses were more likely to drop the courses than those who took the same course in person. Assessing students in various subgroups who enrolled in such courses, they found that members of all groups performed less well than they did in traditional courses, but that the impact was most severe for men, African Americans, and those with weak academic credentials.[51] These results are particularly troubling because such individuals are already underrepresented among college graduates. This suggests that as public universities move to online education, graduation rates among students who already face challenges in college completion may continue to fall, unless substantial efforts are made to provide student support.

The Growth of For-Profit Schools

Meanwhile, a rapidly growing proportion of American college students, particularly those from less advantaged backgrounds, have been flocking to for-profit colleges.[52] The earliest degree-granting private for-profit institutions were founded in the late nineteenth and early twentieth centuries, such as Strayer University in 1892 and DeVry in 1931. In the

1970s, they enrolled only 0.2 percent of students and still in 1993, just 1.6 percent. But by 2005 their share had grown to 5.1 percent and then soared to 9.6 percent in 2010.[53] There were only 343 for-profit colleges in 1990; by 2009 that number had risen to 1,199.[54] The largest of them, owned by the Apollo Group, is the University of Phoenix, which enrolled 395,361 students in 2008–2009—nearly eight times as many as the largest traditional campuses such as Arizona State, Ohio State, the University of Texas–Austin, or the University of Minnesota.[55]

What has driven the growth of this sector? Advocates explain that it is addressing unmet needs, serving the educational needs of an underserved population. Not everyone possesses the aptitude to succeed at a traditional college, it is argued, but they still require skills training to make the transition from high school to employment. According to this narrative, the for-profits step into this void by offering practical training in areas such as criminal justice, information systems and technology, and health-related fields. They strive to accommodate their student bodies, which consist of a higher percentage of older students, those already shouldering employment and child care responsibilities, as well as many from minority groups and disadvantaged backgrounds. They have accommodated these students' busy schedules and learning needs by providing opportunities to take just one or two courses at a time, making extensive course offerings available year round, and finding enough instructors to teach as many students as wish to enroll in a particular course. Kaplan CEO Andrew S. Rosen says in his book *Change.edu: Rebooting for the New Talent Economy* that "private-sector institutions have shown more nimbleness, more innovation, and more commitment to learning outcomes than just about any institutions on the American higher education scene."[56]

Unfortunately for many students, the reality of these schools has not matched the rhetoric. They have had experiences like that of Sandra Muniz, of Davis, California. In 2007 the forty-three-year-old emergency room clerk decided to pursue additional training. "I needed some skills so that if I got laid off I'd be able to find another job." She enrolled at Heald College, a for-profit institution, borrowing $10,000 to pay for a three-month program in office skills. But when she finished the program, she couldn't find a new job that would use the skills she had acquired. No problem—Heald enabled her to borrow again so that she could enroll in a criminal justice program, with the intent of transferring to Sacramento State to finish her degree. But then she discovered that Sacramento State would not accept most of her credits from the for-profit institution. Afterward, with no degree, $19,000 in student loan debt, and a job that barely allows her to pay the interest on her loan, Muniz says of the college she attended, "I feel very scammed. They pay more attention to the profit for them, not the students' education."[57]

How do the for-profits fail so to live up to their promises? For one thing, the tuition they charge, typically much higher than the cost of comparable programs at public sector colleges, vastly surpasses what students can repay after acquiring their degrees. The nonprofits and public institutions, not being driven by the profit motive, invest extra revenue back into their operations—for example, in the form of student financial aid, new buildings, or enhanced programs. For-profits invest only $2,659 per student in instruction, compared to $9,418 by public colleges and $15,289 by private nonprofits.[58]

The for-profits instead focus on recruitment, seeking to enroll as many students as possible. Various investigations, including undercover operations by the Government Accountability Office (GAO), revealed that these schools have often lured students through high-pressure and deceptive practices, and sometimes outright fraud.[59] Out of fifteen colleges investigated by the GAO, thirteen provided deceptive information to applicants, implying guaranteed jobs for their graduates or inflated earnings for those employed in the fields for which they offered training. One college told an applicant for an associate's degree in criminal justice that he would be poised for a job with the Federal Bureau of Investigation or Central Intelligence Agency—both organizations that strongly recommend at least a bachelor's degree for candidates to be considered for positions as special agents. A beauty college informed an applicant that barbers earn $150,000 to $250,000 annually—whereas in fact 90 percent make $43,000 or less.[60]

Once enrolled, almost all students at for-profits—94 percent of those who attain bachelor's degrees and 97 percent who earn associate's—borrow federal student loans in order to afford the tuition, as shown in Table 1.1. This compares to 33 percent of students at community colleges, 58 percent at four-year publics, and 69 percent at four-year private nonprofits. Moreover, the students at the for-profits borrow much larger sums: in the case of bachelor's degrees, 2008 graduates had gone in debt by $32,700 on average, compared to $17,700 by students in private nonprofit colleges and $22,400 by those in public institutions.[61] Among those in associate's degree programs, the for-profit graduates incurred more than twice as much debt as graduates of community colleges: $18,800 on average, compared to $7,100.

In spite of this price premium, there is little evidence that the training students receive at for-profit institutions does much to enhance their earnings. Contrary to recruiters' promises of high job placement rates and future pay, those who attend for-profits—as evidenced by recent studies—experience higher unemployment rates than those who pursue training in the same subjects at other institutions. And when they do attain jobs, they make lower wages. Defenders of the for-profits have argued that such outcomes simply reflect the fact that their institutions serve students who are more disadvantaged from the start. Yet some studies controlling for such differences found that students who attended for-profits fared worse in the job market later on.[62] One found that comparing two students with the same backgrounds, the one who attained her training at a public or not-for-profit institution reaped significantly higher wages later on, while the one at the for-profit college failed to experience increased earnings.[63] We do not know the extent to which these differences may be the result of superior training in the traditional colleges compared to the for-profits; they may emanate primarily from the stronger reputation that more established, better-known institutions enjoy in the eyes of employers. And at least one study found no evidence of an earnings gap between those who attended the different institutions.[64] What we can say with certainty, however, is that even if graduates of for-profits fare as well as others in the job market, they face greater financial challenges given the much higher debt levels they have assumed in acquiring their education.

Not surprisingly, therefore, students who acquire their education at for-profit colleges are more likely to default on their loans. Nearly one in four borrowers who attends a for-profit defaults on his or her student loans within three years; over time these students account for nearly half of all defaults, with taxpayers left bearing the responsibility.[65] Student loans are a form of debt that, since 1998, may not be forgiven in bankruptcy. As a result, a large proportion of those who attended for-profits find their lives in financial ruin.

These problems of the for-profits are not limited to just a few bad apples among them. High levels of student borrowing and default pervade the sector. To put this in perspective, of the 1,635 private nonprofit colleges, 2 percent have default rates over 30 percent, and 6 percent over 20 percent; by contrast, among the 1,806 for-profits, 15 percent have default rates over 30 percent, and 44 percent over 20 percent.[66] In fact, it is difficult to find sterling examples of for-profit schools that genuinely serve low income students well. The *Washington Monthly*, which provides rankings of colleges and universities, scoured its list of 1,572 and came up with a group of 349 that they call the "best-bang-for-the-buck" colleges, because they "do the best job of helping nonwealthy students attain marketable degrees at affordable prices," as indicated by the percentage of students with Pell grants, graduation rates, and default rates relative to actual prices student paid for tuition. Only one for-profit college, Trident University International in California, made it onto this list, ranked 170th.[67]

As colleges grow more stratified, more differentiated in their accessibility to different socioeconomic groups and in what they offer them, they are generating greater inequality in American society. At the upper end, the elite private universities and colleges and the nominally "public" flagships that benefit from ample private donations attract affluent student bodies. For most students, the high costs they charge are quickly offset by the high value and high returns they offer. The wide middle tier of public colleges and universities, those attended by nearly three out of four of the nation's college students, are under duress. These traditionally "low cost, good value" alternatives to the elite institutions have suffered from sharp reductions in state funding, forcing tuition hikes and straining resources. The developments have greatly impeded the nation's ability to improve educational attainment, particularly among low to moderate income young people and the growing proportions of African American and Hispanic students who enroll in public colleges.[68] The bottom tier of for-profit colleges, like the nonprofit privates, charge high costs but, unlike them, invest little in students. And students can pay these costs only by taking on debt, at amounts that the jobs their degrees attract leave them struggling to pay.

In sum, the debate over the value of college is meaningless unless these distinctions of cost and value are taken into account. Even at their high cost, degrees in the private nonprofits offer high value for most graduates, although exceptions exist. Conversely, the students most likely to be left with enormous debt and limited job prospects are those who attend for-profits. Students thus emerge from these different institutions even more unequal than before. And for those who attend the schools at the bottom rungs, typically students who hoped that they could improve their lives if they pursued an education, the experience and its impact are an egregious affront to the legacy of expanded opportunity through education.

———

The nation's growing concern about student loan debt and about the value of a college degree blind us to what has really gone wrong in higher education. We are not producing too many college graduates but too few, especially from the bottom three-quarters of the income distribution. Low and middle income Americans are more likely than ever to enroll in college, but only those in the top income group boast strong completion rates. And even among those who do graduate, the growing disparities between different types of colleges and universities further exacerbate inequality. The higher education crisis in the United States points to the demise of opportunity and the emergence of a society with caste-like characteristics. This bodes ill for the nation's economic future, indicating that we will likely fall short in meeting the demand for a highly educated workforce. More fundamentally, if Americans born to privilege are guaranteed to maintain their status but those born on the margins of society have little hope of improving their circumstances, the American dream is called into question. Because education powerfully affects who exercises a political voice, the quality of our democracy itself is at stake.

A SUPPORTIVE PUBLIC

Given that our political representatives in the past supported policies that promoted higher education, we might think that their unwillingness to continue this tradition in recent decades reflects the public's desire to reverse course. But poll after poll shows a consistent level of support. In 2012, 81 percent of Americans told pollsters they agreed that "our government needs to invest more in America's higher education system." This included majorities of both Republicans (64 percent) and Democrats (91 percent). Sixty-six percent also concurred that "cuts in funding to public universities and colleges have lowered our country's standing as a global leader in education."[69]

Over time, Americans' support for government's role in helping students to afford a college education appears to be holding steady and, by some counts, growing stronger. A 1986 poll asked respondents, "If you had a say in making up the federal budget this year, for which of the following programs would you like to see spending increased and for which would you like to see spending decreased?" Thirty-nine percent of Americans answered that "federal spending on financial aid for college students" should be increased; by 1996, that number had increased to 53 percent.[70] In 2007, 70 percent told pollsters that "spending tax money to provide a college education for those who can't afford it is a good idea"; 59 percent of Republicans and 69 percent of high income people concurred.[71] This may reflect the fact that the vast majority of Americans today believe that a college education is important for "finding a good job" (75 percent) and for "having job mobility and success throughout life" (74 percent).[72]

Favorable views about policies that facilitate college-going fit squarely into the broader framework of American public opinion. Scholars have found that while Americans generally express little enthusiasm for a widespread redistribution of wealth or for policies that aim to ensure equal outcomes, they consistently support the idea that everyone, regardless of their social group, should have an equal chance to achieve.[73] For instance, majorities of Americans have consistently agreed over time that "our society should do whatever is necessary to make sure that everyone has an equal opportunity to succeed."[74] Education generally is viewed as a "key ingredient in equality of opportunity and as a public good, not just a benefit of individual citizens," and support for spending on it has grown over time.[75] Graduating from college is viewed, by the vast majority of Americans, as "definitely part of the American Dream," as indicated by 75 percent of respondents in a 2011 study.[76]

Even after the economic downturn that began in 2008, Americans continue to prioritize government financial aid for college students over other spending. Forty-four percent of those responding to a 2011 survey believed that federal spending on financial aid for college students should be *increased*—a greater percentage than those who favored increases for most other options, including health care (41 percent); energy (36 percent); antiterrorism defenses (33 percent); Social Security (41 percent); rebuilding highways, bridges, and roads (38 percent); scientific research (36 percent); economic assistance to needy people (42 percent); military defense (31 percent); government assistance for the unemployed (27 percent); combating crime (39 percent); and environmental protection (36 percent). The only areas that gained higher support for increased spending were "the public school systems" (56 percent) and veterans' benefits and services (51 percent).[77]

In sum, the public has consistently believed that government has a critical role to play in making college affordable and accessible. Americans do not condone developments that place the attainment of college degrees beyond the reach of so many. To understand why the nation has abandoned its policy legacy in higher education, we need to look elsewhere.

THE POLICYSCAPE AND POLITICS

We are left with a puzzle: Americans continue to value higher education and government support for expanded access to college, and yet trends in the United States indicate that the system is in crisis and that it is exacerbating inequality. More puzzling still, higher education policies that functioned quite well in the past still exist, and yet on balance they are failing to achieve the steady upward progress in ensuring opportunity that they did in the mid-twentieth century. When I began this study, I approached this conundrum like a detective who needed to examine possible culprits and rule them out one by one. I considered factors such as the growing role of money in politics; powerful industries promoting their own agenda; and the demise of broad-based civic associations that in the past helped to articulate the voices of ordinary Americans in politics. Each of these, it turns out, has a role in explaining what has become of higher education policy today, but none of them as leading actors. Neither is this a classic story of the challenges posed by traditional features of the US political system, such as the separation of powers and federalism, although those features do complicate reformers' plans in this issue area, as they typically have in American politics. None of these factors by themselves explains much about the changes that have occurred in higher education policy in recent decades.[78]

Policy Effects

The current policyscape, a political landscape cluttered with policies created in the past and dense with the organizations and industries they have promulgated, has fundamentally changed the task confronting elected officials. Policymakers of yesteryear, whether Rep. Justin Smith Morrill of Vermont advancing the land-grant college law in 1862, or

President Lyndon Johnson promoting the Higher Education Act of 1965, faced both the challenges and the opportunities of pioneers. They created such policies at a time when relatively few comparable policies existed. Of course, American public officials—at least since the later colonial period—have always dealt with an established system of higher education and the legacies of existing policies. But today's lawmakers confront circumstances that differ by several orders of magnitude— maintaining a vast, complex array of policies and ensuring that they continue to accomplish their goals effectively. At first blush, this might appear to be an easy task, as if they are merely policy superintendents. Inventive work is typically required, however, to update policies and keep them functioning well.[79]

But remember that every policy, when implemented, produces its own new political dynamics, as discussed in the Introduction. Characteristics inherent in policy design may cause policies to evolve in ways that, decades later, reduce their capacity to achieve their goals to the extent they did earlier on. Policies may foster unintended consequences, for good or ill, that change the resources, power, or incentives of some individuals or organizations, and sometimes—through feedback effects—even alter the political landscape. Policy development may be influenced by other, unrelated policies through lateral effects. Or some combination of these dynamics may ensue. In whatever manner policies develop, their existence creates new work for future political leaders.

Almost everything requires upkeep. Anyone who has bought an older house knows that period charm and beautiful woodwork are usually paired with an outdated kitchen and dangerous wiring. An inventive and able renovator, however, can overhaul the house in a manner that preserves its beauty and the integrity of its structure, while repairing problems and updating features that have not withstood the test of time. Such is the case with public policy—it requires maintenance to continue to function as intended. And in the case of higher education, we will see that once-effective policies have evolved, or the context around them has changed, in ways that have undermined their effectiveness and created obstacles to reform.

So policies today need the attention of good renovators. But what if the renovators face the challenge of not just updating but also convincing a polarized body to support the renovations? One of the unrecognized downsides of the great partisan polarization that has developed in recent years is not its effect on passing new legislation, which has already been the subject of much scholarship, but rather on maintaining and revising older laws. And this has created an atmosphere in which only those with political connections to both parties can bring together enough Democrats and Republicans to support their priorities. Those who can accomplish this feat, more often than not, represent the affluent. In this manner, partisan polarization makes our political system lean toward plutocracy.

The Rise of Polarization

The rise of partisan polarization in Congress is a real phenomenon that has been demonstrated by numerous political scientists.[80] Members vote with and form coalitions with those in their own parties more consistently than they did in the mid-twentieth century, or even as recently as the 1980s, and they are less likely to cooperate across party lines than in the past. As a result, the voting records of members of each party have grown more ideologically homogeneous and distinct from that of the other party: the most liberal Republican in each chamber is more conservative than the most conservative Democrat, with no overlap between them.[81] In addition, everyday proceedings in the Capitol have grown bitter and adversarial, as members resort to the routine use of arcane rules to obstruct the other party at every turn.[82] Take the Senate filibuster, for example: in the 1950s, the minority party used it an average of once per session to prevent an issue from coming to a vote; that number rose to seventeen in the 1980s, and to fifty-four in 2009–2010.[83] Individual senators also make frequent use of their privilege of putting secret holds on bills, preventing them from coming to a vote by objecting to some issue privately to the Majority Leader and insisting on a personal response to it before they will drop the issue.[84] The House began to abide by the so-called Hastert Rule whereby the Speaker would only bring legislation to the floor for a vote if it had the support of the majority of the majority party—a clear impediment to bipartisan lawmaking.[85]

Note too that contemporary polarization has an asymmetric quality: since around 1980, the Republican Party has veered far more sharply to the right than the Democrats have moved to the left.[86] Democrats had already drifted in a more liberal direction in since the 1960s, particularly as they lost the conservative southerners who dominated party leadership posts in the mid-twentieth century. After President Lyndon Johnson signed the historic the Civil Rights Act of 1964 into law, his aide Bill Moyers found him surprisingly melancholy. Johnson offered a prescient rumination: "'I think we just delivered the South to the Republican Party for a long time to come."[87] This transformation did not happen instantly but over time, as most southern Democrats in Congress were replaced by Republicans. Other dynamics were also involved in altering the base of the two parties. For example, since 1980 social conservatives have allied with fiscal conservatives in the GOP while northerners have increasingly identified as Democrats.[88] The Democratic Party today remains a "big tent," a diverse coalition of moderates and liberals. Republicans, by contrast, have lost nearly all of their moderate members, and those who remain in office—whether newly elected or, in many cases, old-timers such as senators John McCain and Orrin Hatch—have become more extreme in their policy positions and voting behavior over time.

Republicans' rightward shift accelerated after the 1994 midterm elections, when the GOP won control of both houses of Congress for the first time since 1954. Speaker Newt Gingrich and other leaders sought to preserve their victory by adopting an aggressive approach to party discipline.[89] The rapid decline in the ranks of moderate Republicans became evident, said former senator Lincoln Chaffee of Rhode Island, in the size of a group who lunched together: "It started in the 80s and 90s with a much more robust lunch of moderate Republicans, but through time fewer and fewer, and it got down—when I got there in the late 90s—to five of us."[90] After the election of Barack Obama, Republicans moved still farther to the right. In Congress the party adopted the priority articulated by Senate Minority Leader Mitch McConnell—to make

Obama a one-term president—by insisting on party loyalty on major policy issues.[91] For those who failed to comply, the Tea Party threatened a primary challenge by an even more conservative candidate; in this way several long-serving Republicans lost their seats.

A polarized body that includes an extreme party has little incentive to care for and upgrade existing policies. Many conservatives in Congress and state legislatures today conclude that the way to deal with policies they don't like is to permit them to deteriorate over time. Congressional Republicans often resort to a "take no prisoners" stance, abdicating responsibility for policy maintenance and in effect ceding the task to Democrats. Democrats often play the role of centrists, but, even when in the majority, they typically lack the internal unity necessary to forge the supermajority needed to pass regular legislation in the Senate today. When they do succeed in legislating, it is without the benefit of engagement with a loyal opposition—one that could offer different approaches to the task. These dynamics occurred in Obama's first term, when the Democratic leadership sought to end bank-based student lending and to use the savings to expand Pell grants. The plan easily passed the House, but a few Democrats in the Senate—under pressure from bankers in their states—equivocated, and the party lacked the sixty votes necessary to withstand a filibuster. Ultimately they managed to bundle the plan with health care reform through special procedures that require only a majority of fifty-one votes in the Senate, and it became law. Republicans, solidly united against the plan, never attempted to shape it in ways that would have made it more satisfactory to them—for example, by considering how to manage either the future fiscal feasibility of Pell grants or administrative issues that might emerge in direct student lending. As this example illustrates, the American public is deprived of the value of a constructive two-party system.

The Rise of Plutocracy

The second political dynamic affecting US policymaking today is the rise of plutocracy, as lawmakers are responsive to the needs of powerful industries and wealthy households, and less so to those of the vast majority of Americans. Scholars have observed that elected officials' votes in recent decades have mirrored the preferences of their wealthy constituents more than others, and that they have taken their cues on various issues from elites and powerful vested interests.[92] Certainly the dramatically rising income of the wealthiest Americans in recent decades give them abundant resources to invest in politics, and so it is unsurprising that their voices would be most audible to elected officials. By the same token, the cost of running political campaigns has risen steeply, leading public officials to rely on their biggest contributors. The amount organizations invest in lobbying, like their spending on electoral politics, has escalated sharply.[93] Although the precise mechanisms are not clear, it appears evident that "money talks" in American politics, as those with wealth manage to overcome the otherwise paralyzing effects of polarization and have their voices heard.

To be sure, neither the role of money in politics nor public officials' tendency to respond to powerful vested interests is a new phenomenon in American politics. Historical examples abound of "rent-seeking" by industries, as they seek to promote, protect, or expand public policies that increase their profits. For example, since at least the mid-twentieth century, the real estate industry and home builders have routinely lobbied to protect the home mortgage interest deduction and other features of the tax code that provide people with an incentive to purchase homes instead of renting.[94] The farm lobby and oil and gas industries regularly exert their influence to protect subsidies that benefit them. In addition, scholars have investigated possible instances of "regulatory capture," meaning that government agencies tasked with regulating the private sector in the public interest are, instead, coopted by those interests. Agencies suspected of catering to the concerns of those they are required to regulate include, for example, the Interstate Commerce Commission, charged with regulating railroads in the nineteenth century and the Securities and Exchange Commission, presently responsible for overseeing the financial sector.[95]

It is a surprising and contemporary development, however, for higher education policy to become in many ways beholden to the interests of the affluent and those motivated by profit. Until the past two decades, American colleges and universities consisted nearly entirely of nonprofit private institutions and public institutions; the for-profit sector involved barely 1 percent of all students. Student aid policies and public institutions helped low and moderate income Americans attend college. Responsibility for reversing that scenario does not belong exclusively to one political party or the other. In the 1980s, most congressional Democrats turned a blind eye as banks and Sallie Mae began to make considerably larger profits from student loans and as the trade schools seized greater opportunities to take advantage of student aid funds. Then by the mid-1990s, Republicans, though ostensibly still the guardians of fiscal conservatism that they were in the Reagan era, abandoned their prior skepticism about the use of government funds by bankers and for-profit colleges, and instead became its ardent defenders. In both instances, they found key Democratic allies who were also willing to channel vast public funds to private entrepreneurs. Meanwhile, on the state level, lawmakers have sanctioned scaling back support for public universities and colleges by refusing to ask those with high incomes to pay more in taxes. The cost of obtaining a college degree has thus been shifted from higher income residents to young people from low to moderate income families, who make up the majority of students at public institutions and are now required to pay much higher tuition. In these ways and others, the political system exhibits plutocratic tendencies as officials act in the service of the powerful and the privileged, sometimes in a bipartisan fashion.

Whereas polarization means that lawmakers leave the policyscape in a state of neglect, plutocracy generates even more invidious consequences. Existing policies offer a treasure trove of opportunities for public officials, even those who were once foes. It can provide them with a source of "patronage," resources to bestow on those whose financial political support and loyalty they seek. This helps to explain the altered stance of congressional Republicans beginning in the 1990s, when after decades of skepticism toward student aid, they suddenly found a political opportunity in it—the means to cater to banks and for-profit colleges that might in turn contribute to their campaigns. In becoming staunch advocates of student aid—as long as it was channeled through these conduits—they abandoned their prior argument that such organizations were "milking" the federal government for profits. Now they championed them as businesses who embodied the spirit of free enterprise. In an approach to governance that would be repeated in other issue areas, they vociferously disparage government spending in general, far more than their predecessors did in the 1980s, while just as forcefully condoning it when it benefits particular groups. The 2013 House version of the farm bill repeated this formula—by eliminating the Food Stamp program for poor people while approving large subsidies for wealthy farmers. The selective support of government programs that aid the affluent epitomizes how public officials can utilize the policyscape for plutocratic ends.

———

When the Occupy Wall Street protestors turned away from their broad focus on inequality and began to concentrate on student debt, their motivation made sense but how they chose to frame the issue undermined their broader intent. By turning the focus to financial challenges facing college graduates during the Great Recession—a group that even then enjoyed employment rates more than three times as high as those of high school graduates—they cut themselves off from the broader issues of inequality that have emerged in American college-going and graduation rates since the 1980s. Nonetheless, their effort to turn attention to financial issues surrounding college attendance was long overdue. After more than two hundred years of promoting higher education, the nation's incapacity to do so effectively in our times represents a departure from a historical legacy that is tied to deeply rooted national values. Despite the fact that college degrees are more linked than ever to opportunities over a lifetime, the American public has been largely silent concerning this radical departure. Tuition increases have elicited student protests on individual campuses, particularly in recent years, but typically those are only small events of limited duration. The public's quietude may owe in part to the fact that what's gone wrong emanates not from just one policy but many. In fact, to understand it, we need to consider both national policies and state-level ones, and spending programs as well as regulatory policy governing schools receiving aid. We will begin by examining developments involving some of the major policies that constitute federal student aid.

CHAPTER TWO

DIMINISHING RETURNS

The Transformation of Federal Student Aid over Time

ON NOVEMBER 8, 1965, PRESIDENT LYNDON B. JOHNSON RETURNED TO his alma mater, Southwest Texas State College, to sign the Higher Education Act into law. He explained that during college, "I worked at a dozen different jobs, from sweeping the floors to selling real silk socks. Sometimes I wondered what the next day would bring that could exceed the hardship of the day before. But with all of that, I was one of the lucky ones—and I knew it even then." Midway through college, he took a job as a teacher at a school in Cotulla, a nearby town. "I shall never forget the faces of the boys and the girls in that little Welhausen Mexican School, and I remember even yet the pain of realizing and knowing then that college was closed to practically every one of those children because they were too poor." Johnson continued, "And I think it was then that I made up my mind that this Nation could never rest while the door to knowledge remained closed to any American. So here, today, back on the campus of my youth, that door is swinging open far wider than it ever did before."[1]

The law Johnson signed that day was the most far-reaching and comprehensive higher education law ever created in the United States. It featured grants for low income students, guaranteed student loans subsidized by government, and an enhanced work-study program, as well as aid for struggling institutions of higher education, including the historically black colleges and community colleges. The president told the audience, "The rest is up to you . . . to the teachers and the citizens and the educational leaders of tomorrow. . . . You are witnessing an historic moment. You should carry the memory and the meaning of this moment with you throughout your life. And when you look into the faces of your students and your children and your grandchildren, tell them . . . that a promise has been made to them. Tell them that the leadership of your country believes it is the obligation of your Nation to provide and permit and assist every child born in these borders to receive all the education that he can take."[2]

Landmark policy achievements in the mid-twentieth century, from the GI Bill through Pell grants, helped the United States become the world's leader in college graduation rates. Together, for a time, these policies breathed life into the American dream. They helped individuals from across the income spectrum attain college degrees. But after 1980 the nation fell away from this successful trajectory. Student aid policies became less effective in expanding the ranks of college graduates across the income spectrum. The problem is not that landmark policies were terminated or abandoned; to the contrary, they remained intact but required maintenance and updating. Just when lawmakers began to ready themselves to engage in these tasks, partisan polarization soared and undermined their ability to do so effectively.

For example, the Higher Education Act (HEA) has been reauthorized eight times since 1965. The number of individual programs has proliferated, and the number of students assisted has exploded—Pell grant recipients, for example, have increased from 567,000 in 1974 to 9,444,368 in 2011–2012.[3] Yet progress has stagnated even while the law has remained intact and appropriations for it have mushroomed over time. Early on, the average student received considerably more in grant aid than he or she borrowed in loans—five times as much in 1975–1976, for example. By the mid-1980s, however, students typically borrowed at least as much as they received in grant aid, and loans and grants have remained at comparable levels ever since.[4] Figure 2.1 shows the developments underlying these trends. In the 1970s, soon after Pell grants were established as part of the HEA, the value of the average grant actually surpassed that of tuition at a four-year public university, providing enough to assist with room and board. After 1980, however, tuition began its long, steady ascent to a rate that is now 3.5 times higher in constant dollars than it was then. Meanwhile, Pell grants stagnated in real terms; by 2011 they covered only 54 percent of the value of tuition, not including room and board.[5] To make up the difference in paying their tuition bills, students took advantage of increased borrowing leniency and took on greater amounts of debt in order to attend college, a trend that has continued since then. As of the 2010 school year, average student loan debt at graduation was $22,011 among borrowers who obtained degrees at four-year public universities, up from $12,157 in 1992, in 2010 dollars.[6] These developments discourage many students from staying in college

FIGURE 2.1. PELL GRANTS FALL BEHIND AND STUDENT BORROWING SOARS AS TUITION RISES AT FOUR-YEAR PUBLIC INSTITUTIONS (2010 DOLLARS)

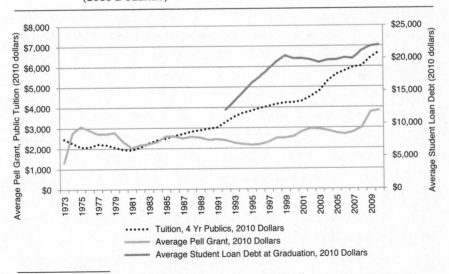

SOURCE: US Department of Education, *2010–2011 Federal Pell Grant Program End-of-Year Report*, http://www2.ed.gov/finaid/prof/resources/data/pell-data.html; *2012 Digest of Education Statistics*, Table 349, http://nces.ed.gov/programs/digest/d12/tables/dt12_349.asp; Mark Kantro-witz, "Debt at Graduation for Bachelor's Degree Recipients (Public Colleges)," FinAid.org.

long enough to graduate, and they promote rising indebtedness among those who remain enrolled. As a result, no longer is Johnson's "door to knowledge" still "swinging open far wider than it ever did before."

What went wrong? How could lawmakers permit these developments? To begin with, we will see that public policies, even after being signed into law, are not static and unchanging; rather, they evolve over time, in part due to effects that they themselves help to generate. Features of policy design made Pell grants more vulnerable to deterioration and student loans more prone to expansion. Unintended consequences also emerged, particularly as government subsidies available to banks provided them with an increasingly attractive incentive to lend money to students. Then in turn, the profitability of the enterprise led the banks to engage in rent-seeking behavior, mobilizing to protect the student loan system and to make its terms all the more favorable to them.

But these policy effects are not constant over time; rather, they vary with the political context, as the capacity or incentive of public officials to update policies waxes or wanes with the political winds, and their preferred strategies fluctuate as well. As the long period of progressive policymaking of the mid-twentieth century came to an end in 1980 and the country shifted in a conservative direction, initially policies ran on autopilot, as lawmakers proved unwilling and unable to work together to update them. By the late 1980s, however, public officials began to make progress toward bipartisan policy maintenance, working "across the aisle" to update the GI Bill and to generate ideas to reform student loans. Such constructive efforts proved to be short-lived, however, as partisan polarization suddenly grew much more extreme, particularly after 1994. Polarization brought an end to the era of landmark lawmaking, and it led to an intensification of conflict over routine maintenance of laws, such as the periodic reauthorizations of the Higher Education Act. These trends are illustrated by Figure 2.2: the lines depict the rising levels of partisan polarization in the House and Senate, and the bars show the growing partisan gaps on votes on higher education laws in the House. Not only did lawmakers cease creating bold new policies on behalf of students, as they had done successfully when polarization hovered at low levels, but

FIGURE 2.2. RISING PARTISAN POLARIZATION AND THE DEMISE OF
LAWMAKING FOR FEDERAL STUDENT AID, 1941–2009

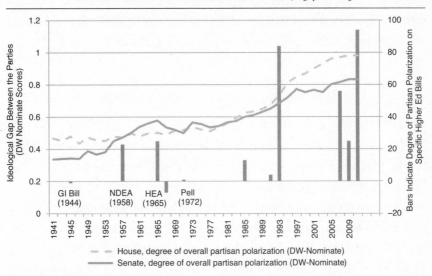

NOTE: For Montgomery GI Bill in 1987, the differences between the percentage of Democrats and Republicans supporting the bill was 0 percent, so it does not appear on the graph.

SOURCE: Voteview.com; author's analysis of roll call votes on twelve major higher education bills.

they also found it much more difficult to perform routine maintenance on existing laws.[7]

Partisan polarization, in turn, ushered in the rise of plutocratic governance. As lawmakers found it increasingly difficult to work together on behalf of their constituents, the policy initiatives that could command sufficient bipartisan support in Congress became fewer and farther between. In the realm of higher education, with few exceptions, those policies that managed to garner support across the aisle in the late 1990s and early 2000s were ones in which powerful moneyed industries or affluent people won out, while the needs of students and their families went largely unmet. These circumstances exacerbated rent-seeking efforts by those who stood to make money from federal student aid, amplifying the voice of vested interests relative to that of ordinary Americans.

Before turning to these recent developments, however, we will first examine the formative period in the mid-twentieth century to see how political leaders at that time managed to overcome divisions and create the higher education policies that govern us still today.

THE POLITICS OF PROGRESSIVE POLICYMAKING

Four dramatic episodes between 1944 and 1972 produced the landmark laws that remain the foundation of federal student aid. Bookended by the first GI Bill, which permitted World War II veterans to attend college at government expense, and by Pell grants, which provided aid to low income college students, these pivotal policy developments helped make educational opportunity available to more Americans than ever before. Certainly they shared the progressive ethos of the New Deal and Great Society, aiming to improve the quality of life for Americans across the income spectrum. Yet they were also rooted in two much older traditions: federal support for higher education and, in the case of the GI Bill, social provision for those who had served the nation in the military.

Building the Foundations of Federal Student Aid

When lawmakers enacted the Serviceman's Readjustment Act of 1944, otherwise known as the GI Bill, they built on a policy legacy that had begun with the federal government's provision of pensions to Revolutionary War veterans and later to those who had fought for the Union in the Civil War. By the World War I era, lawmakers opted for a more restricted approach that would bestow benefits immediately after the war rather than for decades later on: vocational education benefits for disabled veterans only. By the time the Depression hit, jobless, impoverished veterans became an embarrassment to the nation. During World War II, therefore, momentum grew for a package of benefits that was more generous and inclusive than the World War I version, but which, like it, prioritized benefits awarded soon after military service and for a relatively short duration, first and foremost for education and training. The American Legion drew on plans circulating in the Roosevelt administration and Congress, but it expanded their coverage and enhanced their benefits and crowned its own proposal with the popular title, "the GI Bill." Once introduced in Congress, the organization's grassroots network helped speed the legislation's enactment.[8]

The GI Bill contained several benefits, including long-term unemployment benefits and low-interest mortgages, but the most popular component of all was the education and training benefit, including coverage of tuition and stipends for college-bound veterans and those seeking vocational training. Of the 15 million returning World War II veterans, 51 percent took advantage of these benefits, one-quarter of them to attend college or graduate school. They included men like Richard Werner, the son of a chauffeur who became unemployed during the Great Depression. "I doubt very many kids in my [high] school ever considered college," he said, "because in those days you had to be very well off to go . . . so I looked upon a college education [as] about as likely as my owning a Rolls-Royce with a chauffeur."[9] The GI Bill made it possible for Werner to attend Queens College and to become a teacher; millions of others had similar stories. One reputable estimate of the law's impact suggested that GI Bill users acquired 2.7 to 2.9 more years of education than they would have in its absence.[10] In addition, those who used the GI Bill for education or training became more active citizens, joining 50 percent more civic organizations and taking part in 30 percent more political activities in the postwar era than comparable veterans. Lawmakers in later years used the World War II bill as a template to extend educational benefits to veterans of the Korean and Vietnam conflicts, as well. With each version, a higher percentage of beneficiaries used the student aid benefits to attend college.

Just fourteen years after enacting the first GI Bill, national lawmakers created the first student aid law for civilians—the National Defense Education Act of 1958 (NDEA). While its applicability to non-veterans seemed a bold departure, the law, like the GI Bill, was justified on the basis of national defense. During the cold war, when the Soviet Union launched Sputnik—the first artificial satellite—into space, Americans grew concerned that the nation was falling behind and needed to improve its educational system in order to compete. The Eisenhower administration proposed a modest scholarship program for those with exceptional grades and solid backgrounds in math and science.[11] Congressional leaders countered with more ambitious plans. The law that ultimately became enacted stated boldly: "We must increase our efforts to identify and educate more of the talent of our Nation. This requires programs that will give assurance that *no student of ability will be denied an opportunity for higher education because of financial need.*"[12] It featured low-interest federal loans for any needy college student, as well fellowships for graduate study, vocational training, and other provisions more closely tied to concerns about enhancing the nation's expertise in the sciences, engineering, and related fields. The law made student loans available on a gender-inclusive basis, in sharp contrast to the GI Bill, for which mostly men qualified. Consequently it was utilized by large numbers of women and men alike.[13] In effect, the national security rationale brought into being a law that began to treat access to college as a right of American citizenship.

In following years, policymakers sought to build on that concept, and President Johnson, in the wake of President John F. Kennedy's assassination, exercised the political will and skill to turn such ideas into law.[14] Johnson made education—both at the K-12 level and beyond—the cornerstone in his grand domestic agenda for the Great Society and related it to the War on Poverty as well. He pursued it aggressively and accomplished what no other president before him ever had. The original HEA contained provisions that continued the nineteenth-century tradition of directly promoting institutional development, in this case through funds for urban universities and historically black colleges. Its student aid provisions, on the other hand, expanded the twentieth-century approach of financial assistance for individual students. They were contained in the law's Title IV and included need-based grants to be offered through colleges, the Guaranteed Student Loan program, and extensions of the loans and work-study programs in the NDEA.

The most significant reauthorization of the HEA occurred in 1972, when Claiborne Pell, a Democratic senator from Rhode Island, successfully promoted the inclusion of "basic grants" for low income students. Unlike the earlier HEA grants, which were allocated by colleges and universities, these would be made to students directly by government. The grants started at a maximum of $1,400 per year.[15] Renamed Pell grants in 1980, they quickly became a primary vehicle of educational opportunity for young Americans. Besides their far reach in covering the cost of education at a public university, as discussed above, they quickly grew to cover, in the mid-1970s, one-third of the cost of tuition at the average private four-year university.

Surmounting Political Obstacles

Each of these landmark student aid laws was enacted through a typical American political drama, complete with struggles between the executive and legislative branches, House and Senate versions, and congressional allies and their adversaries of various stripes. Those controversies, however, did not turn into the kind of intractable conflicts that have become so common in recent years. First, partisan cleavages, though ever present, did not prevent bipartisan compromise. Especially in the creation of the original GI Bill and the NDEA, both of which occurred before the enactment of civil rights, the most searing divisions formed not so much *between* the parties as *within* them, specifically between friends and foes of federal government involvement. The predominant conflicts pitted the southern Democrats who feared that these policies would promote racial integration against others in the party who more readily embraced educational opportunity. Battle lines were also drawn between northern Catholic Democrats, who insisted on the inclusion of religious colleges, and others who viewed such an approach as a violation of the separation of church and state—in essence, the use of taxpayer dollars to support religious sects.[16] But skillful leadership along with inventive approaches to policy design enabled large majorities to coalesce on behalf of the public good. Second, although vested business interests certainly had a voice in higher education politics in the mid-twentieth century, it was much less persistent and powerful than it has become in more recent decades.

In several instances, leadership provided by progressive southern Democrats—a faction that has all but vanished in American politics—helped guide these policies toward their successful enactment. The NDEA, for example, was promoted by two Democratic congressmen from Alabama hill country, populists Lister Hill and Carl Elliott. They managed to steer it past the objections of both southern segregationists, such as Democratic senator Strom Thurmond of South Carolina, and conservative Republicans, including Barry Goldwater of Arizona.[17]

Proponents of these laws also used policy design in ways that effectively circumvented the contentious issues of the era, most obviously surrounding race. Both the NDEA and GI Bill channeled education aid directly to students, rather than to state and local officials to administer. They included no language about race or, for that matter, religion, gender, or other criteria that institutions of higher education routinely used in the admissions process at that time to disqualify applicants. But neither did they require institutions to alter their behavior in these respects as a criterion for use of federal funds—in effect turning a blind eye to both Jim Crow segregation in the South and the use of religious and gender quotas by many schools in other regions. The GI Bill and NDEA funds could be used by any American—but only at a university or college that would admit her.[18] Within a few years of the NDEA's passage, once the civil rights movement transformed American politics and new laws terminated segregation, these same policies could be used by students at any institution.[19]

By the time Johnson promoted the HEA, he did so in a new political landscape in which fewer challenges emerged from within his own party, but more came from Republicans and the banking industry. The partisan battles over the HEA revolved around an approach to student aid that would become commonplace a half century later: tuition tax credits. Already in the creation of the NDEA, the Eisenhower administration had suggested channeling benefits through the tax code, on the basis that it would involve less direct government intervention and would do more for the middle class. The idea fizzled but reemerged in debates over the HEA. The Democratic leadership insisted that such tax credits would be too costly, resulting in sizable lost revenues annually.[20] Republicans continued to push tax credits, and groups such as the Liberty Lobby, a taxpayer association, made the case for them during congressional hearings.[21] The Johnson administration ardently opposed such alternatives, however, and it prevailed.[22] As we will see, thirty-two years later tuition tax credits became an "idea whose time had come" when they were championed by Democratic president Bill Clinton.

The banking industry's fight over student loans in the HEA might appear to anticipate contemporary politics and the rise of plutocracy, and yet it is more striking for its difference from recent student aid politics than its similarity. Ironically, the banks at that time held a position that was 180 degrees apart from the one they defended staunchly in recent decades: they opposed the creation of the bank-based student loan system, and instead argued for a continuation of direct loans from government, as existed under the NDEA.[23] In the early 1960s, young people who failed to qualify for NDEA loans—whether due to higher family income, grades below the requirements, or areas of study outside of the required fields—had trouble borrowing to attend college. Banks generally refused to lend to them, perceiving them as a high risk because they offered no collateral and because an education—unlike a home—cannot be repossessed. When banks did make such loans, they charged exorbitant interest rates of 11 to 14 percent and as high as 26 percent in some instances.[24] Johnson administration officials had hoped that with government offering to subsidize and guarantee loans, banks would become more willing to lend to students. They also expected that such a plan, by addressing the needs of middle class students, would help diffuse the clamor for tuition tax breaks and solidify support for the HEA.[25] The banking industry favored the idea of government subsidies to lenders but resisted the accompanying regulations—government control over loan rates and terms.[26]

The tactics of the banks and lenders in 1965 provide another sharp contrast to recent times. Back then, they managed to be a thorn in lawmakers' sides, and ultimately won a few adjustments to the student loan plans in the HEA, whereas from 1993 through 2007 the industry powerfully dominated student aid politics. While Congress was considering the HEA, representatives of the American Bankers Association (ABA) and related groups testified at hearings and argued that the proposed student loan policy was unnecessary.[27] Johnson attempted to communicate with the ABA through a personal connection, urging the organization to "lie low," but it refused to back down. Finally, the administration convened banking industry leaders at the White House and granted them some concessions in exchange for their support.[28] Within less than three decades, as an unintended consequence of the HEA, the banking industry had become the major player that dictated the direction of student aid politics, ironically by defending the same system it had resisted in 1965. By then, presidential intervention proved powerless in the face of the industry and in fact, as the Clinton administration would learn, actually heightened the level of conflict.

Johnson's powerful leadership, which helped steer the HEA through the legislative process, would be almost unimaginable today. Certainly his personal commitment to the issue, along with his formidable political skills, served as assets. As historian Robert Dallek writes, the president possessed "an almost mystical faith in the capacity of education to transform people's lives and improve their standard of living."[29] He hailed from the hard-scrabble Texas hill country, and public education had been his own "ticket out of poverty." Johnson became renowned by some—and despised by others—for his legendary ability to cajole and persuade opponents to become supporters of his legislative priorities. But political events also rendered Johnson's job in promoting legislation less onerous than it has been for most other presidents before or since. When he resoundingly defeated Goldwater in 1964, his coattails ushered large majorities of Democrats into Congress, including thirty-eight freshmen who displaced Republicans.[30] By contrast to today, furthermore, members in each party were ultimately willing to support a presidential priority. In the House, the final vote on the conference committee report was 313 to 63, with 75 Republicans in favor and 41 opposed, and 238 Democrats in favor and 22 opposed.[31] This concurrence of developments permitted the enactment of sweeping legislation for educational opportunity.

The Educational Amendments of 1972, which included Pell grants, also emerged through a tumultuous process that ultimately united members of both parties in support of expanded educational opportunity. President Richard Nixon himself showed little interest in shaping this major higher education policy but he did not mount any opposition to the measure.[32] As the chief proponent for the grants, Senator Claiborne Pell could hardly have had a personal background more different than Johnson's. He had been born into wealth as a descendent of the original lords of the manor in Pelham Manor, New York, who had received a royal charter of land from King George III of England.[33] Despite the vast differences in their upbringing, Pell shared Johnson's passion for making higher education more accessible to ordinary Americans, and the grants he promoted epitomized the spirit of inclusivity that infused the original HEA.

The 1972 provisions also created the Student Loan Marketing Association (SLM, otherwise known as Sallie Mae), a government-sponsored private corporation that was intended to help draw more capital into student lending, thus reducing the subsidies government paid for guaranteed loans.[34] Sallie Mae, promoted by Republican Peter Dominick of Colorado, enjoyed bipartisan support as it provided legislators with an acceptable alternative to tuition tax credits.[35] Most of the controversy over the amendments concerned whether to replace the HEA's institution-based grants with direct aid to students, and Democrats stood on both sides of that issue.[36] But ultimately members engaged in logrolling and the amendments passed with strong bipartisan support.

The *Washington Post* heralded the bill as a "true breakthrough for higher education," noting that it "would go a long way toward equalizing opportunity." Noting the high degree of bipartisan effort behind the bill's passing, it cited several individual congressmen and senators of both parties who "have all provided leadership and have all been forced at various times to give in on particular points in order to move the legislation ahead."[37] On final passage, as seen in Figure 2.2, there was no difference in rates of Democratic and Republican support—a far cry from the gulf between the parties on most higher education votes in recent years.

The era of progressive policymaking for higher education featured its share of political controversy. At each juncture, however, political leaders found ways to overcome their divisions and create policies that would broaden the ranks of the college-going for Americans across the economic spectrum.[38] They did so through a willingness to work with those in the other party and to part ways with the recalcitrance of some in their own party. They also found approaches to policy design that enabled them to circumvent impassable obstacles while still acting, as far as was possible, on behalf of the common good. Although powerful vested interests were certainly present in the policy process—enough to warrant presidential attention—nonetheless their influence was far more circumscribed that it would be later on. Strikingly too, the main priority of the banks in this period was for government to leave them alone; before long, by contrast, they would evolve into the most vociferous defenders of the very policy whose creation they had resisted once it became clear that it handsomely benefited their bottom line.

FISCAL CONSERVATIVES GOVERN THE POLICYSCAPE

No sooner had Pell grants been enacted than American politics began to undergo a sea change. The economy, which had been flourishing during the post–World War II period, confronted the oil shocks of the early 1970s and stopped growing at its previously robust pace. American workers struggled as good paying jobs in industry, abundant in previous decades, began to disappear. Family incomes, long on the rise, stalled for many and deteriorated for some. In states and localities across the nation, antitax movements gathered steam. Meanwhile, social conservatives mobilized to protest the vast cultural transformation under way in attitudes and practices regarding marriage, family, and sexuality, epitomized for many by the Supreme Court's 1973 *Roe v. Wade* decision legalizing abortion and by the emergent gay rights movement. Economic and social conservatives gained power as they united their forces, an effort that became crystallized by the 1980 nomination of Ronald Reagan as the Republican Party's candidate for president.[39]

Reagan's election to the presidency signaled the ascendance of a new public philosophy that espoused more limited government and unfettered markets, and a larger, reinvigorated Republican Party in Congress that could help make it a reality. Reagan famously announced in his first inaugural address that "government is not the solution to our problem; government is the problem."[40] That view has emboldened Republicans ever since, gaining traction as they became competitive in a larger share of congressional elections and usurped from Democrats their decades-long dominance. Already in 1980, Reagan's victory ushered a GOP majority into the Senate, bolstering his ability to promote his agenda on Capitol Hill. Although Democrats regained control of that chamber in 1986, nonetheless the new, close margin between the two parties persisted, reshaping political dynamics in Congress. By the 1990s, many Democrats began to frame their own issue priorities in terms of a more conservative approach to governance, with Bill Clinton, for instance, seeking to "end welfare as we know it."

While this history is well known, less well appreciated is the fact that despite the antigovernment ethos that arose during this period, political actors from 1980 right up to the present have governed in a political landscape fashioned by the progressive policymakers of the mid-twentieth century. Its core policies became a force that lawmakers must reckon with, as they decide on funding for them in the course of the annual budget process, oversee their implementation, and in some cases—such as the HEA—periodically update them through routine reauthorization procedures. The policymakers of the mid-twentieth century, in a sense, had "set the table" for their successors, shaping both the political opportunities and challenges they would confront, even as they attempted to govern in a changing political and ideological context. In the realm of student aid, policymakers took different approaches to this task. Reagan, who viewed Johnson's legacy as the epitome of excessive government spending, sought to claw back existing policies but met resistance from Democrats. During his two terms in office, the parties settled into a contentious stalemate that left policies to drift and decay. By the end of the decade, however, they began to find ways to work together and deal with existing policies more constructively.

Reagan entered the White House emboldened by a landslide victory in the Electoral College and immediately set out to dismantle numerous social policies, including several concerning education. As an opening salvo, his 1981 budget proposed substantial cuts in student aid, and it passed through Congress with striking ease given the new Republican majority in the Senate and the presence in the House of a number of southern Democrats—led by Phil Gramm of Texas, who soon after switched to the GOP—who supported his approach. Congress approved several policy changes he endorsed: making eligibility for loans subject once again to a means test; requiring student borrowers to pay a costly origination fee at the time they take out a loan, simply as a means of reducing the deficit; and setting new budget spending limits on Pell grants, which meant that many students who qualified for the full amount would fail to receive it.[41] These changes, which went into effect promptly, signaled the end of what had been a nearly forty-year effort, through higher education policy, to make college-going affordable for a broader cross-section of the American public.

Many Americans did not welcome this new direction. Colleges, students, and parents objected, strengthening the resolve of congressional Democrats to defend the landmark policies they had enacted in the past.[42] Pat Williams, a Democrat from Montana, remarked in 1984, "For a quarter of a century we passed out needed roses. For the past three years we've been passing out the thorns. Our role in the last two years has been to stem the hemorrhaging caused by the [budget cuts imposed in 1981] and Reaganomics."[43] Even with the American public calling on lawmakers to defend existing policies, however, Democrats remained flummoxed about how to govern effectively in a transformed political environment.

Policy Design and the Politics of Drift

Gradually a new normal emerged over student aid, as annual budget skirmishes led to deterioration in the value of Pell grants and, indirectly, to the growth of student loans. Democrats pointed to rising tuition on college campuses and argued for increases in Pell grant levels. Some, such as William D. Ford, sought to make the grants an entitlement— meaning that receiving them would be considered the right of people who fit the eligibility criteria, in this case college students from house- holds below a particular income level—and to make benefits rates tied to the Consumer Price Index, so they would increase automatically with inflation, just like Social Security. Conversely, officials in the Reagan and George H. W. Bush administrations and congressional Republicans, motivated by fiscal conservatism, worried about growing government deficits and sought to scale back Pell grant spending. The compromises between these positions did not decimate the grants, but they took the entitlement option off the table and left benefit rates dwindling in real terms and falling well behind average tuition costs.[44] Politicians in both parties found common ground instead on the expansion of student loans because that only required them to lift borrowing limits and waive restrictions on who could borrow.[45]

At first blush, these policy developments might be summed up as "drift," a term coined by political scientist Jacob Hacker to connote "changes in the operation or effect of policies," due to changes in envi- ronment "that occur without significant changes in those policies' struc- ture."[46] By the late 1980s, colleges had increased tuition, and student aid policies no longer functioned as effectively as they had in the 1970s to assist students in attending and completing college. Yet this transforma- tion did not owe simply to changes in the context *surrounding* student aid policies; it also emanated in part to changes in the policies *themselves*.

Understanding what transpired requires attention to how the poli- cies evolved, and how their internal characteristics and dynamics set in motion by them caused them slowly and gradually to veer off course. These shifts did not occur in a vacuum; rather, they were hastened by the new political context that emerged in the 1980s. During the Reagan administration, it was not only college tuition that changed; the programs within the HEA changed also, and they developed along different trajectories from one another. Since Pell grants lacked cost-of-living adjustments, maintaining their value would have required lawmakers to engage annually in budget deliberations—a long, complicated, and contentious process involving several committees in each chamber—and to coalesce around increased benefits. Amid concerns about rising deficits, lawmakers could more easily forge agreement on student loans—allowing more students to borrow more money and become more indebted—than concur to elevate spending for grants. The expansion of loans offered the "path of least resistance."[47] In other words, innate policy characteristics and the politics of fiscal conservatism *combined* to promote both the escalation of student loan borrowing and the deterioration of grants. This dynamic helps explain why by the mid-1980s students typically borrowed as much or more in loans than they received in grants, reversing the circumstances of just one decade prior. The rise of tuition coupled with policymakers' failure to guide policy development effectively had led to the demise of educational opportunity.

Leaning Toward Bipartisan Reform

Yet within a few more years, some policymakers began to develop new ideas about how to govern the policyscape effectively. Republicans in the late 1980s, attempting to trim the deficit through budget cuts in domestic programs, grew alarmed by the growing size of government subsidies, in the form of hundreds of millions of dollars annually, to banks that made loans to students. Initially Democrats continued to defend these arrangements, still believing as they had in 1965 that banks needed inducements from government if they were to lend to students.[48] By the end of the decade, however, two developments altered their views. First, it became increasingly apparent that student loans had spawned a lucrative industry that yielded financial benefits for numerous banks that made loans, guaranty agencies that insured the loans, and most of all, for government's own creation, Sallie Mae—by then a member of the New York Stock Exchange that boasted assets of $41.4 billion.[49] Second, officials learned of the rapid increase in the percentage of borrowers defaulting on their loans—up from 12.5 percent in 1980 to 14.9 percent in 1990. Government had to pay the cost of these defaults, to the tune of $2.4 billion in 1990, up from just $200 million in 1981. The liberal lion of the Senate, Democrat Ted Kennedy, remarked, "The American taxpayer is not going to support that program unless we get a grip on it."[50] Several in his party began to depart from their long-term support for the program as they became more concerned that it was creating private profits at public expense while jeopardizing many students.[51]

Conservative Democrat Sam Nunn of Georgia fueled further criticism of the existing system when he conducted a yearlong investigation into student loans. Extensive hearings revealed a system that delivered financial benefits to lenders and for-profit schools but served students and taxpayers poorly. Nunn observed, for example, that Sallie Mae made profits of several hundred million dollars annually from the program, and he questioned whether the corporation should be required to offer some portion of those profits to pay for it.[52]

And so in 1991 a bipartisan group hatched plans for "direct lending," an arrangement through which the US Treasury would make loans directly to students' universities and colleges, circumventing the banks and lending agencies and thus eliminating their subsidies. This idea had originated from a policy adviser to George H. W. Bush, his undersecretary of education, Charles E. M. Kolb. In Congress, proponents for an alternative hailed from both parties, including congressmen Tom Petri, Republican of Wisconsin, and Robert E. Andrews, Democrat of New Jersey, and senators Paul Simon, Democrat of Illinois, and Dave Durenberger, Republican of Minnesota.[53] In the 1992 HEA reauthorization, they won provisions for demonstration projects to test the approach. Within a few short years, however, the issue became subject to growing partisan polarization, making the bipartisan spirit of these efforts, not to mention the fact that the idea for direct lending originated with a Republican administration, seem incomprehensible.

Meanwhile, if Congress in the 1980s lacked the capacity to update student aid provisions for civilians, this was not the case when it came to veterans. The Montgomery GI Bill, enacted in 1987, epitomized the most constructive aspects of late-twentieth-century policymaking for higher education. Congressman G. V. "Sonny" Montgomery, a conservative Democrat from Mississippi who had served in World War II, began to champion the idea of a new, permanent GI Bill for the All-Volunteer Force (AVF) in 1980. His aims were twofold: first, to ease the transition back to civilian life for members of the AVF—just as the nation had done for earlier generations of veterans—and, second, to create a recruiting tool for the AVF. The Department of Defense opposed the idea, fearing that such benefits might incentivize service people to muster out in order to pursue education.[54] But Montgomery persisted, arguing that to the contrary, the promise of an education would attract more young people, particularly college-oriented ones, to enlist, thus strengthening the AVF.[55]

A group of fiscal conservatives on both sides of the aisle steered the new GI Bill toward final passage. Besides Montgomery, the most active leaders included Sam Nunn of Georgia, Republican senator John Tower of Texas, and Republican congressman John Paul Hammerschmidt of Arkansas. Montgomery believed that "being 'bipartisan' and truly listening to the views of the minority party takes work; work in the form of time, effort, and earnest commitment," but he also felt that it produced both "ownership" of the outcome and a better product. He recognized that this made for a messy and cumbersome legislative process, which he described as "slower than a snail on crutches."[56] It took seven years and involved consideration in multiple committees in both chambers and a total of nineteen congressional hearings. Montgomery worked assiduously to facilitate that process, acting, in the words of one staffer, as "a calming force because—based on what I saw—both sides of the aisle respected him. He typically was like an island of reason in a sea of dispute when things boiled over."[57] Such bipartisan efforts meant that when the bill was finally enacted in the House, only two members in the entire chamber voted against it; absent partisan divisions, it does not even register on Figure 2.2.

The Montgomery GI Bill demonstrates that even in the altered political environment, it was possible for members to work together across party lines and create major legislation. Perhaps it shows, at the same time, that such cooperation occurred only when it could be directed to the compelling case of benefits for those who had been willing to put themselves in harm's way on behalf of the nation. Even then, it did not occur quickly or easily. It took Sonny Montgomery's tenacious leadership to bring members together. Nonetheless, in an era when lawmakers strained to adjust to their jobs of maintaining the policyscape, the enactment of the Montgomery GI Bill, which performed ably for years to come, was a noteworthy achievement.

These bipartisan initiatives demonstrated a path along which contemporary policymaking could have developed, not only in the realm of student aid but in other issue areas as well. It involved both Democrats and Republicans recognizing the value of existing programs and their constituents' reliance on them, and uniting to maintain, modernize, reform, and upgrade them as needed. Rather than one party taking all responsibility, both parties engaged in the process, and the country benefited from the broader array of viewpoints and the deliberation, contestation, and give-and-take that was brought to the policy process as a result. On student aid for civilians, this approach was epitomized by the way in which Democratic senator Ted Kennedy and Republican senator Nancy Kassebaum worked together as chair and ranking majority member of the Senate Education and Labor Committee. They held extensive hearings on issues and used strategies to keep senators present and engaged in deliberation; they worked together to enlist equal numbers of sponsors on bills from both parties; they coordinated efforts to each dissuade colleagues in their own party from adding amendments to a bill that could kill it; and they reached out to the House in an effort to garner cooperation.[58] From the vantage point of 1990, it would have been reasonable to anticipate that governance of the policyscape over the next quarter century would follow these general patterns. The moment of such constructive bipartisan policy efforts would prove, however, to be short-lived.

Showdown

In 1993, newly elected president Bill Clinton took the idea of the bipartisan reformers and sought to replace the current system of student
loans with direct lending. The controversy that ensued evolved into a
showdown. Lenders—who had been privileged by federal policy since
1965—mobilized in full force to protect their profit-making interests.
The Consumer Bankers Association took the lead in the fight, bringing
representatives from more than ninety banks from all over the country
to Washington, DC, and sending them forth on Capitol Hill with book-
lets listing members of Congress serving on committees responsible for
direct lending legislation and offering tips on how to approach them.[59]
Sallie Mae launched a major public relations campaign to defend the
existing system.[60] The banks and lenders promoted campus activism
to oppose direct lending, in some cases hiring students to initiate such
efforts.[61] Ultimately Congress enacted a weakened version of Clinton's
plan, adopting direct lending but only on a limited basis and at a slower
pace than its proponents had hoped.[62]

When the dust settled, it became apparent that the direct lending
battle had been a turning point in student aid politics and indicated a
broader transformation under way in American politics. It ended the
fragile bipartisanship in higher education policy that had survived the
Reagan and George H. W. Bush eras. It also signaled the beginnings
of plutocracy in this issue area, of policymaking driven by the fierce
mobilization of an industry that benefits from government spending,
and the ardent efforts by members of Congress to represent it. Neither
student aid politics nor American politics have been the same since.

THE RISE OF POLARIZED AND
PLUTOCRATIC GOVERNANCE

As recently as 1992, policymakers seemed to be on the brink of constructively governing the policyscape in the higher education arena.
Democrats no longer mounted an unbending defense of the policies

their party had created; they began to recognize that some components had gone astray and needed to be reformed. Republicans blended their fiscal conservative leanings with concern for managing government programs effectively and efficiently. Plenty of potential existed for cooperation between these two positions, and some in each party were discovering how to engage in such efforts. After the direct lending fight in 1993, however, this moment of political possibility would be replaced by strident polarization on one issue after another. And the lenders' powerful role in that struggle turned out to be a preview of what was to follow, as they came to dominate the debate over student aid policy—dictating developments concerning student loans and consuming so much of policymakers' attention that consideration of other policy alternatives could not even receive a hearing. With lenders setting the policy agenda, plutocracy flourished as the twenty-first century began.

The 1994 midterm elections gave Republicans a majority in both chambers of Congress for the first time in forty years, and they seized the opportunity to solidify their gains. The House elected as Speaker Newt Gingrich, whom many credited as the intellectual and organizational force behind the GOP victory. He adopted an aggressive new leadership style, using congressional rules and procedures in unorthodox ways to strengthen the party's hand. For example, he abandoned the traditional approach of selecting committee chairs based on seniority, and in some instances he passed over members perceived to be too accommodating to Democrats and selected more conservative leaders instead. The party advanced a far-reaching policy agenda, the Contract with America, aiming to overhaul core aspects of domestic programs and adopt term limits and a balanced budget amendment.[63]

This moment turned out to be a political juncture that was just as consequential as 1980, not least because partisan polarization escalated rapidly. Polarization had already been on the rise in the Senate since 1980, which had been losing the comity for which it had long been known. Procedures such as the filibuster were increasingly being used to prevent bills the minority disliked from coming to a vote. After 1994, both chambers grew markedly more divisive.[64] But while these generalities have been much analyzed, the concrete implications of such divergence for the policy process have not been. Figure 2.3 reveals the implications for higher education policy by showing across time the rise of the average differences in party support for amendments to bills to reauthorize the Higher Education Act and other higher education bills. While elected officials have a large incentive to support final passage of education bills, votes on amendments can be both more divisive and more consequential for the actual content of bills. Figure 2.3 demonstrates that it has become more and more difficult, in both the House and Senate, to forge bipartisan cooperation around student aid.

Between 1995 and 2008, a dramatic change occurred in the content of bills put forward and the substance of policy developments. As polarization worsened, the government became more dysfunctional and less capable of managing existing policies effectively. But it's not simply that polarization led to stalemate and inaction. Instead,

FIGURE 2.3. Growing Partisan Gaps in Support for Amendments to Higher Education Laws, 1971–2008

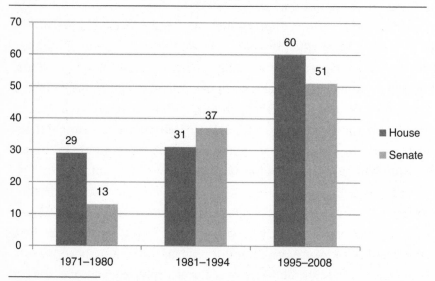

Source: Author's congressional roll call vote analysis of all amendments to reauthorizations of Higher Education Act of 1965 and other higher education bills. N = 65 in the House; N = 26 in the Senate.

plutocratic governance filled the void, as only moneyed interests managed to overcome the gaping partisan divisions and to compel bipartisan cooperation—on behalf of the privileged.

Rent-Seeking Reciprocity

The new, more strident, and highly energized GOP leaders would take a vastly different approach to the policyscape than had the fiscal conservatives who dominated their party in prior years, and this would terminate hopes for constructive bipartisan policy maintenance. A number of moderate Republicans had served in Congress in the 1980s and early 1990s, in many cases playing leadership roles, and they typically sought to manage public programs efficiently and effectively. Since 1995, these individuals have all but disappeared, whether through retirements or by changing their orientation to governing. Without them, the new Republican Party has evolved in a Janus-faced manner. In its public persona, the party now exhibits little interest in managing public programs, speaks vociferously about defunding and dismantling them, and aims to do so in most instances. Simultaneously, however, the GOP also practices what could be termed the art of conservative state building, aiming to use federal power and government funds to pursue selected policy goals in a manner that their more fiscally conservative forebears would not have allowed. They still speak the language of deficit hawks and praise limited government, but belying such talk, they have aggressively cultivated as political allies interest groups whom they defend and whose financial assistance they seek. This strategy, termed the K Street approach in reference to the area of Washington where most lobbyists' offices are congregated, meant that GOP leaders encouraged favored industries to hire party loyalists in key lobbying positions, and promised in turn that their demands would be heard on Capitol Hill.[65] Serving those entities became integral to their policy agenda, and made them willing to channel public resources to them, with the expectation that the industries would reciprocate with campaign contributions. The policyscape provided political opportunities for them to develop such relationships.

In this new political environment, Republicans ceased criticizing bank subsidies as excessive government spending and turned into staunch advocates of the bank-based system, redefining student lending as a "private" or "market-based" approach. Most Democrats, by contrast, became increasingly disturbed by the large profits lenders were gaining at the expense of students and the American public and stopped defending the industry. By the end of the 1990s, the two parties had reversed the positions they held on the issue in the previous decade. Further, indicative of growing polarization, the gap between their stances widened as more Democrats lined up in support of direct lending and Republicans unified around better terms for the lenders. With Republicans in control of both houses of Congress and then by 2001 of the White House, the lenders' star was on the rise.

Republicans in particular, as well as a few Democrats, became accomplices to student lenders as they sought to facilitate what could be termed rent-seeking reciprocity. Typically interest groups are assumed to initiate relationships with public officials as a means to pursue policy developments that favor them. But what was new in student aid politics after 1994 was the extent to which politicians took the initiative to reach out to powerful groups. They did so by finding ways to capitalize on existing policies—both by offering lenders their advocacy in the policy process and by requesting campaign donations from them. Not only was an industry seeking rents, but elected officials—in a codependent fashion—sought to extract benefits themselves from the relationship. The bond between the lenders and the GOP tightened.

The shifting terrain of student aid politics became manifest in the 1998 reauthorization of the Higher Education Act, which offered increased financial incentives to banks to engage in student lending.[66] The Consumer Bankers Association lobbied Congress extensively, threatening that its members would cease lending unless Congress applied a more favorable subsidy formula. Months of partisan wrangling ensued as Republicans pushed for higher subsidies for the lenders and Democrats argued against them. Finally House chairman Buck McKeon, ranking minority member Dale Kildee, and Clinton administration officials arrived at a compromise, though the White House later complained that the outcome—assuring lenders rates of 7.96 percent—was too generous.[67]

Policymakers had to find in the bill the hundreds of millions of dollars required to finance the increased subsidies for the banks, and in a little noticed maneuver in conference committee, they placed the burden on student borrowers: those who declared bankruptcy could no longer discharge their student loan debt.[68] This change put student loan debt in a category different from credit card balances and nearly all other forms of debt, which can be waived in bankruptcy, and comparable only to such obligations as child support. It slipped under the radar of public awareness. Democrats, on the defensive given the recent revelation of Clinton's affair with a White House intern, also rallied in support of the bill on final passage. As McKeon explained, "They want a signing ceremony badly. If you were President Clinton, would you want to sign a higher education bill or talk about Monica Lewinsky?"[69]

While the student loan industry benefited from the energetic new advocacy Republicans provided, it also gained from the occasionally plutocratic tendencies of many Democrats. This became evident in the Clinton administration's effort to privatize Sallie Mae. Executives for the government-sponsored enterprise had been urging privatization since the fracas over direct lending in 1993. In 1996, Clinton administration officials quietly permitted Sallie Mae—which had become tremendously profitable, worth $45 billion and with stocks traded on the New York Stock Exchange—to retire its federal charter and to reorganize as a private company.[70] Remarkably, they neglected to require that in the process the organization, which owed its existence and profits to government, make substantial contributions back to the federal budget.[71] One long-term lobbyist on higher education issues explained that Clinton, as a centrist Democrat, wanted to obtain credit for pursuing privatization, and Sallie Mae appeared to be a reasonable locus for such efforts.[72] Even after privatizing, Sallie Mae continued to benefit from government subsidies and the government-guaranteed status of its loans.[73] Such support permitted it to expand the scope of its activities, for instance to include loan servicing and guarantor services, such that it increasingly dominated the student loan market and was able to buy out several smaller lenders.[74]

Not surprisingly, as tuition continued to climb and grants dwindled, student borrowing soared and lending generated bigger profits than ever. Sallie Mae had become the nation's largest student loan company, managing more than $126.9 billion for over 10 million borrowers, and it employed 12,000 individuals.[75] A CNN report noted that between 1995 and 2005, Sallie Mae's stock returned nearly 2,000 percent, compared to the S&P 500's average 228 percent gain, and that between 1999 and 2004, CEO Al Lord received $225 million in total compensation.[76] As of 2006, the next CEO, Thomas J. Fitzpatrick, was the most highly compensated CEO in the nation according to the *Washington Post*, gaining compensation (salary, bonus, stock awards, etc.) of approximately $37 million.[77]

As the volume of student loans escalated, lenders grew even more active in politics to defend their gains, creating several new organizations to advocate on their behalf. Only one of their major organizations that lobbied to protect student loans, the Consumer Bankers Association, predated their enactment in the HEA; another had followed two years afterward, the National Council of Higher Education Loan Programs. In the 1990s through 2000, additional associations formed to represent lenders' interests in Washington, DC: the Education Finance Council, the Student Loan Serving Alliance, and America's Student Loan Providers.

Many lending organizations employed their own lobbyists. In 2006 College Loan Corp maintained twenty-six registered lobbyists; Sallie Mae, eighteen; and the Education Finance Council, eight. In addition, some lenders hired lobbying firms to advocate on their behalf. Even accounting only for its in-house lobbying costs of $1.6 million, Sallie Mae ranked third in its spending on lobbying in 2006 among all finance and credit companies: it spent less than Visa and HSBC Bank, but more than MasterCard and American Express.[78] By 2007, it outspent all other finance and credit companies in lobbying, devoting over $5 million to such activities.

The industry also commenced involvement in campaign financing, an activity that distinguished it from the trade and professional associations that represent traditional universities and colleges and their employees. Sallie Mae first created a political action committee in 1998. By 2006, it emerged as the top donor within the entire finance and credit industry; fellow student lender Nelnet took fifth place.[79] Relative to all other finance and credit companies, Sallie Mae ranked as high as fifth and as low as eighth in the generosity of its soft money contributions. Sallie Mae's company leaders and their spouses also made substantial individual contributions to candidates.[80]

The precise effect of such spending on lawmakers' advocacy on behalf of an industry is difficult to pin down, but evidence indicates that Republican leaders at least conveyed to lenders that they would protect their interests and that they took action to do so. House Education and Labor Committee chair John Boehner had received $172,000 from student lenders in 2003 and 2004. In 2005, soon after Hurricane Katrina, Republicans put forward a budget reconciliation plan that angered lenders by imposing stringent new origination fees on loans as a means of making more government funds available for rebuilding New Orleans and the gulf coastal region. In a speech to the annual meeting of the Consumer Bankers Association, Boehner appeared to assure the industry, "Know that I have all of you in my two trusted hands . . . I've got enough rabbits up my sleeves to be able to get us where we need to."[81] Shortly thereafter, the final bill emerged and it contained sharply reduced penalties for lenders as well as some other features they had been seeking.

Reckless Responses

Meanwhile, President Clinton took it upon himself to promote the approach to student aid that Republicans had been advancing since the Eisenhower era: tax breaks to offset families' college tuition payments. Previously, Democratic presidents Lyndon Johnson and Jimmy Carter had fought the idea, arguing that it would not expand access to college and would not be an effective use of resources. But in 1996, President Clinton—in the midst of his campaign to win reelection—took the initiative to move it onto the policy agenda.[82] This development surprised both policy experts in the organizations representing institutions of higher education and long-term Hill staffers who worked on student aid; none of them had been promoting the approach or thought much of it. Rather, it was campaign manager Dick Morris who hatched the plan to promote the tax credits upon finding that the issue polled well in a public opinion survey. When he told Clinton about it, the president grew excited, envisioning it as a policy that could help encourage more Americans to attend college.

The president's advisers were not enthused. As Morris reported in his own account, national economic adviser Laura D'Andrea Tyson and Treasury secretary Robert Rubin "felt it was opening the Treasury door to pass out goodies before the election." Rubin "didn't see the point of giving the aid through a tax cut or credit," as he believed that benefits channeled through the tax code are not well targeted to those in need and are an "inefficient way of providing help." He said to Morris, "If we want to help people go to college, let's just increase the scholarship program." Morris replied, "Politically, people want us to downsize government, so we are developing ways of cutting taxes but achieving social good at the same time." He added that more scholarships would "add to bureaucracy, that we needed to seize the public's imagination." But "Rubin dismissed the idea as 'political'—the most venal word in his vocabulary."[83]

Morris acknowledged that the primary motivation for the tuition tax credits was political: it provided a way to trump tax-cut plans that Republican opponent Bob Dole would put forth. "'Politically,' I argued, 'we need a tax cut to beat the tax cut we expect Dole to propose. We can't outbid him because we're not willing to cut taxes without identifying how to pay for them. But a college-tuition tax credit will be a whole lot cheaper and a lot more attractive than an across-the-board tax cut.'"[84]

Most of the president's advisers continued to cast doubt on the plan, but after one of them, Gene Sperling, prepared a memo defending the idea, Clinton embraced it. He announced it during his commencement address at Princeton University, and it became a major tenet of his reelection campaign.[85] Soon after his victory at the polls, Clinton delivered on his promise. The Taxpayer Relief Act of 1997 included both the

Hope Scholarship tax credit and the Lifelong Learning tax credit, the first aimed at full-time students and the latter at those taking courses less than half-time. Each permitted families to deduct up to $1,500 per eligible student annually from their taxes.

The lack of partisan acrimony surrounding the tuition tax policies sets them apart from other types of student aid in the past twenty years. Once created, they quickly accounted for nearly as much total aid as Pell grants—remarkable after all of the years Democrats had spent struggling unsuccessfully to increase spending for that program. They did so by placing an immense drain on federal resources: already in 2000, they cost $5.4 trillion in lost revenues, 71 percent of federal outlays in Pell grants that same year.[86] Studies by economists show that tuition tax credits fail to expand access to higher education; rather, they permit students who were already planning to attend college to attend more expensive institutions than they would otherwise, and they give colleges an incentive to increase tuition prices.[87] Tuition tax policies can be termed a "reckless response" to the nation's higher education crisis: expensive and ineffective at best and counterproductive at worst.

Such policies fit into the larger patterns of policymaking over the past quarter century, as lawmakers have found it far more politically expedient to channel new social benefits through the tax code than to package them as direct grants from government. They are more palatable to the public, as Morris observed and scholars have found, likely because they give the appearance of reduced taxes.[88] They also face fewer hurdles in Congress: after receiving approval from a tax committee in each chamber, they are typically tucked into a large tax bill and adopted with relative ease. Unlike direct spending approaches such as Pell grants, they do not face the multistage budget process—a formidable gauntlet at the best of times and all the more so as polarization has increased.[89] From an accounting perspective, there is no difference in the impact of direct spending versus policies run through the tax system: either one reduces what's available in federal coffers. And both qualify as social policies: they are targeted to a particular group that policymakers deem worthy of assistance, and not to other Americans—who effectively pay the cost.

Political scientist Christopher Howard terms such policies, collectively, as the "hidden welfare state," and they are the biggest share of what I have termed "the submerged state."[90] As of 2012, their cost surpasses $1.1 trillion dollars.

Once tuition-related tax expenditures were in place, they were easily expanded. When George W. Bush became president, he endorsed an enlargement of them in the Tax Relief Act of 2001. That same law also expanded another innovation from the 1997 law, tax benefits for education savings plans, which became known as Coverdell Education Savings Accounts. These benefits permitted parents with incomes up to $220,000 to contribute up to $2,000 per child per year to a college saving account for each child. Funds may later be withdrawn from it for educational expenses, and they are not subject to income tax.[91] These new innovations in student aid policy not only fail to expand access to higher education, but they also shower extra benefits on the affluent. Economist Susan Dynarski finds that their advantages rise with income. Households with the highest incomes and tax rates gain the most from such programs in both absolute and relative terms.[92]

In sum, these reckless responses of tuition aid through the tax code, though so easily enacted and expanded upon, fail to broaden the ranks of college graduates and they rob the US Treasury of funds that could be used far more effectively to make college degrees attainable. They exacerbate the growing tendency of federal student aid to become more costly than in the past but less effective in expanding college graduation rates and mitigating inequality.

Voices Heard and Unheard

As lawmaking around student aid policy seemed to become increasingly dominated in the late 1990s and early part of the twenty-first century by the concerns of business interests and the affluent, the voices of ordinary Americans were barely audible. Only two mass membership organizations speak on behalf of college students: the United States Student Association (USSA) and the Public Interest Research Group (PIRG).

Both have staff and offices in Washington, DC, as well as members and chapters on college campuses. Between 1994 and 2007, they advocated for a shift to direct lending, but their message was not heeded. Conspicuous by their absence were the voices of other Americans—the parents of students, potential students, and borrowers—who lack organizations that could speak on their behalf about student aid matters.

The most visible actors on student aid policy have long been the numerous trade associations that represent universities and colleges, and a vast number of professional organizations speak for groups of employees associated with them. Most of these groups maintain offices in the same building—the National Center for Higher Education at 1 Dupont Circle. The oldest among them, the National Association of State Universities and Land-Grant Colleges, began in 1887 in response to the Morrill Act. The American Council on Education, founded in 1918, hired staff in the 1970s to engage in policy analysis and governmental relations, and by the 1980s it coordinated such efforts on behalf of several of the other major higher education trade associations so that they could speak to Congress with a unified voice.[93] Meanwhile, many public and private nonprofit universities and colleges hired their own lobbyists to advocate on their behalf.[94]

But while these entities—collectively, the higher education establishment—often take positions that overlap with students' interests, they failed to stem the tide as the amount of student aid grew increasingly inadequate. This may owe in part to the fact that they are, first and foremost, trade associations, which exist to represent their members' interests. The primary concern of these organizations is with the sustainability of the institutions they represent, not broader issues such as access to college or college completion rates. They have put a priority on preserving their member institutions' strength and autonomy, rather than pursuing broader goals and new approaches. In addition, several organizational representatives complained that their associations have failed to act together in a coordinated manner, becoming more reactive than proactive.[95] One lobbyist explained, "I think the higher education associations are pretty good at blocking things that we believe would be harmful to the institutions. It is not clear how successful we are at making things happen that we really want to make happen."[96] Amplifying this critical view, one assessment of the higher education lobby, published in *Washington Monthly,* was subtitled, "Welcome to One Dupont Circle, Where Good Education-Reform Ideas Go to Die."[97] And meanwhile, these organizations' power became outgunned by that of the lenders, who have hired more lobbyists and engaged in an activity that One Dupont Circle has collectively shunned—campaign financing. The policyscape, as it developed amid polarized politics, energized especially the active proponents of the status quo; opponents remained largely unorganized and voiceless.

POLICIES OFF COURSE

In the early years after the enactment of the federal student aid policies, Lyndon Johnson's dream—that the nation would "provide and permit and assist every child in these borders to receive all the education that he can take"—seemed on the way to being realized as college graduation rates climbed and the ranks of those attending became more diverse. In recent decades, however, federal student aid policies yielded unforeseen effects that have undercut their success.

Problems emerged first because of policy design effects that made student loans more easily sustainable than Pell grants, particularly under changing political circumstances. As a result, as tuition soared, policies evolved to become less helpful to those with low incomes while leaving middle income students increasingly in debt. For the banks, meanwhile, student lending—the policy they had opposed in 1965—became highly lucrative, and they mobilized politically to protect the arrangements from which they had benefited.

For a brief period, it seemed that policymakers might work effectively across the aisle to address these problems and manage the policyscape effectively. Reform ideas circulated in the late 1980s and early 1990s and won some support across the aisle. But then polarization widened further, and it brought a close to such possibilities.

Instead, the unintended consequences of policies became a new form of political spoils, useful to public officials and interest groups alike. By the late 1990s, lenders with soaring profits provided a ready source of cash to fund the campaigns of public officials who were negotiating in an increasingly polarized and competitive political climate. Meanwhile, lawmakers who could agree on little else came together for the purpose of promoting tuition tax credits. These policies, which scholars have deemed ineffective in promoting opportunity, reduced federal revenues, leaving less available to fund programs that could make a difference.

Student aid policies needed public officials who could revise, update, and reform them, but instead polarization and plutocracy, in combination, ran them farther off course. Vibrant political participation by young Americans might have helped to call attention to the crisis, but their voices were muted and few and far between on Capitol Hill. In their absence, rent-seeking reciprocity and reckless responses by policymakers ensued, and the dream of educational opportunity—articulated so clearly by Lyndon Johnson when he signed the Higher Education Act into law—faded from view.

Meanwhile, it was not only the student lenders who sought to benefit from federal student aid, but also an emergent group of colleges that operated for the purpose of making profits. They saw, in the largesse of student aid, a golden opportunity.

CHAPTER THREE

"Unscrupulous Profiteers"

The Struggle to Reform the For-Profit Colleges

US Congresswoman Maxine Waters, who has represented the poorest district in Los Angeles for over twenty years, learned about for-profit colleges from her constituents. "I have seen young person after young person who simply wanted to get trained for a trade, for a job, get ripped off," she explains.[1] Waters first became aware of the problems caused by "trade schools" or "proprietary schools" back when she was serving in the California State Assembly during the 1980s. At that time, she created a job training program for unemployed young adults in public housing who had, she felt, "been dropped off of everyone's agenda." She discovered that most of them had at some point been recruited into a private postsecondary school, which typically seized their student loan money and left them in debt but did little else, offering inferior instruction and sometimes not even holding actual classes. When she tried to introduce legislation to regulate the schools, she quickly encountered powerful resistance from the industry.[2]

Once elected to the US Congress in 1991, she resumed her efforts at the national level, introducing an amendment to the 1992 reauthorization of the Higher Education Act that required for-profits to obtain at least 15 percent of their funds from sources other than the Higher Education Act. The concept, borrowed from a long-standing rule used in the implementation of the GI Bill, was based on the principle that federal student aid should not be granted to a school unless at least a minimum threshold of its students paid for tuition themselves, indicating some modicum of program quality. "I and some of the members of the Congressional Black Caucus have taken on this issue because our communities have been harmed," she said. Referring to the schools as "a rip-off," she noted that for many of her constituents "the jobs that were promised were never forthcoming and (the students) ended up having to pay back the government those loans."[3]

Although the Waters amendment won approval, over the next two decades the for-profit colleges continued to exploit federal student aid funds, and the stakes involved grew bigger than ever. Congress actively permitted this development by loosening the few regulatory restrictions that had been applied to the sector, including the Waters rule, thereby making it easier for the schools to use more federal funds than ever before. It was at this juncture that total for-profit enrollment soared from only 1.6 percent of all students in higher education in 1993 to 9.6 percent in 2010.[4] It was also in this period that fourteen of the schools mushroomed into multistate businesses, and when investors took notice, they became publicly traded on Wall Street and profits soared. For instance, the Apollo Group, owner of the University of Phoenix, the largest among them, earned revenues that grew from $12 million to $1.34 billion between 1994 and 2003, as stock prices skyrocketed from $0.72 per share to $63.36 per share.[5] Meanwhile, the industry's cost to the federal government exploded, and its share of student loan defaults rose to nearly half of the total—even as evidence accumulated that the schools often violated existing federal regulations and left a good share of their students worse off than if they had never enrolled. Yet aside from Waters, few in Congress questioned how things could have gone so far wrong.

The weak record of the for-profit colleges is no longer news, but still to be explained is how they became so reliant on the federal government, even as they generated substantial private profits. This raises questions about how they emerged in the first place, and why they have continued to thrive—and gain substantial federal support—despite poor results. Even more perplexing, why have bipartisan efforts to regulate them in the past been replaced in recent years—in the midst of sharp political polarization—by bipartisan efforts to deregulate them? The answers to these questions help explain how existing policies have collided with polarization and plutocracy, and why the results have further stratified higher education and spurned the hopes of the least advantaged.

When lawmakers in 1944 and again in 1972 designed public policy to make federal money available to students seeking technical and vocational training, it was hardly their ambition to provide a bonanza for entrepreneurs. Yet time and again, existing policies yielded unintended consequences as opportunists seized the chance to use student aid money to reap handsome profits. As lawmakers made it easier for students to borrow more in student loans during the 1980s, it exacerbated the situation further. With each new generation of student aid to the for-profits, the emergence of problems eventually stimulated efforts at reform, to create restrictions that would enable the policies to function more effectively. As recently as 1992, Congresswoman Waters was a member of a bipartisan trio trying to rein in the excesses of the schools.

But no sooner had she and others accomplished modest policy changes than circumstances changed completely, and the for-profit colleges engaged in greater abuse of federal funds—and unsuspecting students—than ever before. Beginning in the early 1990s, forces materialized for a "perfect storm" that unleashed unprecedented profitability for the schools. At its center stood a new generation of entrepreneurs who led the for-profits, and alongside them, a newly emerging technology, the Internet, in which they recognized a means to revolutionize higher education and a business opportunity to be seized. Changes roiling the American political scene—as it lurched toward polarization and plutocracy simultaneously—helped make more public resources available to the for-profits than ever. A reinvented Republican Party dispensed with its reservations and became the sector's ardent defender. Meanwhile, many Democrats remained steadfast in their support, still convinced that the schools provided meaningful opportunities for low income and minority students. With this bipartisan alliance doing its bidding, the industry found itself one of the most successful of the era.

The origins of today's for-profit education sector lie in the nation's historic tradition of providing public support for veterans. To understand how it evolved to its present state, therefore, we must begin right after the end of World War II.

THE GI BILL SPURS TRADE
SCHOOLS THAT MILK THE SYSTEM

Today the original GI Bill is best remembered for providing financial aid to veterans who attended traditional colleges and universities, but more than two and a half times as many, 5.6 million, pursued vocational and on-the-job training, primarily by attending what were then called "trade schools." They gained skills in areas ranging from construction and architecture to auto mechanics, refrigeration, electrical work, pipefitting, glasswork, barbering, tailoring, and numerous others. The GI Bill was not the first federal policy to promote advanced education for Americans not seeking to attend a traditional college. Progressive Era reformers had achieved modest beginnings with the Smith-Hughes Act of 1917 and the vocational rehabilitation services offered to disabled World War I veterans beginning that same year. The World War II policy dwarfed the earlier ones in terms of both the number of students it reached and the amount of spending.[6] It reaped highly positive results, making advanced education accessible to far more Americans than would have attained it otherwise, and better jobs and higher income followed.[7]

But the nation's first large experiment in providing federal aid to trade schools quickly revealed the difficulties that can arise when entrepreneurs seize opportunities to profit at government expense. After the law was created, thousands of new schools and programs suddenly sprang into existence and began offering training to veterans with GI Bill benefits; almost instantly their numbers increased more than threefold, from 2,400 to 8,000.[8] The development of this new sector of advanced education is a classic example of an unintended consequence of public policy—a result that lawmakers had not set out to achieve—and it introduced unexpected implementation issues. While many of the new schools were reputable, reports emerged of fly-by-night ones that offered shoddy training and appeared to exist only, in the words of Senator Paul Douglas (D-IL), to "milk the system."[9] Some rewarded veterans with a bonus on enrollment. Others inflated their tuition prices to take advantage of the full amount the federal government would cover. By the late 1940s, the Veterans Administration, aiming to limit such abuses, began to require the schools to file financial statements, which exposed the fact that 58 percent of the programs engaged in price gouging, charging excessive, unfair rates for their training.[10] Congress intervened in 1950 with new legislation, introduced by Republican senator Robert Taft of Ohio, that tightened up requirements for such schools.[11] But in 1952, when a special House committee chaired by Texas Democrat Olin Teague conducted an in-depth investigation of programs under the GI Bill, it concluded from the evidence, "We wasted millions and millions of dollars on the thing."[12]

These investigations prompted a bipartisan outcry against the trade schools for what lawmakers perceived as their outright abuse of federal funds. In particular, the Teague committee's scathing report about "unscrupulous school operators" influenced how Congress, that same year, went about designing a new GI Bill for veterans of the Korean War.[13] The process reflected what is called "political learning," meaning that public officials derive lessons from earlier policies and mold new policies accordingly, attempting either to replicate past success or in this case, to avoid past problems.[14] In fashioning the new GI Bill, lawmakers came up with the approach that shapes debate around for-profit colleges to this day: they required schools to have at least some minimum threshold percentage of students whose tuition was *not* paid for through GI Bill funds.[15] The debate revolved around what percentage of tuition paying students, in this case nonveterans, was sufficient to indicate program quality. As historian Melinda Pash has noted, the House Veterans Committee—perhaps influenced by the Teague report—originally agreed on a relatively restrictive ratio of requiring a program to enroll at least 25 percent nonveterans if the remainder were to be financed by the GI Bill. Some senators worried that this threshold would unduly limit veterans' options, and they recommended a less restrictive ratio; the final legislation established a ratio of 85 to 15, requiring at least 15 percent nonveterans.[16] In 1978 the Supreme Court upheld the principle Congress had established in 1952, explaining that it was a "device intended . . . to allow the free market mechanism to operate and weed out those institutions [which] could survive only by the heavy influx of Federal payments."[17]

Forty years later in 1992, when Congress again agonized over opportunistic uses of federal student aid funds by trade schools, it confronted the same issues that had arisen in the implementation of the original GI Bill. Once again, unintended consequences emerged as for-profit schools hustled to make profits. It was then that Maxine Waters introduced the 85 to 15 ratio derived in the earlier period and promoted its application to the use of federal student aid in the Higher Education Act. But the application of that rule would engender far greater controversy in the 1990s than it had in the middle of the twentieth century, and it continues to do so today.

Bringing For-Profit Institutions into the Higher Education Act: The 1972 Reauthorization

The expansion of civilian federal student aid laws to trade schools emerged at the high water mark of American liberalism, as policymakers sought to foster opportunity for those who had previously been left behind. When they were created, the major laws—the National Defense Education Act of 1958 and Higher Education Act of 1965 (HEA)—did not extend to study in such schools and discussion of them was not part of the debate. The momentum for their inclusion began when Republican president Richard M. Nixon, in 1970, sent a message to Congress that began, "No qualified student who wants to go to college should be barred by lack of money."[18] The administration recommended a two-pronged plan for expanding access to higher education: first, student aid that included grants for the poorest and easier access to loans for all; and second, career education in nontraditional venues, including technical institutes.[19] Members of the Democratic-controlled Congress took the initiative to link these two goals by expanding student aid under Title IV of the HEA to include students in accredited proprietary schools, just as the GI Bill already had for decades.[20] In effect, the 1972 amendments, according to chroniclers Lawrence Gladieux and Thomas Wolanin, amounted to a "broadening of the educational mainstream to include types of students and institutions that have generally been excluded or given second-class status in the past."[21] The provisions epitomized the inclusive spirit of progressive policymaking for higher education that was so commonplace in the mid-twentieth century.[22]

The long-term effects of extending Title IV to the for-profits diverged sharply, however, from the intentions of policymakers in 1972. They aimed to broaden access to advanced education.[23] There is no evidence to suggest that they would have condoned the accumulation of immense debt loads for low income students who attended proprietary schools—higher even than at traditional colleges. Lawmakers in 1972 seemed to expect the for-profits to be held to a different standard, indicated by their stipulating in the law that they must "provide training for gainful employment in a recognized occupation" in order to qualify for federal student aid. But that requirement lacked an enforcement mechanism, and it became meaningless as the implementation of the law proceeded. Only during the Obama administration, as we will see in Chapter 6, did officials attempt to attach teeth to such language, strengthening its enforcement capacity.[24]

BIPARTISAN EFFORTS TO REGULATE THE FOR-PROFITS, 1980S TO 1993

In a déjà vu evoking memories of the original GI Bill's implementation, new concerns about trade schools emerged soon after civilian students began to use the HEA funds that had just been became available to them in 1972. Within the next few years, public officials began to question the schools' marketing practices and low graduation rates. The Federal Trade

Commission held hearings and officials pushed—unsuccessfully—for regulations.[25] The amount of Title IV money going to such schools escalated rapidly: their share of Pell grant dollars increased from 7 percent in 1973–1974 to almost 30 percent in the late 1980s, when they also utilized 22 percent of student loans.[26] Journalists began writing about for-profits in terms that echoed those used thirty-five years earlier—lambasting the "unscrupulous operators" of "diploma mills," who were "in the business of skimming benefits from financial aid programs."[27] They chastised the schools for their "questionable recruiting practices," their tendency to "enroll students who lack the skills to complete their courses," their corrupt accreditation procedures, and the fact that their graduates often could not find work in their field of study.[28]

Yet for all the similarities to the past, the problems generated by the for-profits in the 1980s overshadowed those of the postwar years. World War II veterans did not need loans to attend public or private nonprofit colleges, not to mention the for-profit trade schools; the GI Bill benefits covered their tuition at any institution, including the nonprofit private universities, which typically charged the most.[29] By the 1980s, however, tuition at for-profits often exceeded that charged by nonprofits, and their students readily borrowed, taking on debt they would later have trouble repaying. The US Department of Education, alarmed by the number of borrowers from such schools who defaulted on their loans, announced in 1982 that 528 schools had been deemed ineligible for new loan funds because they had default rates of 25 percent or above.[30] But borrowing by students at the trade schools kept growing, particularly as lawmakers adopted more lenient lending guidelines, and default rates continued to increase as a result.

Groping Toward Reform

Meanwhile, in a development that mirrored the emergence of bipartisan efforts to reform the bank-based student loan system, as discussed in Chapter 2, some public officials in both parties began to seek ways to manage student aid to the for-profits more effectively. Here again, the need for policy maintenance was articulated early on by Republicans in the Reagan administration, fiscal conservatives who were disturbed by the misuse of government funds. On the trade schools, it was William Bennett, secretary of education, who led the charge, in 1987 assailing them as "diploma mills designed to trick the poor into taking on federally backed debt, milk them for their loan money and then wash them out or 'graduate' them ill-prepared to enter the job market and pay off their loans."[31] He put forward a proposal to terminate student aid to any school with default rates higher than the average, at that time 20 percent. Democrats in Congress acknowledged some implementation problems, but they still applauded most of the trade schools for their mission and inclusivity and did not want them harmed by an overly aggressive solution. Senate Postsecondary Education Subcommittee chair Pat Williams (D-MT) likened the Reagan administration's approach to "a sledgehammer opening a peanut."[32] Many also worried that the new rule would cause many historically black colleges to close.[33] Ultimately congressional leaders and the Reagan administration agreed to hold off on action until the following year.

By then, even some Democrats who had long defended for-profit schools had grown concerned that they were not policing themselves effectively. Congressman William D. Ford, a Democrat of Michigan, was a World War II veteran who still appreciated the opportunity the GI Bill had provided to him to attend trade school. In Congress, he had vociferously defended both student aid and for-profit colleges. But by 1989, he said, "I've worked on these student-aid programs for 25 years, and I'm not about to see them destroyed by schools abusing this program."[34] The education committees faced pressure to reduce spending throughout the annual budget process, and after years of enduring cuts to student aid programs generally, lawmakers felt they had little choice but to force discipline on the for-profits, which were, in Williams's words, "getting out of control."[35] They imposed restrictions on use of one particular program, Supplemental Loans for Students, which had unintentionally evolved into a primary source of aid for students in trade schools and had led to hundreds of millions of dollars in defaulted loans.[36]

None of these small policy changes solved the larger problems, however, as the for-profits readily adapted to them by finding still other means of accessing federal student aid. In 1990 the George H. W. Bush administration proposed stringent new regulations on the sector, with Republican senators Phil Gramm of Texas and Bob Dole of Kansas introducing the bill. The far-reaching plan, which would have prohibited schools from hiring commissioned sales representatives to recruit students, required lenders to offer repayment plans for borrowers that varied with their earnings, and made schools refund tuition to students who left the program before completing coursework. But the for-profit industry put up strong resistance through extensive lobbying and the proposal never made it out of committee.[37]

At this juncture, one congressional subcommittee launched the first ever in-depth probe of the for-profit sector, investigating how it conducted business and the amount of federal aid it used. Normally such a task would fall under the jurisdiction of the education committee in the House or Senate, but being full of defenders of the trade schools, they had not undertaken the responsibility. Instead, the inquiry emerged from an unlikely source in Congress—the Permanent Investigations Subcommittee of the Senate Governmental Affairs Committee, which was chaired by Sam Nunn, a moderate Democrat from Georgia who was widely regarded as an impartial and thoughtful statesman. As Chapter 2 notes, Nunn's subcommittee set out to investigate student loans, for which the costs to the federal government for defaults had grown from 10 percent of the total spending on the program in 1980 to over 50 percent in 1990. The investigation focused on the trade schools because they were primarily responsible for the problem: 39 percent of their borrowers defaulted compared to 10 percent of those in the public and nonprofit sectors.

After eight days of hearings during which nearly fifty witnesses testified, the subcommittee issued a damning report, explaining that it had uncovered "overwhelming evidence that the GSLP (Guaranteed Student Loan Program), particularly as it relates to proprietary schools, is riddled with fraud, waste, and abuse, and is plagued by substantial mismanagement and incompetence."[38] The subcommittee had heard about federal student aid going to an auto repair school in Ohio that was actually run out of a fruit stand, to a school for travel agents in Florida that recruited at public housing projects and in welfare offices, and myriad other such instances.[39] It leveled a bold indictment of the program, saying that its intended beneficiaries, "hundreds of thousands of young people, many of whom come from backgrounds with already limited opportunities" had "suffered further" because they became "victimized by unscrupulous profiteers and their fraudulent schools." It lambasted the poor quality of the training in such schools and the high level of debt students incurred. In addition, the subcommittee added, "the American taxpayer has suffered, both in terms of footing the bill for billions of dollars of losses in defaulted loans and the ultimate costs of the program's failure to provide the skilled labor force our Nation needs in the increasingly competitive global marketplace." Conversely, it noted that schools themselves as well as lenders, loan servicers, accrediting bodies, and others had "profited handsomely, and in some cases, unconscionably."[40]

This devastating report was signed by the subcommittee's bipartisan membership, a group that included a large number of both Republican and Democratic senators with strong records of working constructively with those in the other party.[41] It concluded with twenty-seven recommendations for an overhaul of federal procedures. Nunn expected that either the House or Senate education committee would pick up where his subcommittee left off, using their findings and responding with policy solutions. Instead, those groups ignored the report. As one education advocate explained, they "circled the wagons and saw Nunn as an outsider" to their issue jurisdiction. Senator Kennedy, chair of the Labor and Human Resources Committee, viewed Nunn as a disloyal conservative southerner, and he "fought him tooth and nail."[42] Meanwhile, in the House, before even seeing the report, Chairman Ford announced that "the government has no business telling students that one type of school is better than another."[43] He resumed his prior posture as a defender of for-profits. Both committees in effect dismissed the report. Two decades would elapse before Congress once again conducted a thorough investigation of the for-profit sector.

If You Can't Tie One Good Knot

In 1991, with another reauthorization of the HEA looming, Congress confronted the question of whether the proprietary schools, given their high default rates, should be excluded from the student loan program, or whether they should remain eligible but made subject to special restrictions.[44] The first option remained untenable, but the House Education and Labor Committee did put forward some changes, such as prohibiting schools from providing commissions or bonuses to recruiters. It was at this juncture, on the House floor, that the for-profits came under attack from an unlikely bipartisan trio of representatives. Liberal Democrat Maxine Waters was joined by Bart Gordon, a Democrat from Tennessee who had once gone into a trade school incognito with a hidden video camera to film an exposé for television, and by Marge Roukema, a moderate Republican from New Jersey.[45] The three of them banded together and offered several amendments to regulate the sector.

Waters drew on the regulatory principle devised for the Korean War GI Bill, and proposed a new 85/15 rule: at least 15 percent of a trade school's revenue must be accrued from sources outside the federal student aid programs in Title IV of the HEA. Like its predecessor, the rule aimed to deter schools that existed solely to pursue federal funds and preyed on vulnerable groups in the process. It made the for-profit sector subject to a market principle, in essence requiring that tuition not surpass what at least some students, who lacked federal aid, were themselves willing to pay.[46] Congress affirmed Waters's amendment and each of the others in voice votes, with names unrecorded. The final legislation, signed into law by President George H. W. Bush, included what became known as the 50/50 rule, which forbade the use of federal financial aid at schools that enrolled more than 50 percent of students in correspondence classes, meaning those conducted online or through the mail.[47] It also regulated the recruitment practices of the for-profits, in an attempt to discourage their use of high-pressure sales techniques to attract students solely for the purpose of gaining student aid dollars.

The piecemeal reforms fell far short of the sweeping overhaul called for by the Nunn report. As one observer characterized what emerged, "If you can't tie one good knot, tie lots of bad ones."[48] Still, from a contemporary perspective, what is most striking is that policymakers managed to engage in some actual maintenance of the policyscape governing for-profit colleges. At that juncture, enough members of both parties both shared concerns about policies gone awry and considered it worthwhile to make them function better that they were willing to join together in the attempt to do so. The "bad knots" they tied, however, would not endure, particularly as the political winds shifted and put new momentum in the sails of the for-profit industry.

POLARIZATION AND PLUTOCRACY
PROMOTE THE FOR-PROFITS, 1994–2008

For fifty years, the pattern of events surrounding for-profit schools had involved unintended consequences of federal student aid policy followed by bipartisan efforts at policy reform, but in the 1990s, circumstances changed entirely. When the industry made major initiatives to promote its own growth, the political system, itself in transformation, coalesced around the sector as a worthy cause to promote. As ideological polarization increased, the Republican Party shed its prior concerns about the industry and championed it as a paragon of the private sector. GOP leaders led a campaign to weaken the few loose regulatory restrictions that existed. But unlike most policy issues in recent years, the cause of the for-profit colleges still appealed to many Democrats as well, and they worked together with Republicans to do its bidding. Together, these developments created a perfect storm that fueled industry profits—and accelerated the devastation for low income students.

An Industry Prepares for Growth

Already in the early 1990s, the for-profit industry made strategic plans for a new era of growth. It abandoned its old "mom and pop" business model and traditional approach to politics and became more savvy and aggressive on both fronts. In 1991 its two older trade associations merged to become the Career College Association (in 2010, renamed the Association of Private Sector Colleges and Universities), which promptly started a political action committee (PAC) and hired lobbyists with ties to both parties.[49] Some of the individual for-profit universities emulated the CCA's example by themselves contributing to campaigns and lobbying.[50]

The Apollo Group created its first PAC in 1998 and later added three additional ones. John Sperling, its founder, spoke forthrightly in his autobiography about what he perceived as the necessity and value of the company's political involvement. "None of the Apollo companies would exist without the ability to protect them from regulatory and political attack," he said. In the early 1970s, he had done the company's lobbying himself, and eventually he hired lobbyists to protect the company's interests on the federal level and throughout the states.[51] "Yes, we use money to get their [politicians'] attention—our American system of campaign finance gives us no other alternative. Sadly, it's the only way to do it when you are from out-of-state and the forces against you have money, votes, and even football tickets!"[52] Sperling reflected, "Now Apollo itself is on the money treadmill. I have never done a full accounting of the annual cost of maintaining the political capability that helps ensure our survival and future growth. It would be very depressing if I did."[53]

Private industries in the United States have long contributed to campaigns and engaged in lobbying, but the for-profit colleges' involvement in these activities set them apart from other institutions of higher education. By contrast to public or private nonprofit colleges and universities, they donate substantial amounts of money to political candidates.[54] Although the actual amount any particular for-profit school donates pales compared to candidates' formidable war chests, in combination the sector offers substantial contributions to key congressional leaders and other supporters. Like the student lenders, the for-profits possess resources to invest in politics precisely because existing federal student aid policies have already provided them with significant business opportunities. They, in turn, have channeled a portion of those funds back into the political system, seeking the influence to protect and expand the policies that have enabled them to flourish. The public at large, meanwhile, is largely unaware of the issues at stake, remains unorganized around them, and therefore lacks the opportunity to be part of the debate.

At his eightieth birthday party in 2001, Sperling announced that he aimed to increase enrollments at the University of Phoenix from 124,800 to 470,800. Soon after, the Apollo Group announced a corporate goal called "5-5-5," meaning "Five Years, Five Million Students, and Five Billion Dollars."[55] The for-profit industry was prepared to soar.

Elected Officials Ready to Assist

Lawmakers, for their part, energetically pursued the opportunity to support the for-profit sector. In some respects, such advocacy was nothing new, merely reflecting how the decentralized organization of most for-profits happens to dovetail with the representative structure of Congress. Geographically, the for-profits are located in states and congressional districts all over the country, and therefore they form a natural constituency that public officials from far-flung localities seek to represent. In 1994, when assistant education secretary David Longanecker spoke at a Senate hearing, he said, "Every Congressman I have talked to wants us to manage this program more tightly. On the other hand, when it comes down to an institution that happens to be in their general jurisdiction, it is a different story. That is obviously a more legitimate institution than the others we should be shutting down."[56] The senators in attendance reportedly broke into nervous laughter; it was commonplace for even critics of the trade schools to seek special treatment for those with high default rates if they happened to operate in their own localities. Such dynamics reflect the old adage articulated by Congressman Tip O'Neill, House Speaker in the 1980s, "All politics is local." In a legislature in which representation is based on geographic units, lawmakers' responsiveness to local constituencies is simply "politics as usual."

Besides the natural appeal of their local ties, the for-profits have also long attracted widespread support because they seemed to epitomize different values that each of the two political parties believed they each stood for. Said Thomas Wolanin, longtime aide to Bill Ford, "Republicans tend to see these institutions as businesses and say therefore we ought not to be too harsh on someone who's trying to make a buck. Democrats tend to see them as points of access to training for some lower-income students."[57]

As partisan polarization intensified, the pull of these ideologically grounded rationales grew stronger, prompting Republicans to emerge as newly zealous advocates for the sector. As early as the culture wars of the 1980s, some in the GOP voiced distrust of traditional institutions of higher education, believing they offered little of value and indoctrinated students with liberal ideas—all at considerable expense to the federal government. Once the party claimed the majority in Congress in 1995, it defined its issue agenda on more stridently ideological grounds. It came to identify the for-profit sector's approach to education as one it could endorse: straightforward job training, absent the courses of study that seemed superfluous, and provided by organizations that belonged, as least nominally, to the private sector. In addition, some Republicans championed the schools as serving the needs of less advantaged Americans. Their most vocal proponent, Republican Congressman John Boehner, then chairman of the House Committee on Education and the Workplace, observed that "statistics show proprietary schools tend to serve larger populations of needy, high-risk, minority, and non-traditional students [who are] the students most in need of federal assistance."[58] Support for the for-profits offered a policy solution to inequality that fused with the free market orientation the GOP preferred, comparable to contemporaneous initiatives of the George W. Bush administration to promote home ownership.

Finally, the rising costs of reelection campaigns made potential donors increasingly attractive to members of Congress in both parties. For Republicans, efforts to court the for-profit sector and to do its bidding fused with the K Street approach that party leaders promoted in the 1990s. Republicans did gain larger contributions from the industry than Democrats during the 1990s and the early 2000s, but this is not surprising because donors typically favor those expected to hold the majority and especially congressional leaders. In fact, in keeping with traditional patterns of campaign contributing, the for-profits distributed their donations widely to members of both parties.

Even as polarization grew, politicians' need for cash fused with both the ties of localism and ideological rationales in a manner that transcended the partisan divide. The for-profits proved masterful at winning support on both sides of the aisle.

Congress Loosens Restrictions

Lobbying by the for-profits, combined with elected officials' readiness to do the industry's bidding, led to an unprecedented era of policy activity as lawmakers quietly loosened the regulatory framework put in place in previous years. The Clinton administration mostly turned a blind eye to the sector's activities, but Republican leaders began to advocate energetically on its behalf. Although the sector did not receive much overt attention during the 1998 reauthorization of the Higher Education Act, policymakers took the opportunity to make critical changes. The General Accounting Office had recently released a report suggesting that the many of the for-profits still used high amounts of federal student aid and, compared to other schools, had worse outcomes among their students— lower degree completion and job placement rates, and higher loan default rates.[59] Yet Republican leaders argued that the schools had improved their performance since the tougher rules were adopted in 1992. A few Democrats in the Black Caucus bolstered the case by claiming that they aided those who were less privileged. On that basis a bipartisan majority agreed to relax some of the restrictions on the schools.[60]

Most significantly, Congress diluted the 85/15 principle to 90/10, such that proprietary schools could gain all but 10 percent of their revenues from the federal government, specifically from Title IV of the HEA.[61] Boehner justified the loosening of the 85/15 restriction by arguing that it would help to alleviate inequality in higher education. The existing rule, he argued, "creates an incentive for proprietary schools to raise tuition or move away from urban areas where students are more likely to depend on federal aid."[62] Congress approved the change with little controversy and it became part of the legislation signed into law by President Clinton. It remains in place to this day.

Agency Assistance to the Industry

Next, under the George W. Bush administration, the US Department of Education softened its approach toward the for-profit colleges by weakening its interpretation of the rules applied to them. This effort began when Bush, in an unprecedented step, nominated a former lobbyist for the for-profit colleges to fill the role of Assistant Secretary for Postsecondary Education. For the three decades the position had existed, presidents had filled it with individuals from public and non-profit colleges, state higher education boards, or private industry. But Bush named Sally Stroup, former chief Washington lobbyist for the Apollo Group that ran the University of Phoenix—thus placing her in the position to oversee regulations applying to her previous employer.[63] Subsequently, when the department received complaints from the for-profits about the regulations governing them, it engaged in administrative rule making and interpretation that relaxed those policies.

Ever since Congress in 1992 had restricted the recruitment practices of the for-profits, the Department of Education had complied by requiring the schools to adhere to the same ethical principles that public and non-profit colleges have long enforced voluntarily, such as providing applicants with clear and accurate information about their institutions and about the costs of attendance and financial aid.[64] The newly staffed department in 2001 declared that approach to be inappropriate, and it eviscerated the regulation by developing what it termed "safe harbors," loopholes that permitted schools to circumvent the restrictions.[65] Department deputy secretary William Hansen issued a memo explaining that unlike the agency's past practice, in which schools lost access to financial aid funds if they violated the "incentive compensation" prohibition and rewarded recruiters who enrolled higher numbers of students, in the future a milder "remedial" approach, such as a fine, would suffice.[66]

Such leniency permitted the for-profits to pair the basic recruitment approaches they had used since the 1940s with the more aggressive techniques utilized by call centers. Investigative journalists began to cast a spotlight on such practices. The *Allentown Morning Call* newspaper reported, "Telemarketing—that's how enrollment at Lehigh Valley College often begins. Recruiters must make 125 calls and schedule five appointments a day, and enroll 10 applicants a month. Top performers get vacations to the Bahamas. Those who fail to sign up enough applicants are asked to resign." The *San Francisco Weekly,* describing the California Culinary Academy observed, "Many former students say admissions representatives told them whatever they thought the applicants needed to hear to get them to sign on the dotted line. The students claim admissions actually accepts anyone eligible for a student loan. The graduates say they were misled about the terms of their loans; many have since realized that by the time they finish making payments, they'll have paid more than $100,000 for just 15 months of school."[67] In time, both *60 Minutes* and *Frontline* ran major exposés, revealing how the schools instructed recruiters to use any measures to get "asses in classes."[68]

In 2003 two former employees for the University of Phoenix became whistle-blowers by bringing a false claims lawsuit against the company, claiming that it violated the ban on compensating employees based on the number of students they recruited. In response, the Department of Education conducted a program review of the university. Its findings, issued in a searing thirty-two-page document, described recruitment procedures far removed from the professionalism associated with traditional college admissions and clearly aimed to access as much as possible in federal student aid funds. Managers pressured call center workers to recruit aggressively, routinely reminding them that their salaries depended on the number of students they enrolled. They rewarded those who met their targets with free trips, gifts certificates, spa packages, and cash. They also used intimidation techniques; most notoriously, they placed them in a glass-enclosed red room, "a place viewed with fear and dread" by recruiters with whom the reviewers spoke. There "senior recruiters and managers hovered over" them until they had "attained the required number of enrollments."[69]

The department responded in 2004 by charging the University of Phoenix a fine of $9.8 million—a small cost to the company with net revenues that had soared to $1.34 trillion in 2003.[70] Investigations between 1998 and 2009 found that thirty-two other schools also violated the incentive compensation rules, but given the parameters set by the Hansen memo, the department only required two of them to pay a fine. Most simply received requests to cease violations.[71]

The restaffed Department of Education had put itself on the side of the for-profit sector and lowered the barriers to its use of government-provided student aid funds. What transpired next would make all of the previous instances of the for-profit sector's growth pale by comparison.

Congress Unties Another Knot

Back on Capitol Hill, with a mere eight lines of text buried in a bill of 82,000 words, Congress changed policy in a new way that opened the floodgates of for-profit enrollment—and the sector's use of federal aid funds.[72] In the 2006 budget bill, it dropped the 50 percent rule that had been adopted in 1992 to require colleges to hold at least half of their classes on campus in order to qualify for federal student aid. Originally this rule affected primarily correspondence classes, but as the Internet made distance learning possible, the restriction had applied also to online classes and curtailed their growth. Once lawmakers disbanded with the provision, completely online colleges became eligible for Title IV funds, and their growth took off.[73]

The termination of the 50 percent rule represented the fruition of a concerted effort by the industry, agency officials, and congressional leaders. Stroup's office at the Department of Education had prepared several reports that recommended that Congress abolish the rule for online courses. The department's own inspector general criticized the analysis, saying that it understated the problems with online courses, including cases in which the rapid enrollment led to financial aid fraud. On Capitol Hill, John Boehner, from the time he became chair of the House Education and Workforce Committee in 2001, had been co-sponsoring bills that would end the 50 percent rule as well as others of the 1992 regulations. He was joined in these efforts by Congressman Howard "Buck" McKeon, who took over the education committee chair from Boehner, and Senator Mike Enzi, who chaired the Senate education committee.

The for-profit colleges had done their part to court these Republican leaders. Between 2002 and 2006, Boehner, McKeon, Enzi, and each of their PACs attracted one out of five dollars in campaign contributions made by the industry.[74] Boehner's PAC, Freedom Project, received more than half of its funding from the for-profit colleges and private student lending companies; it provided him with $2.9 million to distribute to his Republican colleagues to support their campaigns.[75] The party leadership in turn eased the school's access to federal dollars, using the resources in existing policies to reward these political allies.

In the next five years after the demise of the 50 percent rule, enrollments nearly doubled in the for-profit sector, and revenues soared. Wall Street investors, impressed by the industry's rapid online growth, made initial public offerings. The compensation of industry executives climbed into the millions. The Apollo's University of Phoenix and Kaplan, owned by the *Washington Post,* doubled their revenues—and the default rates of their students climbed at the same pace. Enrollments at colleges owned by the Education Management Corporation, backed in part by Goldman Sachs, increased by 500 percent between 2006 and 2009. Capella Education Company went public immediately after the rule's demise and more than doubled its enrollment, from 18,000 to 40,000. Several others saw comparable growth rates. New colleges also flourished. In 2005 Bridgepoint Education of San Diego, founded in 1999, purchased a failing college in Iowa—the Franciscan University of the Prairies—renamed it, and by 2010 had elevated enrollment from 350 to 76,000.[76]

If the enormous increase in enrollments at the for-profits had advanced educational opportunity, it would be an achievement to celebrate. But as the sector grew, complaints from students about mistreatment at the hands of these schools proliferated, leading to scores of investigations nationwide by state attorneys general. Evidence mounted that the schools emphasized recruitment far above pedagogical goals as they sought to gain access to as much student aid as possible. But now the sheer amount of money involved vastly surpassed that of prior periods as the percentage of all Pell grant dollars used at for-profits increased from 13 percent in 2000 to 25 percent in 2009, student loan spending by the sector increased by a comparable rate, and default rates soared.[77] Online degrees enabled the schools to provide educational services at a much lower cost than brick and mortar colleges, and now it enabled them to reap more than ever in federal financial aid money. The American public was left with the bill.

OPPORTUNITIES FOR SHAREHOLDERS

The cozy relationship that developed in the late 1990s and early 2000s between Congress, the for-profit college industry, and the US Department of Education resembles the kind of "iron triangle" that political scientists have long noticed in relationships between industries, agencies, and public officials. Indeed, analyses of the for-profits offered by critics in Congress make it sound indistinguishable from any other industry that seeks to channel government resources toward its bottom line. Congressman Michael N. Castle of Delaware, a Republican who defied his party's leadership in 2005 by opposing the termination of the 90/10 rule, commented that the for-profits "have a full-blown lobbying effort and give lots of money to campaigns. In 10 years the power of this interest group has spiked as much as any you'll see."[78] As Congresswoman Waters explained, such schools are "very sophisticated" in their approach to politics, and "they actually have members of Congress who protect them."

What is unusual is that the industry at the center of this story is a sector of higher education. It is not the manufacturer of goods such as weaponry for the US armed forces, or the provider of services such as transportation or communication that facilitate commerce. Rather, these political relationships emanate from a service sector that is associated with the provision of a basic right of citizenship: education. The ample federal funds provided to it belong to policies created with the intention of enabling Americans—including the least well-off—to pursue opportunities associated with cherished national values, with the American dream. And yet today, the political relationships that have developed between public officials and the industry have promoted, above all else, extensive profits for company owners and shareholders, at the expense of students and taxpayers.

For a half century, from 1944 through 1994, political developments surrounding the for-profits involved repeated controversies and occasional battles. Time and again, new student aid generated unintended consequences that facilitated the proliferation of the sector and inadvertently led to abuses by school operators who were in business primarily to take advantage of available federal money. Eventually, however, in each instance public officials sought to fix existing policies so that they would no longer generate such outcomes. Politicians of all stripes numbered among those leading such efforts, including southern Democrats in the 1950s, fiscally conservative Republicans in the Reagan and George H. W. Bush administrations, and conservative and liberal Democrats and moderate Republicans in Congress in the early 1990s. Lawmakers worked across the aisle to fashion regulations, employing some of the same strategies decades apart.

Since 1994, however, these long-standing cycles of unintended consequences and reform have been replaced by politics driven by polarization and plutocracy. As ideological divergence between the parties grew, Republicans chose the for-profit colleges as a cause to champion and they lined up behind the sector. Yet in what is a surprising development in a polarized age, many Democrats continued their long-standing advocacy for the for-profits, as well. Public officials of both parties have worked together to promote the schools' autonomy from federal regulations and their access to financial aid. As the amount of public money involved has exploded, instead of tightening restrictions, lawmakers have loosened them. It is clear that the demands of business owners are being met, enabling them to channel public money to their own private gain; by contrast, the hopes of students to improve their lives appear to have been ignored.

The result, bipartisan efforts at plutocratic governance, generate a self-reinforcing character. As the industry profited, it enhanced its ability to communicate with lawmakers. During the 2007–2008 election season, for example, the Apollo Group played a prominent role. Not only did it lead the for-profit colleges in campaign contributions, but by donating over $11 million, it ranked twenty-eighth among *all* organizations and businesses nationwide. It spent approximately twice as much as Goldman Sachs, JP Morgan Chase, Bank of America, Time Warner, and Walmart, among others, and three times as much as the US Chamber of Commerce.[79] The loud political voice of the for-profits remained unmatched by that of their critics, and ordinary Americans remained outside of the debate entirely. Around 2005, a coalition of Washington, DC–based consumer, education, and student organizations formed in an attempt to defend the federal rules established in 1992 and to prevent their further evisceration.[80] Yet those whose interests were most directly affected by the policies—the students of the for-profits and American citizens and taxpayers who expected government dollars to be spent wisely—lacked an organization that offered them a strong and coherent voice on these matters, and they remained unheard.

CHAPTER FOUR

FROM PIONEER TO SLACKER

The Rise and Decline of American Public Higher Education

IN THE MIDDLE OF THE TWENTIETH CENTURY, WHEN THE UNITED STATES led the world in the educational attainment of its citizens, the state of Colorado led the nation, boasting the highest rate of young adults with bachelor's degrees. By 2010, however, Colorado had fallen to the middle of the pack nationwide, and even more striking, today its young adults are less likely to hold college degrees than its older residents. In the intervening years, between 1970 and 2010, the state pulled back on its support for higher education: spending per full-time college student dropped from $5,726 to $2,978 in 2010 dollars, and it also declined per capita from $281 to $242.[1] The story of what happened in Colorado is emblematic of how a once proud achievement—a vast system of public universities and colleges that opened the doors of education to generations of ordinary Americans—has been left to deteriorate.

As economic inequality grew in the United States from the 1970s onward, Colorado attracted many new residents, typically individuals who had higher rates of education than long-term residents but less allegiance to supporting local public universities and colleges. Antitax sentiment galvanized in the state beginning in 1986, when conservative activist Douglas Bruce moved there from Los Angeles and drafted the Taxpayer Bill of Rights, which came to be known as TABOR. This provision would amend the state constitution so that state and local elected officials could not enact tax increases without voter approval. Bruce and taxpayer groups led a statewide campaign to promote it. Political leaders in both parties opposed it, as did many interest groups, but after two unsuccessful attempts, TABOR passed in 1992 with approval from 54 percent of voters. Once the state economy hit a recession in 2001, the budget contracted and the states' public universities and colleges paid the price. Circumstances worsened in subsequent years, leaving these institutions funded at far lower levels than one would have predicted a half century ago.[2] Similar developments have occurred in many other states, with severe consequences for the nation's college graduation rates and its ability to broaden degree attainment beyond the ranks of those born into upper income families.

Starting soon after the nation's founding, the federal government provided resources to the states to assist them in promoting higher education, and they responded willingly. For the next century, this cooperative federalism fostered the rapid establishment of public universities and colleges. Then in the middle of the twentieth century, it led to soaring increases in the number of Americans attaining college degrees. States followed up on the federal government's provision of student aid, described in Chapter 2, by greatly increasing their own spending on their institutions of higher education. In 1900 fewer than one in four college students in the United States—just 22 percent—attended public institutions; by 1975, the proportions had reversed themselves, as more than three out of four, or 79 percent, did.[3] As enrollments in state-run schools escalated, the composition of college graduates grew increasingly representative of Americans in terms of income, race, and gender. The states further expanded their investments in higher education even after the economy slowed in the 1970s and federal efforts contracted in the 1980s.

Since 1990, however, states have once again followed the lead of the federal government, this time in rolling back their commitment to higher education. They have asked public colleges and universities to do more with a good deal less.[4] Actual costs at these institutions have increased sharply, recently by 3 percent annually, twice as fast as inflation, but the revenues they obtain from government have stagnated in real terms in most states and deteriorated in others.[5] They have had little choice but to raise tuition; between 1980–1981 and 2010–2011, it escalated by 244 percent in constant dollars at four-year public universities, growing from $6,381 to $15,605, not including room and board; at two-year public colleges, it increased by 156 percent on average, from $5,072 to $7,925.[6]

States vary, however, in the extent to which they have supported public higher education over time and in their continued willingness to do so. We will see that it has not been economic factors alone that have influenced the degree of state-level commitment in this area, but rather that the policyscape has also been highly consequential, as existing policies have generated their own effects in ways that have proven harmful to spending on public universities and colleges. The historic development of public universities in the states yields a long-run impact, as states that established them before private colleges emerged still demonstrate a higher level of commitment to funding public universities and colleges today. Other present-day policies that would appear unrelated to higher education have influenced funding for it through "lateral effects." Medicaid and prisons, for example, have imposed heavy and growing financial burdens on state budgets, and lawmakers have funded them at the expense of public universities and colleges. Revenue policies, along with restrictions that make it difficult for public officials to raise taxes, such as the TABOR provision in Colorado, have also undermined higher education spending. Plutocratic governance at the national level has therefore been mirrored by many states as they have in effect shifted costs from affluent citizens to students at public universities, who must now pay a much higher percentage of the costs of attending than in the past.

Cumulatively, the nation's shrinking commitment to public higher education contributes significantly to the rise of economic and social inequality. Students from families with low to moderate incomes are price sensitive consumers of higher education, and therefore these increases in college costs can make enrollment prohibitive, and affect whether once enrolled they complete their degrees or fail to graduate. In addition, as public institutions confront leaner budgets, the gap widens between what they, compared to private nonprofit institutions, are able to provide for their students. Universities and colleges that not long ago provided broad avenues of opportunity are being transformed into more costly and resource-poor institutions, with severe consequences for the vast majority of American college students who hope to graduate from them.

PIONEER OF HIGHER EDUCATION POLICY

Public support for higher education is an American tradition even older than the nation itself. Nine colleges were established during the colonial period—Harvard, William and Mary, Yale, Princeton, the University of Pennsylvania, Columbia, Brown, Rutgers, and Dartmouth—and even they emerged through a combination of public and private support.[7] After the Revolution, the nation's first government, operating under the Articles of Confederation, opted to settle states' conflicting claims over western territories by asking them to cede such land to the federal government to be used for national purposes. From 1783 onward, several individuals petitioned Congress to set aside a portion of these lands for the purposes of education, including the development of institutions of higher learning.[8] The Northwest Ordinance, enacted in 1787, did just this, noting that, "Religion, morality, and knowledge, being necessary to good government and the happiness of mankind, schools and the means of education shall forever be encouraged."[9]

This pioneering legislation initiated the development of the nation's system of public universities and colleges. States that took advantage of these early land grants could either use the land as the location on which to establish a university or sell it and use the profits to help support colleges elsewhere in the state.[10] States seized the opportunity, and the number of universities proliferated rapidly: between 1782 and 1802 alone, nineteen new colleges were established—more than twice the number that had existed in the colonial era.[11] After 1802, the federal government explicitly granted land for the creation of a university to every new state that entered the union; several received as much as 100,000 acres for this purpose.

Strikingly, the South took the lead in opening the very first public universities, including the University of Georgia in 1785 and the University of North Carolina in 1789, and several others that followed soon afterward.[12] In fact, the region possessed 57 percent of the nation's public institutions established prior to the Civil War.[13] This may seem surprising, given that the South proceeded more slowly than other regions in developing social welfare policies, and its presence has been cited as a reason why the United States proceeded more slowly than Europe in establishing such policies at the national level. That the region took the lead in developing public institutions of higher education underscores the depth and pervasiveness of support for higher education in the American past.[14]

As the nineteenth century proceeded, states across the nation continued to follow the federal government's lead in promoting higher education as they energetically developed their public universities and colleges. In order to attract settlers from the east and to avoid losing young residents to neighboring states, they competed to develop the best institutions they could.[15] In 1851 an editorial in a Minnesota newspaper opined that "not a single youth of either sex should be permitted to leave the territory to acquire an education for want" of a public university. Some set aside additional land themselves, beyond what the federal government provided, for the establishment of public universities and colleges.[16]

The federal government offered even greater incentives to states to develop public universities and colleges in 1862, during the Civil War, when President Abraham Lincoln signed into law the Morrill Land Grant College Act. In the words of Congressman Justin Smith Morrill of Vermont, who promoted it, the aim was "to promote the liberal and practical education of the industrial classes in the several pursuits and professions of life."[17] Until then, most institutions of higher education were established as liberal arts colleges; in creating the land-grant approach, reformers sought a new model that would blend traditional course offerings with education in the emergent agricultural and mechanical professions and the sciences. By their very nature, these new public institutions were associated with expanding access to higher education. Their spirit is epitomized by the words of Ezra Cornell in 1868, "I would found an institution where any person can find instruction in any study." Each state then belonging to the Union gained 30,000 acres of federal land for each senator and representative it had in Congress.[18] Once again, states could use the land as the site for a university or sell it and use the proceeds for that purpose. Some eastern states gained and developed land in the West; for example, New York made a profit on timber land in Wisconsin and used it to establish Cornell University.[19] Ultimately, through this first Morrill Act, the federal government distributed over 17 million acres of land for the purposes of higher education.[20] The second Morrill Act, created in 1890, included the states of the former Confederacy; by requiring states either to show that race was not a criterion for admission or to develop separate land-grant colleges for persons of color, the law gave rise to most of the historically black colleges.[21]

Regions varied in the extent to which they developed more public or more private sector universities, depending on the timing of when they were settled relative to the creation of the land-grant policies.[22] In the Northeast, most of the institutions that were developed during the colonial period evolved into private institutions, and thereafter the region continued to develop mostly private institutions. On average, states in the region did not establish their first public universities until 1840, ninety-four years after founding their first private university. By contrast, the public and private sectors developed almost simultaneously in southern states, where the average public university was established in 1809 and private university in 1812, and in the Midwest, where those years were 1847 and 1845, respectively.[23] The West represented the opposite extreme from the Northeast, as the average public university took root in 1884, thirteen years *in advance* of the average private university.[24] The variation in these historical patterns, we will see, bore long-term consequences for more recent developments in public higher education.

Although the early establishment of so many universities and colleges throughout the United States was a remarkable achievement, it did not immediately make higher education broadly accessible. State legislators typically favored the land-grant approach to education, with its emphasis on practical and professional training fused with goals of economic development, but they were hard-pressed to find adequate financial support. At that time, states still lacked the taxing capacity necessary to provide ample revenues to such institutions; they were already stretched to pay for common schools and roads.[25] Even in the era of the Morrill acts, therefore, about five times as many private institutions were established as public institutions.[26] The growth of colleges and universities was curtailed, also, by the fact that only a small portion of the population actually graduated from high school. As of 1910, fewer than one in ten young Americans completed high school; not surprisingly, only half of them—about 5 percent of all eighteen- to twenty-one-year olds—enrolled in college, in either a two-year or a four-year institution.[27]

These circumstances began to change dramatically between 1897 and 1940, when the proportion of all college students in publicly controlled institutions shifted from 22 percent to nearly 50 percent.[28] In a sweeping transformation, by 1930 half of young Americans outside of the South graduated from high school, and the increases were most dramatic in the Midwest and West—regions of the country with strong public institutions of higher education. Already tuition at private universities averaged four times the cost of in-state tuition at publics, so as more Americans of moderate means became college ready, they sought admission, primarily to the publics.[29]

During this era, states also established a new type of public institution to accommodate a larger number and wider array of students: two-year colleges. These "junior colleges," which were nonexistent in 1900, grew to 258 in the first four decades of the twentieth century.[30] Initially they served as feeder schools for those seeking to start college close to home before attending a four-year institution elsewhere, but increasingly they provided a means of attaining a terminal degree with training in the skilled trades and semiprofessions. States also transformed many of what they had previously called "normal schools," those used for training teachers, into the branch campuses of state university systems.[31]

In sum, the history of US higher education policy over the nation's first century and a quarter is a story of innovation and rapid diffusion. The federal government's crucial role was not that of a meddling regulator or the deliverer of unfunded mandates. Rather, in keeping with its role in other policy areas in that period, it simply provided resources to the states, with few strings attached.[32] Through such largesse, it effectively stimulated the states to respond in turn, competing with one another to establish public universities and colleges.[33] During the same period, interstate economic competition deterred states from developing extensive social welfare policies or labor protections.[34] In the case of higher education, by contrast, the federal government set the process in motion, and states willingly and eagerly joined in. American federalism sparked a "virtuous circle" that led the national government and the states in tandem to develop an extensive system of public higher education, with all varieties of colleges and universities springing up in far-flung locations throughout the nation.

THE ZENITH OF MASS
PUBLIC HIGHER EDUCATION

When the federal government further strengthened its commitment to higher education in the mid-twentieth century, it once again stimulated state governments to respond in kind. Within a few decades, higher education underwent what University of California president Clark Kerr termed "the great transformation," and public universities and colleges served as the locus of change.[35] The number of college students nationwide grew from 3.5 million in 1960 to 12 million in 1980, and the vast majority attended public institutions, where enrollment soared from 2 million to 9.5 million students. The number of public institutions more than doubled, increasing from 700 to 1,500, outpacing the growth of private institutions, where 400 new ones joined 1,300 that already existed.[36] Public community colleges multiplied also, from 405 in 1960 to 1049 in 1980, and their enrollments skyrocketed, from 400,000 in 1960 to 4 million in 1980.[37]

High school graduation rates had continued to climb during the Depression and World War II, and the end of those events unleashed a new zeal for college attendance. In addition, college tuition costs actually declined relative to family income in the 1940s and 1950s, and held steady until about 1980.[38] The baby boom generation came of age during this period, making for more Americans who were college ready than ever before.

These new masses of Americans prepared to attend college could not have enrolled on the same scale without government's role in accommodating them. The federal government stimulated attendance through its student aid policies, and public institutions helped absorb the swelling ranks of students. In 1947, fully 49 percent of all college students in the nation were veterans on the GI Bill; half were enrolled in public institutions and half at private institutions.[39] As subsequent landmark laws extended federal student aid to civilian students, they too stormed the public universities and colleges.[40]

Besides student aid, other federal policies also goaded states into improving their public university systems or required them to broaden access to more students. A plank of the 1972 Education Amendments provided funds to states to create coordinating agencies to oversee their systems of public higher education; by the early 1980s, nearly all states had done so.[41] As well, the Civil Rights Act of 1964 and Title IX, which forbids discrimination in admissions, opened the doors of colleges to minorities and women as never before.

In retrospect, public higher education achieved its zenith in this period. Not coincidentally, this was the same era in which US college graduation rates escalated most rapidly and, as we saw in Chapter 1, the nation's young adults led the world in degree attainment. Public colleges and universities, assisted by federal aid for their students and direct support from state governments, bore major responsibility for this success.

Emulating Retrenchment

If the period between 1960 and 1980 saw public higher education flour-ishing, the years since then have seen it languishing. Federal sources of student aid such as Pell grants diminished in real terms, and overall the share of public higher education costs financed by the federal gov-ernment decreased from 15 percent to 12 percent. Initially, states re-doubled their own efforts, offering generous support that helped make up the difference. By the late 1990s, however, they allowed their con-tributions to fall behind as well.[42] Ever since the founding the federal government had taken the lead in promoting higher education and the states had followed; now it was the first to scale back its commitment and the states, in time, did the same.

As the "virtuous circle" of American federalism turned into a "vicious cycle," state support for higher education diminished on every measure other than absolute dollars spent. Enrollments at public universities and colleges grew by 38 percent over the period, due to the entrance of the millennial generation, with its high school graduation rates that ex-ceeded those of preceding generations.[43] But states offered less to these new students, in real terms, than they had to previous cohorts: spending per student declined by 26 percent between 1990–1991 and 2009–2010, from $8,608 to $6,360. States' per capita commitment to higher educa-tion dropped as well, from $283 in 1990 to $268 in 2010.[44] Overall na-tional income rose by 66 percent during this period, but states reduced what they collectively invested in colleges and universities from $8.75 per $1000 income in 1990–1991 to $6.12 in 2010–2011.[45] The share of state budgets devoted to higher education dropped from 8 percent in 1980 to 4 percent in 2010.[46] Meanwhile, colleges' expenses per student grew in real terms, particularly for student services and academic sup-port, though both increased at much lower rates in public institutions than in private institutions during this period.[47]

Public universities and colleges have made up the difference by raising tuition during a period when wages for low to moderate income families have stagnated. The increases in college costs impose the greatest burden on those who can least afford them and are most dependent on public colleges and universities. As seen in Figure 4.1, for those in the highest income quintile, the average cost of attending public four-year institutions (including tuition, room and board, and fees) as a percentage of family income increased from 6 percent in 1971 to 9 percent in 2011. But both this increase and the actual cost remain negligible relative to their income. For those in the bottom three-fifths of the income distribution, however, these increases are quite severe. For those in the middle income quintile, they have grown by 123 percent, to 29 percent of income, and for those in the lowest income quintile, by 171 percent, to 114 percent of income.[48] These same tuition increases have also fallen most heavily on African American and Hispanic families compared to whites and Asian Americans.[49]

FIGURE 4.1. The Unequal Impact of Rising College Costs: Proportion of Family Income Required to Pay Costs of Attending Public Four-Year Institutions, by Income Quintile, 1971 and 2011

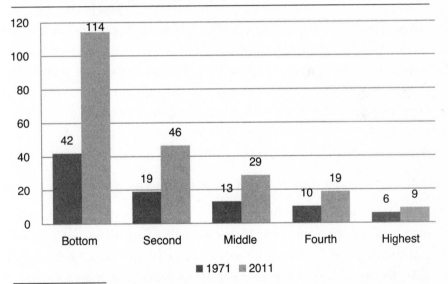

SOURCE: Donald E. Heller, "Trends in the Affordability of Public Colleges and Universities," in *The States and Public Higher Education* (Baltimore: Johns Hopkins University Press, 2011), 22. Updated with College Board, *Trends in College Pricing, 2012*, http://trends.collegeboard.org/sites /default/files/college-pricing-2012-full-report_0.pdf; US Census Bureau, Table F-3, Mean Income Received by Each Fifth and Top 5 Percent of Families, http://www.census.gov/hhes/www/income /data/historical/families/index.html.

As a result, "public" education has become, in reality, increasingly "private" in its actual funding. As recently as 1987, states contributed the lion's share of the costs of running public universities and colleges, covering 77 percent of the costs per student. Over the next two decades, students and their families picked up more and more of the tab. By 2012, the average state's share had fallen to 53 percent, with students' contribution nearing the halfway point.[50] Several institutions have long since crossed this 50 percent threshold. Flagship state universities took the lead in privatizing; for example, states finance less than one-quarter of the expenses of the University of Colorado, University of Michigan, and University of Virginia. More surprisingly, a growing share of community colleges, such as those in Iowa and South Carolina, rely on students to cover more than half of costs.[51]

The nation's system of public higher education is increasingly financed privately and through a system that is inherently regressive. Public institutions lack enough high income students to use price discrimination—charging the sticker price for those who can afford it and lower rates for others—as private institutions do. Elite private institutions and a few of the flagship public institutions are also able to raise funds from annual giving and from endowment growth.[52] The vast majority of public institutions lack these alternatives and have no option except to increase tuition for everyone. Their students compensate through increased borrowing, and those who graduate do so with greater indebtedness.[53]

GOVERNING THE POLICYSCAPE IN THE STATES

While the overall pattern of recent years has been that states are spending less in real terms on public higher education than in the past, considerable variation exists between them in the extent of their support. As of 2010, the spending per full-time student in public universities and colleges ranged from $2,978 in Colorado to $10,197 in Hawaii, and higher education spending per capita varied between $105 in New Hampshire to $556 in Wyoming.[54] During the period from 2007 to 2012, educational appropriations per full-time student declined by 23 percent on average across all states, but this ranged from a 51 percent decline in New Hampshire to a 31 percent increase in North Dakota, which distinguished itself with Illinois as one of the only two states to raise funding.[55] In sum, most states have left their public systems to deteriorate, but to varying degrees, while a few retain stronger commitment.

The relationship between the characteristics of individual states and their level of support for higher education reveals a great deal about the general patterns driving the abandonment of public higher education nationwide. I have examined this relationship by conducting statistical analysis of the attributes associated with states' per capita spending on higher education from 1960 to 2010.[56] Some might assume that richer states spend more on higher education and poorer states spend less. In fact, it turns out that on average, states with lower per capita incomes devote a significantly greater share to supporting higher education. Massachusetts, the second wealthiest state, comes in thirty-third in spending per full-time student; Colorado is the fourteenth richest state, but it ranks forty-sixth in per capita spending and dead last in per student spending. Conversely, some poor states commit a proportionately higher share of their funds to higher education: New Mexico is the fourth poorest state in the union, with per capita income of $33,000, but it ranks eighth in per capita higher education spending and thirteenth from the top in spending per student; North Carolina is the fifth poorest but ranks fifteenth by college spending per capita and fourth in its generosity per student.

If affluence isn't a central factor, what is? It is reasonable to expect that state spending on higher education would fluctuate with the business cycle. One might assume that when unemployment is high, lawmakers will expand support for higher education, given that many of the jobless go back to school at this juncture and educating them provides states with an opportunity to create a more highly skilled, recession-resilient workforce. Yet one of the best-established findings indicates the reverse: by contrast to how states treat many other policy priorities, they offer greater support to public colleges and universities when the economy is thriving, and less when times are hard.[57] This explanation accounts for less of the variation between states in the past decade, however, because even when the economy was stronger, funds for higher education have stagnated.

If there is one broad, overall finding of more recent and nuanced research, it is that politics matters. When lawmakers face budget constraints, they must make choices about how to respond—and they have done so in different ways across states. Those with professional legislatures—with more full-time staff, higher pay, and more time spent in session—devote more resources to higher education.[58] In addition, those with a higher percentage of active interest groups generally spend less on higher education, presumably because their activism drowns out the voices advocating on behalf of funding for colleges and universities.[59] Conversely, however, states with more higher education lobbyists spend more on public universities and colleges.[60]

What has received less attention in earlier considerations of variation in state support for higher education has been the significance of policy effects. Dynamics emanating from the policyscape, both those associated with the legacy of higher education policies and also the "lateral effects" of unrelated policies, turn out to be crucial.

The early policy history of higher education within states—specifically the sequencing of the establishment of their first public colleges and universities relative to their first private ones—generated long-term consequences that affected their level of public support in the late twentieth century. States that established their public sectors in *advance* of their private sectors—those in the West—evolved to become stronger funders of their public sectors long afterward. However, those in which private sector development took root earlier—particularly in the Northeast—continued to lag behind.[61] The early timing and sequencing of public and private institutional development set in motion enduring historical processes that privileged whichever sector led the way, far into the future.

Various policy mechanisms might explain why the path states set out on at the start—more private or more public—became self-reinforcing over time. Perhaps success bred success, as colleges and universities that received more resources early on developed well as a result and gained strong reputations, enabling them to garner additional funding from state lawmakers over time. Such institutions may also have stimulated the emergence of interest groups, which subsequently advocated successfully on their behalf.[62] In addition, lawmakers may have derived lessons that made them protective of the public system, particularly if they themselves obtained degrees from it. One recent study considered the educational background of 6,517 state senators and representatives, and found that state legislatures containing a higher percentage of lawmakers who had themselves attended public universities and colleges invested more generously in those institutions than those who had smaller percentages.[63] Similar to beneficiaries of Social Security who advocate on behalf of program benefits even for younger generations, these lawmakers seek to maintain or improve the public benefits they had utilized themselves, ensuring they would be available for future students.[64]

Over the past few decades, state funding of higher education has also been influenced by policies that would appear to be completely unrelated to it. In the state budgeting process, it has been subject to intense competition, especially from Medicaid, K-12 education, and prisons, as seen in Figure 4.2. Medicaid has grown more expensive as health care costs have ballooned, and states have been required to provide funds for those who qualify. K-12 education costs rose as the children of baby boomers filled the schools and as states opted to prioritize it.[65] Incarceration rates exploded in the United States over these decades, quadrupling between 1980 and 2000, in part due to changes in sentencing policies for crime.[66] While spending in these areas increased, higher education funding at first stagnated and then deteriorated. Several studies find evidence that these other budget priorities, especially Medicaid and corrections, have indeed squeezed out spending on public universities and colleges.[67]

Differences in policy design help explain why, in the face of fiscal crises, lawmakers favored funding for these issue areas over higher education. Medicaid, K-12 education, and corrections involve mandatory spending: states are obligated by law to provide funds to cover costs. When a downturn hits and revenues fall, they are excluded from cuts.

FIGURE 4.2. Higher Education Squeezed Out in State Budgets:
Average State Spending and Tax Revenues, Per Capita,
1950–2010 (2010 Dollars)

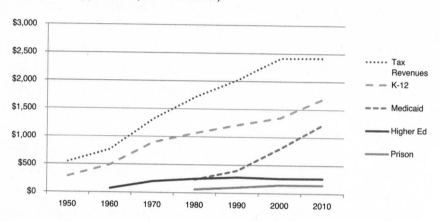

SOURCE: Centers for Medicare and Medicaid Services, Health Expenditures by State of Resi-
dence, Summary Tables, 2009, http://www.cms.gov/Research-Statistics-Data-and-Systems
/Statistics-Trends-and-Reports/NationalHealthExpendData/NationalHealthAccounts
StateHealthAccountsResidence.html; Center for the Study of Education Policy, Grapevine
Reports, Various Years, http://grapevine.illinoisstate.edu/historical/index.htm; State and
Local Government Finance Data Query System, http://www.taxpolicycenter.org/slf-dqs
/pages.cfm; Urban Institute/Brooks Institution Tax Policy Center, Data from US Census Bureau,
Annual Survey of State and Local Government Finances, vol. 4, and Census of Governments,
2010; Kaiser Family Foundation State Health Facts, Medical Spending, http://statehealthfacts
.org/comparemaptable.jsp?ind=.

Higher education, by contrast, is the single largest discretionary item in
state budgets. These differences help explain why it has been vulnerable
as lawmakers struggle to find ways to balance state budgets.

But competing costs are not the whole story either. Theoretically at
least, state lawmakers, when faced with mounting fiscal obligations,
have the option to increase revenues. The most powerful finding of the
statistical analysis I conducted was that states that tax their citizens
more are able to spend more on higher education. This is the case regardless of the cost of their other spending commitments. Some states,
faced with growing expenses across the board, raised taxes—and then
instead of facing a trade-off between higher education and other demands, they were able to support funding for each of these areas.[68]

Although nearly all state budgets have been on a collision course of growing expenses in recent decades, state lawmakers have varied in their willingness to raise revenues. As Figure 4.2 indicates, overall tax revenues grew from 1960 until 2000 on average and then stagnated in real terms. But between 1990 and 2010, only fourteen states increased their revenues by more than $500 per capita in real terms; in most states increases were much lower, and eight states actually dropped the amount they collect.[69] The combination in most states—of rapidly growing expenses and tepid or nonexistent revenue increases—has required lawmakers to find budget areas to cut, and higher education—given its discretionary nature—has presented itself as an easy target.

Here again, additional lateral effects of other policies help explain why funding for public universities and colleges has been shortchanged. The reasons for states' weak revenue-raising efforts emanate not only from antitax sentiments of recent decades but also from policy changes in many states, such as Colorado, that have "cast in constitutional concrete" an inability to increase taxes.[70] States have long differed from the federal government in that all except Vermont have balanced budget provisions that prohibit spending that exceeds revenues. Their ability to raise revenue became more constrained after the 1970s, when tax revolts broke out in many states and localities. The antitax advocates pressured state governments to adopt procedures that would limit the likelihood of future tax increases. Twenty-three states adopted the Tax and Expenditures Limitation, a rule that restricts state revenue growth to some indicator such as the growth of personal income. Thirteen states also adopted supermajority requirements for their legislature's approval of state tax increases. A study by two economists, Robert Archibald and David Feldman, found that these provisions are "very robust predictors" of variation in state appropriations for higher education, as states abiding by such rules offer significantly less funding than others.[71] They conclude, "Our results imply that turning the clock back to the early 1970s is a difficult enterprise. Attacking the tax and expenditures limitations or the supermajority requirements would require a pro-tax coalition that is stronger than the anti-tax forces that implemented them. But there is no evidence that support for these explicit limitations is waning."[72] These antitax rules have become a critical part of the policyscape, and they make a change of course difficult to achieve short of widespread popular mobilization for reform. That state lawmakers are more willing to force tuition increases on students in public universities than raise taxes on those with higher incomes implies that the dynamics of plutocracy which we have seen at the national level also operate at the state level.

Finally, we may wonder how the dynamics of polarization have affected state legislatures and the impact on higher education funding. I find some evidence that nationwide, states with more polarized legislatures are less likely to support higher funding levels for public universities and colleges.[73] Political scientist Luciana Dar, who found similar results in a study focused on California, explains that widening political polarization makes the political system less responsive to the "median voter" who was long assumed to be sought after by politicians in both parties in a two-party system. She argues that polarization changes higher education politics by limiting the scope of debate so that it occurs solely along redistributive lines, focusing on who should pay for it. In the past, such discussions revolved more broadly around higher education as a public good that improved social and civic life in communities. That framing captured the support of moderates who saw it as a means to promote economic development.[74] These analyses of polarization are preliminary, but they suggest that state legislatures too may be subject to some of the polarizing dynamics that have become so apparent on the national level, undermining lawmakers' ability to maintain higher education policy effectively.

Undermining Public Higher Education

The nation's public universities and colleges have educated the majority of Americans who have pursued higher education over the past sixty years. They include many of the nation's top-flight research universities—indeed, some rank as world class—and a vast network of institutions granting bachelor's and associate's degrees. They have welcomed Americans from across the income spectrum and students from a wide diversity of backgrounds that are reflective of the nation's population. They have offered quality education in every discipline of study and field of training available. When it comes to explaining the nation's historic legacy in higher education, their role fits front and center.

But these public institutions have been under siege for the past two decades, victims of competition for funds from other unrelated policies and draconian prohibitions on raising revenues to pay for state priorities. The state-level resources that supported them so well in the past have diminished just as costs have increased and the number of students seeking to attend college has grown. The problem is not that the public universities and colleges are shutting their doors; rather, they are becoming something different than what they have always been—they are being transformed into institutions that are, in reality, increasingly private. As state support atrophies and tuition escalates as a result, their inclusivity is becoming limited to those who can afford the rising costs.

Reduced resources threaten the quality of the education available at public institutions. The gap has widened between the amount they invest in educating each student and what private nonprofit institutions spend.[75] In order to trim their budgets, public institutions must pack more students into classes; the faculty-to-student ratio—which was already much larger than that at four-year private nonprofit colleges—has expanded further.[76] The disparities in faculty pay have widened dramatically, adding to the hiring and retention challenges at the publics. Public colleges have cut costs by hiring part-time and non–tenure track faculty to teach more of their courses, rather than hiring full-time faculty, and by embracing online teaching, whether by offering such courses themselves or by accepting credits that students take from large online vendors.[77] The extent of student learning in such formats remains unclear, but studies so far indicate that students who are less well prepared are served least well by the impersonal, remote nature of online learning.[78] In short, the gutting of public universities and colleges is leading to further stratification in higher education as the value of their offerings increasingly pales compared to those at private nonprofit institutions—for students who can afford them.

Increasing costs, large classes taught by adjuncts, and limited enrollments also discourage students from completing their degrees. One
study found that the increased time that students are taking to complete bachelor's degrees is almost entirely attributable to the growth
of such rates at public institutions; completion rates have changed little at private institutions. These increases are concentrated primarily
among low income students. Investigators found no evidence that differences in college preparedness or demographic attributes explained
the disparity in completion rates. Rather, as resources for public institutions dwindled, students were attempting to balance more hours in
the workforce with their role as students, with a detrimental impact on
their ability to complete their degrees in a timely manner.[79] Another
study revealed that a 10 percent increase in part-time faculty at four-
year public universities was associated with a 3 percent decrease in the
five-year graduation rate, and a comparable increase in the non–tenure
track faculty generated a 4 percent decrease.[80] These findings are remi-
niscent of the adage "you get what you pay for." Investing less in higher
education appears to be undermining the nation's aspiration to increase
college graduation rates and mocking the hopes of many members of
a generation of young students who enrolled in recent years, but who
have yet to complete their degrees.

In addition to the policy effects already described in this chapter,
state higher education spending also confronts an "unintended consequence" of federal student aid policy that exacerbates legislators'
difficulties when they face daunting budget decisions. Paradoxically,
states that try to maintain lower tuition levels for public college and
university students, particularly poorer states in the South and West,
receive *less* overall in federal aid than wealthier states in the Northeast
and Midwest. This is because most federal policies are now channeled
toward individuals on the basis of their need relative to the tuition at
the institutions they attend; as a result, states that charge higher tuition
of students benefit from greater federal aid infusions.[81]

Compounding the problem of reduced state aid for universities and
colleges, many states in recent decades have channeled public dollars

to students who are better-off. This has occurred particularly as states in the South have increasingly used higher education funds for merit-based financial aid for individual students with the strongest academic records, rather than as institutional aid that assists all students or as need-based individual aid. Whereas in the 1970s states made grants to college students only on the basis of need, in 1981 several began to issue merit-based grants, and as of 2010–2011, the percentage of funds allocated for need had diminished to 71 percent on average. Some of these changes occurred through major policy initiatives.[82] For example, in 1992 Georgia governor Zell Miller proposed what became known as the Helping Outstanding Pupils Educationally scholarship program (HOPE). Florida followed in 1997 with the Bright Futures scholarship program; now thirteen states offer such programs, with eight of them concentrated in the Southeast.[83] Economist Susan Dynarski found that while the Georgia HOPE program genuinely boosted college attendance rates, such advances have been concentrated among moderate to high income youth; she concluded that such programs will exacerbate the already large gaps in attendance between low and high income individuals and between blacks and whites.[84]

A once proud national achievement—a widespread system of public higher education—still attracts the vast majority of the nation's college-going students, but it no longer offers them the path to the American dream as it did for earlier generations. In large part, spending for other areas has crowded out higher education. This trend has not gone unnoticed. In 2010, California governor Arnold Schwarzenegger observed, "The priorities have become out of whack over the years. I mean, think about it, 30 years ago, 10 percent of the general fund went to higher education, and 3 percent went to prisons. Today, almost 11 percent goes to prisons, and only 7.5 percent goes to higher education. What does it say about any state that focuses more on prison uniforms than on caps and gowns? It simply is not healthy."[85] In the main, however, such trends have continued without state lawmakers intervening to manage development of existing policies in ways that could preserve and revitalize our national legacy in public higher education.

CHAPTER FIVE

OPPORTUNE MOMENTS

Reform on the Agenda

IN FEBRUARY 2007, CONGRESSWOMAN NANCY PELOSI SPOKE TO AN OVERFLOW audience of hundreds of students at Arizona State University. Just weeks earlier, Pelosi had been sworn in as Speaker of the US House of Representatives, and now, to spotlight her party's new policy agenda, she announced: "The key to it all—to a better future individually and to a stronger America—is education."[1] Citing Thomas Jefferson, she argued that education is essential to democracy, to creating an informed electorate, and further, she said, it is essential to the self-fulfillment of every person and to American competitiveness as a nation.

The event was not the first to signify that change was afoot. Just weeks before, President George W. Bush had endorsed increases in Pell grants. Reversing his administration's stance to date, he also advocated reducing government subsidies provided to lenders. In the next two years, Congress focused more attention to student aid issues than it had since 1993. During that time, it enacted a major new GI Bill and engaged in some crucial policy maintenance for Pell grants and student loans.

The election of Barack Obama brought with it the promise of reforming higher education policy that would help restore it to its role of expanding opportunity for low to moderate income Americans seeking to better their lives. Candidate Obama frequently cited education as a key area of focus. In his 2006 book *The Audacity of Hope*, he described education as "the heart of a bargain this nation has made with its citizens: If you work hard and take responsibility, you'll have a chance for a better life."[2] In his first speech to a joint session of Congress, President Obama proclaimed, "By 2020, America will once again have the highest proportion of college graduates in the world."[3] Observers in the higher education policy community in Washington, DC, commented that never before had a presidential administration placed so much value on education.[4] After nearly a quarter century of stagnation in federal higher education policy, political leaders finally showed signs of trying to change course.

When I began studying higher education policy in 2006, I saw little reason for optimism. The student loan system, designed to help middle income students afford college, had devolved into a system that enabled banks and lenders to collect substantial profits while government bore all the risk. Over time, lenders invested more in developing their political capacity and policymakers focused on negotiating with them, to the exclusion of pursuing alternative approaches that could have helped boost college graduation rates. It seemed like a perfect case of what political scientist Paul Pierson calls "lock in," when the design of a policy adopted at an earlier point in time inadvertently provides incentives for organizations or businesses to behave in particular ways; in turn, those activities reinforce that policy's existence and make a change to a different approach less likely.[5] Why, after more than two decades of bank-based student lending growing increasingly "locked in," did reform become possible?

At any given time, numerous problems confront society, and yet only a small number of them rise to the forefront of lawmakers' attention, making policy change possible. Political scientists have devoted considerable attention to explaining why an issue may or may not get on the agenda, and their explanations typically stress the intersection between social or economic changes on the one hand, and on the other, political developments, such as shifts in which party controls government, how issues are defined, or public opinion. One prominent explanation describes three political processes as separate streams: the problem stream, involving the recognition and definition of circumstances that ought to be addressed by government; the policy proposal stream, meaning the presence of viable alternative approaches to dealing with the issue; and the political stream, or the emergence of political will to address the matter. As this line of reasoning goes, it's only on the rare occasions when these three streams merge together that a "policy window" opens and an issue is likely to command policymakers' attention.[6]

But there's something missing from this explanation: the powerful role that existing policies play in influencing whether reform gets on the agenda or not. The policyscape shapes the very course taken by the "streams" that must converge for policy change: policy effects are likely to figure among the circumstances that need attention from lawmakers; politically feasible alternatives are likely to emerge either in reaction to existing policies or as strategies to build on top of them; and policies that are already in place may offer political incentives for lawmakers to reform them—or conversely, to leave them as they are. Policies can become entrenched and head in a particular direction—including off course—for long periods of time. Yet change is possible when policy effects collide with political and other circumstances in a manner that provides an opening for reform.

It was precisely such a convergence of developments—in American politics, society, the economy, and not least the policyscape—that made reform of federal student aid policy possible once again in the period from 2007 through 2010. Substantial change transpired and led to more generous support for US college students than ever. And yet the sharp partisan polarization that had for so long derailed policies and imperiled efforts to set them straight did not simply dissipate at this juncture; to the contrary, it became exacerbated. Policymakers—in this case, a Democratic majority in Congress—needed to find inventive ways to circumvent immense political obstacles as they promoted reform. They either turned to policy designs aimed to attract bipartisan support, or they embraced legislative procedures that escorted policies through the policy process as quickly as possible, offering minimal opportunities for deliberation. In either case, the dysfunction nonetheless shaped the policies that emerged, in some instances restricting the scope of reform and in others, imperiling the chances for its successful implementation or long-term success.

The Uphill Challenge for Policy Alternatives

We often talk about public problems as if the only thing preventing them from being solved is the absence of the right expert solutions. Our problems in higher education, viewed in this light, require only new techniques for getting those who don't seek to attend college to do so or new schemes that could ensure higher college graduation rates. In reality, however, innovative ideas are rarely in short supply; to the contrary, proposed "solutions" abound. Anyone who peruses the websites of think tanks in Washington, DC, or examines the research of faculty at the nation's many public policy schools will find plenty of alternative approaches to existing policies. For nearly every identifiable problem there are countless "policy entrepreneurs" standing ready to assist. To the contrary, it is politics that typically stands in the way of policy change, and the policyscape itself generates effects that privilege entrenched interests relative to those of ordinary Americans.

In the late 1990s and early years of the twenty-first century, as bank-based student lending proceeded apace, yielding vast profits for lenders while running up indebtedness among students and failing to expand college completion rates, it was not due to a lack of ideas about how to design policy more efficiently. In fact, an initial version of the prominent policy alternative, direct lending—which would have government itself lend to students rather than subsidizing banks to do so, in essence omitting the middleman—had already been enacted in 1993. Throughout the intervening years, however, elected officials allowed bank-based lending to dominate the market, tripling its lending volume in real terms and making 80 percent of all loans, while the fledgling direct lending program struggled.[7]

Why did more students not choose the seemingly better option? As a practical matter, most colleges participated in either the bank-based system or the direct loan system, so students did not often face an actual choice. And the fact that government subsidized the bank-based system meant that interest rates remained relatively low for students in either option—it was American taxpayers who paid the higher costs of the bank-based system, the subsidies required to induce banks to participate. The banks and Sallie Mae enjoyed a key advantage: they possessed the resources and expertise to market their services to universities and colleges, as well as to students and their families. They provided financial incentives for universities to endorse them as their "preferred lenders," offering kickbacks and other incentives in exchange for help in channeling students their way.[8] The US Department of Education, by contrast—even during the Clinton administration, which had promoted direct lending—had no such marketing capacity. As a longtime Capitol Hill staffer explained to me, "How do you compete? I told people, imagine [government] saying, 'We need an advertising and sales budget of $20 million for the program.' They'd laugh at us. Meanwhile, Sallie Mae and the other guys are running around with large advertising forces. They're cultivating aid administrators. These guys would spend, sometimes lavishly, to entertain people: they'd offer some Sallie Mae boat ride that you could go on, Sallie Mae–sponsored horseback riding or whatever. Anyway, the competition didn't work out too well."[9] Under the Bush administration, individuals who had worked for the private lending industry gained posts in the Department of Education to oversee direct lending, and it grew weaker still; between 2000 and 2003 alone, sixty-two colleges and universities dropped out of the plan. Lenders even found a legal loophole that permitted them to use federal money to offer rebates to students who borrowed from them and profits to colleges that switched back to the bank-based system.[10] In short, a policy solution existed and had even been established in law, but the policyscape ensured dominance of bank-based student lending, as the subsidies lenders gained from government permitted them to promote the system that benefited them and continue to dominate the market. The policy alternative stream confronted an uphill trajectory.

Student Aid and the Convergence of the Problem and Political Streams

For decades, political leaders were pressured by Sallie Mae and the banks to maintain the existing system and they faced little countervailing pressure from voters that would induce them to overhaul student aid. Young people in the 1960s and early 1970s, engaged by the civil rights and an-tiwar movements, worked on political campaigns at even higher rates than older Americans and voted at higher rates than in recent decades.[11] Their political participation provided an incentive to lawmakers to cre-ate and maintain the landmark student aid laws. In subsequent decades, however, new generations of young people failed to become as involved, and voter turnout in presidential elections—at 55 percent in 1972—had fallen to 40 percent in 2000. Given the demands being made by more vocal groups, lawmakers had little incentive to prioritize the needs of the young, including on student aid issues.

After 2000, however, young people began to reemerge in political life, shifting the political stream in a direction more favorable to re-form. They turned out at the polls at higher rates in the 2002 and 2004 elections than they had in other midterm and presidential elections, re-spectively, in many years. In the 2006 midterm election they took part at even higher rates than in 2002 and favored Democratic candidates by a wide margin, helping the party gain control of both chambers of Congress for the first time in fourteen years.[12] Democratic Party offi-cials could not help but take note of this newly mobilized constituency and think about how to cement their allegiance to the party.

Meanwhile, information about the boondoggle that the current stu-dent loan system provided to banks and to colleges that played along with them began to leak out. For the decade and a half following the direct lending battle of 1993, student aid policies had hovered under the radar of public awareness. Certainly many "inside the beltway" policy wonks and staffers on Capitol Hill understood the perverse incentives at work, but such recognition was not widespread. Gradually, however, investigative journalists began to expose the intense, mutually support-ive relationship between lenders, politicians, and many campuses. They revealed the stunning profits enjoyed by Sallie Mae and other lenders and their extensive efforts at political influence.[13] One 2003 article in *U.S. News & World Report* detailed the ways Sallie Mae and other lenders ro-manced college financial aid officials. At conferences they invited them to disco parties, golf outings, and a show by the US Olympic ski team, and on campuses they offered special perks. At Tuskegee University, for example, they installed free software and supplied free loan counselors. "It's an endless stream of invitations," said Johns Hopkins financial aid director Ellen Frishberg, after declining tickets from Sallie Mae to see Huey Lewis and the News in concert.[14] Gradually the problems that had developed in bank-based lending gained visibility in the public eye.

As Democratic leaders took note of these twin developments—newly mobilized young supporters and the public's growing awareness that student aid policy had gone awry—they recognized a political opportunity: making student aid reform a priority would enable them to demonstrate their effectiveness, particularly to the young. In January 2007, they unveiled legislation to cut interest rates on student loans and to increase Pell grants, financing the changes by increasing lenders' costs to government and reducing their subsidies.[15] Then Speaker Pelosi's office contacted US Public Interest Research Group (PIRG), one of the student associations, and asked for its assistance in organizing the event in Arizona mentioned above. Its success helped move student aid issues to the front and center of the Democratic Party agenda.[16]

The recognition that bank-based lending was a problem that needed attention continued to emerge, including in locations apart from Capitol Hill and outside the beltway entirely. New York attorney general Andrew Cuomo launched an investigation into the lending practices of Sallie Mae and several others, alleging that they maintained improper relationships with institutions of higher education. Reports surfaced indicating that the US Department of Education under the Bush administration had looked the other way regarding preferred lender practices and that its staff aided universities and colleges even when they circumvented federal rules regarding lending.[17] One of the reports was issued by the Department of Education's own inspector general. As a result, President Bush—to the consternation of members of his own party in Congress—grew less supportive of the lenders and more willing to part ways with congressional Republicans on student loan issues. He replaced several of his political appointees in the Department of Education, particularly those who had worked in the lending industry for years beforehand.[18]

As it became increasingly clear to public officials both that student aid was functioning poorly and wasting taxpayer dollars and also that addressing it provided a political opportunity, the problem and political streams merged, heading in the direction of reform. In September 2007, Congress passed and President Bush signed into law the College Cost Containment and Access Act, a bill that reduced lender subsidies and used the savings to increase student aid.[19] The bill included ample spending increases for Pell grants, enough to raise maximum grant levels from the current rate of $4,310 to at least $5,400 in 2012. It cut interest rates on student loans and initiated the beginnings of income-based repayment and public service loan forgiveness, programs that limited the amount that borrowers working in low-paying jobs or public service would need to repay in student loan debt.[20] In July 2008, in reauthorizing the Higher Education Act, Congress again raised Pell grants rates and imposed new regulations on colleges in their relationships to lenders, and again Bush signed the measure.

These breakthroughs on student aid issues in no way indicated a softening of the sharp partisan polarization that had emerged in Congress. To the contrary, they involved rigid party-line voting and extreme partisan acrimony in congressional proceedings. Republicans, now the minority in both houses, charged that Democrats effectively locked them out of decision making—echoing accusations Democrats had hurled at Republicans just a year prior, when the GOP held the majority.[21] Unlike the situation in the 1980s and early 1990s, student loan issues now divided members almost entirely along party lines, so lenders enjoyed protection while the Republicans ruled and lost the assurance of it once Democrats took power. As the problem of bank-based lending became increasingly apparent, Democrats sought to respond to a newly energized constituency of young voters; addressing the issue offered a political opportunity to the party. In short, polarization in this instance helps explain why reform *could* occur. The wild card, politically, was President Bush, who had become willing to buck his party and support Democrat-sponsored legislation.

The changes that ensued would not immediately restore the promise of equal opportunity inherent in the higher education legislation of the mid-twentieth century, but they were lawmakers' strongest efforts in many years to move in that direction. The lenders' star—though by no means extinguished—no longer burned as brightly as it had for the previous decade and a half. Before engaging in more sweeping changes to student loans, lawmakers found it possible to move ahead to reform student aid for veterans, by creating a bold new GI Bill.

A Victory for Veterans

Like other student aid laws, the GI Bill had become less effective over time and required updating to serve the needs of a new generation of veterans as well as it had those in earlier decades. The original GI Bill for veterans of World War II had covered tuition at any college in the nation and provided subsistence allowances for veterans and their families. By 2005 veterans in the All-Volunteer Force (AVF) faced monthly bills of $1,712 for tuition, room, and board at the average four-year public university or college, but the Montgomery GI Bill gave them $1,034 monthly at most, and National Guard and reserve troops were relegated to a separate policy that covered only one-third as much of their tuition.

Proponents of reform had pressured Congress for many years, without success, before the political climate finally grew more favorable. As early as 1998, the Military Coalition, a group that united thirty military and veterans membership organizations, had called for improvements in veterans' educational benefits. Even after 9/11 and the beginnings of the wars in Iraq and Afghanistan, it made little headway, confronting what one observer called "enormous indifference." Momentum grew, however, as the military sent large numbers of reservists and National Guardsmen from neighborhoods all over the nation to serve in those wars and to do so for longer periods of time and repeated tours of duty. Local media covered their stories, fueling widespread support for improved treatment for returning troops. These factors encouraged political leaders to work on modest alterations to the Montgomery GI Bill.[22]

Jim Webb's 2006 election to the Senate proved pivotal, as he became a catalyst for policy change.[23] While campaigning for office, Webb, a US

Naval Academy graduate who had commanded a platoon of Marines in Vietnam, had worn the combat boots of his son Jimmy, who had performed a tour of duty in Iraq as a Marine. On his first day in office in 2007, he introduced a bill to overhaul the GI Bill. Several veterans organizations endorsed Webb's bill, and both the House and Senate committees began to consider it. The following year, Webb redoubled the effort by teaming up with a bipartisan group of senators that included Chuck Hagel, Republican of Nebraska and a Vietnam War veteran, and Frank Lautenberg, Democrat of New Jersey, and John Warner, Republican of Virginia, both World War II veterans. They seized the moment, taking advantage of the groundswell of organizational and popular support for reform.

Webb's bill gained momentum and prevailed over contenders once veterans organizations, including those representing young veterans, rallied behind it. Already in February 2007, the Iraq and Afghanistan Veterans of America had chosen a World War II–style GI Bill as its top legislative priority.[24] The organization's charismatic young chief legislative counsel, Patrick Campbell, had volunteered for the National Guard soon after September 11, 2001, and had served in Iraq. He and another Iraq War veteran, Bill Ferguson, would spend months in 2007 going door to door on Capitol Hill.[25] They forged an alliance with the Veterans of Foreign Wars, Military Officers of American Association, American Legion, and numerous other veterans groups.

Suddenly, in the midst of a polarized environment characterized by stalemate and mounting fiscal concerns, proponents of an improved GI Bill rapidly accomplished more than they had ever hoped. Within a year and a half, Congress enacted—by nearly unanimous votes in each chamber—and President Bush signed into law the most generous version of veterans' educational benefits enacted in half a century. The Post-9/11 GI Bill permitted service members who were active after September 11, 2001, to earn up to thirty-six months of benefits, including the cost of tuition at a rate equaling that of the flagship four-year public university in their state, a monthly stipend equivalent to housing costs in the area, and a small stipend for books. The government also agreed to match any additional contributions toward tuition provided by private universities or colleges, through what became known as the Yellow Ribbon program. Finally, the same benefits would be extended to reservists, their duration based solely on cumulative active service.[26]

The new law's rapid adoption demonstrates how political polarization now influences policy change even on the rare occasions when circumstances coalesce for reform, in this case making bipartisan co-sponsorship possible. Typically polarization has engendered inaction on myriad issues, not least veterans' educational benefits. As long as Republicans had been in control of Congress, advocating for less government, proponents of reform got nowhere. But after the Democrats took charge and recognized a winning political issue, change came fast and furious—far more so than under the less polarized conditions of the 1980s, when routine legislative procedures presented a maze of obstacles. Before the Montgomery GI Bill was enacted in 1987, Congressman "Sonny" Montgomery spent seven years lining up support for it, and nineteen congressional hearings were held. Webb's bill was enacted within eighteen months of his taking office in the Senate, without a single hearing.

But while the new political environment offered the advantage of speed, it had downsides as well, not least a reduction in deliberation and careful consideration of alternatives. The Post-9/11 GI Bill entirely circumvented the regular veterans affairs committees, venues where those most familiar with such issues could have foreseen problems inherent in its policy design. It also triumphed over Senator John McCain's lower-cost alternative, a version that would have built on—instead of replacing—the existing platform of the Montgomery GI Bill. Just a year or two earlier, proponents of reform would have welcomed the McCain bill, which encompassed all they had worked for since 2000. The Webb approach, which aimed to approximate the generosity of the original World War II GI Bill, stunned them, surpassing their expectations.[27]

Webb and his allies ingeniously designed the bill in a manner that bypassed standard legislative procedures. According to pay-as-you-go rules adopted by Congress in 2007 to promote deficit reduction, a new entitlement program must be financed by new taxes or reductions else-where. But the bill's proponents managed to sidestep those require-ments by arguing, successfully, that veterans' educational benefits in the current era should be considered a cost of war, and therefore could be rolled into a large supplemental war spending bill. They also man-aged to bypass hearings in the House and ushered the bill along under the radar of the Congressional Budget Office, avoiding having it scored for its impact on the deficit.[28] In effect, lawmakers put the cost of the new legislation on a credit card.[29]

Republican leaders were blindsided by the bill's momentum. In late April, staff in Senator McCain's office had summoned representatives of veterans organizations to a meeting to gauge their support for his approach. A testy exchange ensued. The leaders of the veterans' orga-nizations acknowledged that many of them thought Webb's bill had structural flaws that would make it difficult to administer. It proposed calculating benefits, for example, through a complex formula that in-volved the tuition rate at the flagship university in a veteran's state of residence. Their overwhelming sentiment, however, was that the bill en-joyed a "tsunami of support" and that the "handwriting was on the wall" for its enactment, an outcome they would endorse.[30] A few weeks later, Senate minority leader Mitch McConnell caused an uproar when—as a tactic to quell the progress of the Webb bill—he offered McCain's bill as an amendment to unrelated legislation about union rights for fire-fighters and police officers. The Senate voted to table the vote, killing McCain's proposal.[31]

According to those involved in the process, Webb and the Senate Democrats essentially stole the show by dominating "the messaging on who is supporting the troops" away from key Republican leaders in Congress and the Bush administration.[32] They started "stampeding" in their efforts to gain supporters, and once ten Republicans senators signed on, it became clear that the bill could withstand a filibuster.[33] Meanwhile, a venture capitalist who was a World War II veteran fi-nanced ads to be placed in newspapers around the country in support of the bill.

In late June, the House and Senate cast overwhelming votes in support of the measure. Democrats had made the bill a policy priority and supported it unanimously. Although many Republicans would have preferred McCain's less costly approach, they ultimately heeded the advice of House Republican leader, John Boehner: "Members just need to suck it up and vote yes."[34] In an age of sharp polarization, veterans' benefits still had the power to bring members together across the aisle, particularly when they had the full-throated support of veterans' membership organizations—and when their promoters founds ways to circumvent the normal appropriations process.

The Post-9/11 GI Bill's successful enactment and bipartisan support harkened back to policymaking developments of the mid-twentieth century, when other major higher education laws were enacted. However, this bill, unlike the earlier ones, had been enacted hastily and without a thorough vetting from both sides of the aisle. Its passage owed to efforts by congressional proponents, including their strategic use of extraordinary procedures, legislative tricks that steered it past the fray of normal deliberative processes. The consequences would become apparent quickly, as implementation turned into what one observer called "a complete and utter failure," a topic we will examine later on.[35]

OBAMA PROMOTES REFORM

Just after President Bush signed the new GI Bill into law, disaster struck the US economy, as a financial crisis—already percolating for many months—hit its stride and several major banks failed or were rescued by the US government. Standard operating procedures under bank-based student lending would become the first casualty of changing circumstances: the evaporation of private credit sources meant that banks had no way to make loans. Yet while the financial crisis imperiled many domestic policy priorities, it actually created opportunities for student aid reform and coincided with political factors that helped ensure action. Most critically, Obama won the presidency in an election fueled by the active involvement of young people. Once in office, he lost no time in advancing his campaign goal of making college affordable for Americans from low and moderate income backgrounds. Student aid reform, along with health care reform, financial reform, and economic revitalization, represented the major priorities of his first two years in the White House. Within fifteen months, Obama had achieved sweeping changes in federal student aid, including some reformers had pursued for two decades. Yet the accomplishments also contained a few drawbacks, features indicative of their enactment in the context of a highly polarized political climate.

Higher education provisions would occupy a prominent place in the president's first major stimulus initiative, the American Recovery and Reinvestment Act of 2009, which directed federal dollars toward students and colleges in several ways. The bill devoted $15.6 billion to the Pell grant program. It extended grants to 800,000 more students, with the aim of reaching 7 million low and moderate income individuals, and it boosted maximum grant levels up from $4,731 to $5,550.[36] The bill also made available extensive aid to the states that they could use to fund their public universities and colleges. Both of these features represented real accomplishments for promoting opportunity.

In addition, fully 37 percent of the $787 billion dollar stimulus package would be allocated in the form of tax credits, including $49 billion targeted for higher education in the so-called American Opportunity Tax Credit. The policy, which Obama had mentioned throughout his campaign, enlarged upon the Clinton era initiative by allowing tax credits to be claimed for four years of college rather than only the first two. It also increased the maximum annual benefit from $1,800 to $2,500, allowed refunds of up to $1,000 for those with no tax liability, and extended its availability to households with incomes up to $180,000. All of these components were adopted when Congress approved the bill and Obama signed it into law in February 2009.

The idea of helping Americans afford a college education during tough economic times made good sense, but the tuition tax credits— just like those Clinton had endorsed—devoted a huge new portion of federal student aid to purposes that would fail to put college-going more within the reach of low to moderate income Americans. Once again, the approach—expanding student aid through the tax system—lacked grassroots proponents.[37] Given the unimpressive track record of the Clinton-era variants in expanding access to college, neither the usual student aid advocates nor policy analysts greeted it with much enthusiasm.[38] Some were aghast that such assistance would be extended into the upper reaches of the income distribution to families of students who would most certainly go to college regardless of whether or not they received this break.[39] Proponents of social tax expenditures in the Obama administration believed that the refundability feature of the new policy would help make it more accessible to low income people. But the fact that families receive the funds long after they pay tuition makes them unlikely to influence enrollment decisions. The bipartisan appeal of tax expenditures helps explain Obama's emphasis on this approach, as Republicans repeatedly said that more of the stimulus should be in the form of tax breaks rather than in direct spending. Yet given the immense polarization Obama confronted, the stimulus bill—even in the midst of the financial crisis—passed almost entirely along party lines, with only three Republicans in the Senate and not a single one in the House supporting it. In short, it epitomized another reckless response to the challenge of improving the nation's college graduation rates: expensive yet ineffective.

Obama continued to place student aid reform, along with health care reform, at the top of his domestic policy agenda for 2009. His 2010 budget aimed to terminate the bank-based student loan program, which it depicted as "entitlements for lenders," and replace it entirely with direct lending.[40] In addition, the president proposed to use savings that would come from the elimination of the Federal Family Education Loan (FFEL) program to improve other forms of student aid in ways that could assist low to middle income students. He wished to make Pell grants an entitlement, like Medicare or Social Security, so that any student who met the eligibility criteria would receive a full grant rather than the number being determined by the amount appropriated in the budget process. In addition, Pell grants would be increased annually at rates derived from the consumer price index (CPI). Finally, the president planned to provide funds to states and community colleges to foster student readiness and degree completion. To advance these plans, Obama named a key policy entrepreneur, Robert Shireman, to be deputy undersecretary in the US Department of Education. Shireman had been the chief promoter of direct lending from the beginning in the late 1980s, when he worked as a staffer for Senator Paul Simon, and he had also played a major role during the 1993 battle over it, when he served in the Clinton administration. Among advocates of expanded access, he was widely regarded for his cutting-edge ideas and political savvy; among defenders of lenders and banks, he was despised.[41]

The plan to end bank-based student lending was viewed in starkly different terms by proponents and opponents. From the time Obama announced the initiative through its eventual passage in 2010, critics termed it a "government takeover," warning that 100 percent direct lending would undermine "choice and competition" by ending the role of banks and other private organizations in student lending and lead to deteriorating customer service for student borrowers and higher costs for taxpayers.[42] As one Republican staffer put it, "It would make the US Department of Education one of the ten largest banks in the country, but Arne Duncan is not a banker."[43]

Obama's plan to make a complete shift to direct lending received an enormous boost when the nonpartisan Congressional Budget Office released its assessment of the cost savings that would result. The White House had predicted that replacing FFEL would lower federal spending by $47 billion over ten years, but the CBO projected savings of nearly twice as much, $87 billion.[44] In the words of American Council on Education lobbyist Terry Hartle, this announcement was a "game changer."[45] It diffused the arguments of FFEL advocates who claimed that the system rewarded free enterprise and competition, showing it instead to be costlier due to subsidies government provided to lenders. Trade associations within the National Center for Higher Education, some of which had been concerned about their member institutions' capacity to convert to direct lending, dropped their reservations and embraced the change.[46]

Emboldened, Obama delivered a fiery speech in April 2009, speaking out against the ways that the existing system privileged lenders: "Under the FFEL program, lenders get a big government subsidy with every loan they make. And these loans are then guaranteed with taxpayer money, which means that if a student defaults, a lender can get back almost all of its money from our government. . . . taxpayers are paying banks a premium to act as middlemen—a premium that costs the American people billions of dollars each year. . . . Well, that's a premium we cannot afford—not when we could be investing the same money in our students, in our economy, and in our country."[47] He concluded by taking on the lenders directly: "The banks and the lenders who have reaped a windfall from these subsidies have mobilized an army of lobbyists to try to keep things the way they are. They are gearing up for battle. So am I. They will fight for their special interests. I will fight for . . . American students and their families. And for those who care about America's future, this is a battle we can't afford to lose."[48]

Not all Democrats agreed with the president. Those from states whose electoral votes had gone to McCain rather than Obama and those who held unsafe seats were the most likely to defect. Nebraska senator Ben Nelson opposed Obama's plan because the lender Nelnet, based in Lincoln, employed a thousand people in the state. "I think it would be the wrong direction for people to outsource jobs from Lincoln, Nebraska to Washington, DC," said Nelson, whose most generous campaign donor over the past five years had been the student lending organization.[49] Blanche Lincoln of Arkansas also expressed concerns about potential job losses in her state.[50]

But Democratic leaders, cognizant that they were unlikely to attain the sixty votes necessary in the Senate to ward off a filibuster—a refusal to end debate and permit a vote—had planned ahead for that eventuality. Already in April 2009, the budget committees in both chambers had included "reconciliation instructions" in the compromise budget outline, requiring the committees responsible for education policy to reduce program spending by one billion or more.[51] In effect, this would permit the administration's plan for direct lending to be included in a special "reconciliation" bill for which debate would be limited to twenty hours and only fifty-one votes would be required for passage.[52] This foresight would turn out to be essential, as we shall see.

Meanwhile, although student loan reform thus appeared to be on track, Obama's plan to transform Pell grants into entitlements with automatic annual increases encountered unexpected early resistance from congressional Democrats. Senate Budget Committee chair Kent Conrad (D-ND) and House Appropriations Committee chair David Obey (D-WI) objected, not wanting Congress to lose authority over the appropriations process.[53] Neither did chairman of the House Education and Labor Committee, Congressman George Miller (D-CA) push for entitlement status, as he considered the pursuit of full direct lending to be "enough of a fight" already. A large share of the programs in the federal budget already had entitlement status, leaving Congress with little room to maneuver in the budget process; scant enthusiasm existed on either side of the aisle for shifting that ratio further. By legislating a formula for regular increases in grant levels, Miller proposed that Congress could produce essentially the same result of guaranteed rates for students, while retaining "power of the purse."[54]

THE HOUSE TAKES ACTION

Over the next months, lenders, realizing that they were in trouble, put forth their own proposals to restructure student lending.[55] A plan spearheaded by Sallie Mae and promoted in conjunction with Nelnet and a few other large for-profit lenders attracted the most attention because it claimed to offer equivalent savings to the administration's plan. This alternative, implicitly acknowledging that the private lenders lacked access to capital, would eliminate subsidies to lenders and require the federal government to take ownership of loans—as in fact it already had under emergency legislation Congress enacted during the financial crisis as a means to shore up the credit-starved industry. The hallmark of the plan was that it would perpetuate a substantial role for the lenders— in loan origination, servicing, and collection—and would mandate that government pay them fees. The lenders argued that this approach would preserve competition, eliminate the need for campuses to engage in what could be an onerous switch to direct lending, and avoid job losses.

The plan garnered strikingly little support. In what congressional staffers considered a tactical error, Sallie Mae neglected to represent the interests of smaller nonprofit lenders, those to whom members of Congress have far greater allegiance because they are distributed widely throughout states and congressional districts across the nation. The failure to include them, some staffers commented, was in keeping with the organization's self-interested style; even policy actors allied with the lender remarked on its "tone-deaf" attributes.[56] In addition, the alternative did not satisfy congressional Republicans because it did not originate with private capital but with government. From their perspective, it amounted to a "bloated direct loan program," with the added expense of fees paid to lenders.[57]

Within days, Chairman Miller repudiated the lenders' alternative: "It's unfortunate that a small number of lenders are using legislative gimmicks to mask the fact that their proposal would divert $15 billion into their own pockets at the expense of students."[58] Instead, he introduced legislation modeled on Obama's plan, calling for an end to the bank-based lending program and using the savings to strengthen Pell grants and community colleges. The committee approved the legislation that same day in a mostly party line vote.[59]

No member of either party introduced a substitute amendment representing the lenders' alternate proposal. Republicans—after years of working actively in tandem with the lenders—took a passive approach toward policy developments.[60] Their failure to mount opposing arguments owed largely to the GOP's political strategy of unwillingness to compromise with Democrats—evidence of the gaping ideological polarization. As one staffer explained, "If we had been willing to modify some components of the legislation, it would have appeared as it we endorsed others put forward by the majority, when in fact there are wide philosophical differences between us." The party's lack of engagement on the issue also revealed the practical impossibility, given the state of the economy, of devising a feasible alternative to direct lending that both originated with private capital and offered government cost savings.[61] With the opposition effectively silenced, the full House quickly approved Obama's plans.

In mid-September, the full House approved the Student Aid and Fiscal Responsibility Act (H.R. 3221, which became known as SAFRA) by a vote of 253–171. Only six Republicans voted in support and only four Democrats opposed it.[62] The legislation mandated the end of FFEL, requiring all colleges to shift to direct federal lending by July 1, 2010; it permitted lenders to compete to service loans but not to originate them. The legislation used $40 billion of the projected savings from FFEL to boost Pell grants—not by making them a formal entitlement but by ensuring annual increases of CPI plus 1 percent. As such, the maximum award was set to grow from $5,350 to $5,550 in 2010, with additional increases that would bring it to $6,900 in 2019. Obama's plans for community colleges were also included: $10 billion for the American Graduation Initiative, aimed to elevate the number of graduates by 5 million by 2020; plus an expansion of the already existing College Access Challenge Grant program, which awards grants to individual colleges and states that put forward innovative approaches to elevating enrollment and graduation rates.[63]

In effect, the House granted the president everything he wanted with the exception of making Pell grants a formal entitlement. Democratic leaders confidently predicted that the Senate would also pass the legislation within a few short weeks.

Hearing from "The Rest of the Country"

As autumn proceeded, however, Senate leaders delayed action on student aid, hoping to address health care reform first. They wanted to retain the possibility of combining the two issues in a reconciliation package, if necessary, and only one such bill may be enacted per session.

During the delay, lenders mobilized opposition to the shift to direct lending at the grassroots and elite levels. Sallie Mae rallied workers and residents in the towns where it employed the greatest numbers: Fishers and Muncie, Indiana; Lynn Haven, Florida; and Wilkes-Barre, Pennsylvania. In Fishers, over 81,000 individuals signed a petition urging Congress to preserve a role for lenders. At a rally of company employees, hundreds of whom wore T-shirts that read "Protect Indiana Jobs," Sallie Mae CEO Albert Lord attempted to stir populist anger: "There's Washington, and then there's the rest of the country. This is the rest of the country."[64]

Meanwhile, in Washington, DC, lenders aimed to gain support for continuing bank-based lending from at least five moderate Democratic senators. They devoted millions of dollars to lobbying; Sallie Mae alone spent over $4 million on it in 2009, the second-largest amount it had ever spent in one year. To lobby on its behalf, the company hired former Clinton administration official Jamie Gorelick and Democratic fundraiser Tony Podesta, whose brother John had led the Obama transition.[65]

By November, analysts predicted that Obama's student aid proposal lacked the support of enough senators to pass.[66] Democrat Bob Casey from Pennsylvania and eleven other moderate Democrats announced their support for a revised version of the lenders' alternative approach.[67] Yet, according to staffers on the Hill, they never offered "a serious compromise proposal." In fact, some of the rebel senators admitted privately that although they had to speak out about job losses in their states, they would ultimately vote in support of legislation similar to SAFRA.[68]

While lenders struggled to oppose loan reform, the United States Student Association and US Public Interest Research Group (PIRG) worked energetically to promote it. In the midst of the financial crisis, these organizations' membership rolls were on the rise. Their leadership had spent years working to replace FFEL with direct lending, and the chance to promote SAFRA gave them a focal point for rallying their grassroots. And as one organizational leader put it, "Students have been waiting for a while to get behind something they felt would impact them directly." During one week in September, US PIRG and its member groups around the nation collected petitions from students indicating the amount of debt each would have once they graduated and attached each dollar amount to a brick. Displayed in combination, the bricks constituted a Wall of Debt that powerfully depicted the issues students faced. In October, USSA, PIRG, and other associations united forces for Raising Pell Week of activism, as they used social networking sites to reach students and mobilized them for a national youth call-in and FAX-in urging the Senate to pass SAFRA. They recruited numerous organizations to be fellow signatories in an ad to the leaders of the Senate HELP committee that was published on Politico, highlighting the need for student aid reform.[69]

The student organizations generated heightened activity in states whose senators were considered swing votes, often because the student loan industry employed residents. The groups stimulated the publication of newspaper editorials in numerous locations and organized a financial aid hearing with Casey in Pennsylvania. They not only activated students but also, in some locations, coordinated their efforts with labor organizations including the AFL-CIO and SEIU (Service Employees International Union) and with civil rights organizations such as the NAACP and La Raza. In local areas where lenders argued that the demise of FFEL would mean lost jobs, labor organizations probed deeper; in at least one case they revealed that the new servicing activities would actually require Sallie Mae and others to move jobs back to the United States, thus increasing employment.[70]

Both opponents and proponents of student aid reform seemed to be gaining momentum simultaneously and the fate of the president's agenda hung in the balance. But as the holidays arrived the Senate passed health care reform, and early in the new year leaders of both chambers began to iron out a single bill for final passage. It appeared that congressional attention would soon turn back to student aid. But then a special election in Massachusetts upended those plans.

PELL-MELL TO THE FINISH

On January 19, 2010, Republican Scott Brown surprised the nation and won the Senate seat held by the late Ted Kennedy. This development effectively tossed Democrats' plans for health care legislation up in the air and, with it, student aid reform. With Brown elected, the Democratic majority shrank from sixty to fifty-nine—no longer the number needed to withstand a GOP filibuster. Given that no Senate Republicans were expected to support either the Affordable Care Act or the student aid bill, Democrats' only hope for accomplishing the president's agenda was to utilize the special reconciliation procedures that they had planned in advance and that permitted a simple majority vote of fifty-one to pass legislation.

As Senate Budget Committee chair, South Dakota senator Kent Conrad controlled the fate of the student aid legislation because he possessed the authority to deem whether its provisions met the special criteria for inclusion in the reconciliation package. Such bills may not include new programs but only funding for existing ones, and the overall package must achieve budgetary savings. Ironically, the administration had become a victim of its early successes. First, Shireman's efforts in the Department of Education had already pushed many schools to adopt direct lending, and consequently much of the cost savings of the shift away from FFEL had already been realized. Second, the recession had led to soaring college enrollments and more students than ever qualifying for Pell grants, thus elevating demand and program costs.[71] The CBO's lower assessment of savings, now $61 billion instead of $87 billion, would mean substantially less money available for new spending.

In the second week of March, in a stormy meeting in Speaker Nancy Pelosi's office, Conrad told fellow Democrats that higher education should be removed from the bill, delayed for some months and perhaps even until the reconciliation process in the next Congress.[72] Conrad, in whose home state the Bank of North Dakota provided jobs and significant revenue, had never been a strong supporter of direct lending.[73] Now he said, "I think it threatens the health care bill. It would . . . sink them both."[74] Advocates for the higher education provisions were stunned, believing that the legislation would die if delayed beyond the midterm elections.

Days later Senator Tom Harkin, chair of the Senate HELP Committee, and Chairman Miller convened the Democratic Caucus to make the case for including the higher education provisions with health care reform. This was the time, at last, they argued, to terminate the system that channeled so much in federal dollars to banks and lenders, and to redirect the funds to the nation's students. To the leaders' consternation, Conrad did not attend the meeting, citing previous engagements. Six moderate Democratic senators, moreover, sent a letter expressing concerns about job losses in their states if FFEL was terminated.[75]

Conrad finally conceded and agreed to include the higher education provisions on one condition: he insisted on using the new, lower 2010 CBO score for cost savings, meaning tens of billions less for student aid. Perhaps his unwillingness to comply with his colleagues' wishes emanated from his perspective, as budget chair, that the extraordinary reconciliation procedures should be used conservatively; perhaps he meant to rebuke fellow Democrats who had pushed him to drop a special proviso in the bill that would have excused the Bank of North Dakota from compliance, as Republicans were already calling it the "Bismarck Bank Deal."[76] Whatever his rationale, Conrad's decision to use the lower CBO score infuriated other Democrats, who knew that he possessed the discretion to allow either score to be used and that he was willing to use the 2009 scores for determining the health care components of the bill.[77] Nonetheless, they were forced to scale back the proposed increases for student aid. Of the $61 billion in estimated savings from loan reform, the leadership requested $19 billion to help finance health care reform and deficit reduction, with $9 billion and $10 billion directed toward each, respectively. The health care bill, on its own, did not provide sufficient savings to be considered revenue-neutral; combining it with the higher education provisions thus enabled its enactment.[78] These changes left $43 billion—less than half of what policymakers had expected as recently as one month earlier—for the programs aimed to expand access to college and elevate completion rates.

Whereas Obama had hoped to make Pell grants an entitlement and the House had proposed annual increases at the rate of inflation plus 1 percent, the final bill mandated only that the grant levels must increase with inflation. In fact, with the growing demand for Pell grants, one-third of the money allocated for it had to be used to pay for past funding shortfalls, not future increases. As a result, although the House had planned for maximum Pell grant awards to increase to $6,900 (up from $5,350), the reconciliation bill put them at $5,550 for the next two years with gradual increases up to $5,975 in 2020.[79]

In news that devastated community college representatives, negotiators decided to ax Obama's signature American Graduation Initiative (AGI), designed to promote innovative strategies by the sector to improve college graduation rates and to enhance pathways to the workforce. This was a blow, particularly after the House had approved $10 billion for the program in SAFRA, and recent drafts of the final bill were rumored to feature even greater funding for innovation and experimentation. Conrad apparently objected to AGI on the grounds that it was a new program and therefore did not meet reconciliation requirements. Ultimately Democratic leaders managed to find smaller amounts for more modest initiatives for community colleges, but the novel AGI plan was sidelined.[80] As one lobbyist for the community colleges put it, "It was a huge disappointment, after what had been planned."[81]

Remarkably, the termination of FFEL—the most momentous aspect of the higher education provisions—attracted little attention at this final stage, indicating just how much political capital the lenders had lost. Still, when the full Senate voted on reconciliation, three Democratic senators—Nelson, Pryor, and Lincoln, all vocal defenders of the bank-based student loan system and each of whom had voted in favor of health care reform in December—opposed it, as did all Republicans, for a vote of 56–43. This indicated that the higher education legislation likely could not have mustered sufficient support apart from the reconciliation procedures.

When the House approved the reconciliation bill in a vote of 220–211 near midnight on March 21, and the Senate followed a few days later, the occasion was clearly historic because of health care reform, yet it was also noteworthy because of the student aid provisions. It marked the culmination of the two-decade battle to terminate FFEL, a system that had long privileged lenders and inadvertently empowered them more than students. Part of the savings, although less than reformers had envisioned just a few weeks earlier, was directed to programs that would help less advantaged Americans attend college and complete degrees. As one staffer put it, "We have taken money from a vested interest and given it to some of the most low income people in our country. We don't do that very often."[82] On March 30, at Northern Virginia Community College, President Obama signed the new bill into law.

THE SHAPE OF REFORM

In a period of just over three years, between 2007 and early 2010, the president and Congress achieved significant changes in student aid policy. They had successfully engaged in maintaining and updating existing policies, making adjustments so that they would function better for new generations of students. The major accomplishments included the adoption of the generous and inclusive Post-9/11 GI Bill; the increases in Pell grants, and a formula to ensure that the benefits would not dwindle as they had in the past. And of course bank-based lending had been replaced with a cheaper alternative—direct lending. In addition, they had succeeded in reaching agreements about some new policy innovations, including the simplification of federal financial aid applications, to make them easier for more eligible students to complete, and new investments in community colleges.

Why, after all this time, did change suddenly become possible? First, the political stream shifted in critical ways that helped create openings. As those in the all-volunteer military returned from long and often repeated tours of duty in Iraq and Afghanistan, Americans favored efforts to ease their readjustment. Young people participated in politics at higher rates than they had in decades, helping to usher new Democratic majorities into Congress for the first time in a decade and a half, and they invigorated the presidential campaign of Barack Obama and assisted in his victory. Second, complications in existing policies surfaced in the problem stream, coming to the forefront of lawmakers' attention: the inadequacy of GI Bill and Pell grant funding; the channeling of so much federal student aid to banks instead of students; and lenders' often unseemly relationships with campus financial aid officials. These issues presented challenges to be addressed and, simultaneously, political opportunities to respond to key constituencies. Journalists played their part by exposing the shortcomings in the treatment veterans received and highlighted how student loan companies were profiting at students' expense. The bank-based lending program might still have survived had it not been for the financial crisis, which made it apparent even to the system's staunchest allies that it no longer remained feasible. Third, policy entrepreneurs played key roles in promoting policy alternatives. Senator Jim Webb championed the new GI Bill, and Obama and his appointee Robert Shireman played critical roles in advocating for change in civilian student aid. Veterans' organizations and the higher education policy community rallied around the new proposals, providing them with momentum to overcome obstacles along the way. In sum, opportunities for reform arose owing to a combination of shifts in the functioning of existing policies, their interaction with changes in the political environment, and the emergence of savvy individuals ready to promote workable policy alternatives and groups prepared to endorse them.

The result, for American students, was momentous, the largest collective increases in the generosity and availability of federal aid to facilitate college-going since the passage of landmark laws at least four decades prior. Students welcomed the new benefits and took advantage of them quickly. Between 2006 and 2010, college enrollment soared by nearly 7 percent, to the greatest numbers the nation had ever experienced.[83] The number of Pell grant recipients skyrocketed, growing from 5.2 million in 2006–2007 to 9.3 million in 2010–2011.[84] GI Bill beneficiaries escalated over the same period from about 500,000 to 800,000.[85] The American Opportunity Tax Credit was claimed on 13.2 million tax returns in 2010.[86] As for the Republican fears that a "government takeover" of student loans would lead to poor management and that the Department of Education would fail to accomplish it by the deadline just four months after the law's passage, leaving students in the lurch, no evidence emerged. Perhaps the most important take-away from these years is that change is possible; that even with all of the policy effects generated by existing policies and even amid high levels of polarization, lawmakers can manage to achieve meaningful reforms to improve the opportunities of low to middle income Americans and to restore the promise of educational opportunity.

Yet even during this momentous period when reformers triumphed over decades of legislative paralysis, polarization still made policy maintenance and development less effective than they could have been otherwise. Entrepreneurs were forced to adopt extraordinary procedures in order to circumvent the standard obstacles of lawmaking that had become, amid recent partisan divergence, nearly impassable. The GI Bill was pushed forward without congressional hearings that might have found ways to avoid program delivery problems. Without proper vetting and careful planning for administrative dimensions, the new law quickly became the source of vast implementation difficulties. For instance, its formula for covering tuition at a rate of up to the highest in-state public tuition led to inequalities in coverage: a boondoggle for for-profit and private nonprofit institutions with higher tuition and a penalty for public colleges that kept tuition low despite needing extra funds to pay for veterans' services. Congress subsequently dealt with some of these issues in 2010 and 2011.[87]

As for the student aid changes that occurred during the Obama presidency, the new tuition tax credits channeled a vast amount of public resources toward those who were already college-bound but they would likely have little impact on college graduation rates among those who would not complete degrees in their absence. This costly but likely ineffective initiative appeared to be motivated by Obama's wish to court bipartisan support for his priorities—the GOP had championed such tax breaks, after all, since 1965—but in fact the stimulus bill was enacted along strict party lines. Finally, the generous new formula for Pell grants threatened to make them become fiscally unsustainable, yet lawmakers neglected to address such issues. They failed to grapple with the perverse incentives the grants gave to states to neglect their public colleges; they overlooked the duplicity of some private nonprofits that do little to assist Pell grant recipients while using their own funds to court upper income students; and they ignored the rapid increase in Pell grant money going to the for-profit sector, with its poor record in providing opportunity to students. In each of these cases, more careful deliberation might have generated more sustainable and effective policy responses for the longer term.

CHAPTER SIX

HOW MONEY TALKS

Political Influence in the Struggle to Regulate the For-Profits

AS SOON AS REFORMERS EXPANDED FEDERAL STUDENT AID, THE FOR-PROFIT schools seized on the chance to attain a sizable portion of the new funds for themselves. Just as they had after World War II, they aggressively pursued veterans, now those with access to the Post-9/11 GI Bill. Kaplan University, owned by the *Washington Post*, instructed its recruiters, "Veterans' hospitals are another place that you can expect to find veterans . . . many of the facilities allow schools to come on site and set up in a common area, such as a lunch room, and provide an information table." A recruiter from Grand Canyon University reported on her visit to a Wounded Warrior unit, "We were a big hit . . . I consolidated our position with the Army National Guard at this event," and she predicted that several "solid leads that will turn into applications this week."[1] Such efforts paid off in rapid enrollments by veterans and a bonanza in profits. The amount of money that twenty for-profit colleges received from military education benefits increased between 2006 and 2010 by 683 percent, from $66.6 million to an estimated $521.2 million.[2] The sector included eight out of the ten universities nationwide that garnered the largest amount in federal disbursements of Post-9/11 GI Bill in 2010–2011.[3] In short order, a new law that aimed to expand educational opportunities to veterans was providing a windfall to the for-profit college industry.

An unintended consequence of federal policy—the fact that the 90/10 rule, which limits the amount schools can obtain from federal student financial aid, applies only to funds in Title IV of the Higher Education Act, not to the GI Bill and other military-related education funds—means that for-profits have a large incentive to enroll veterans. In effect, for every veteran a college enrolls, it can enroll nine other students who are relying only on Title IV money. This principle, as explained in a *New York Times* op-ed by Holly Petraeus, assistant director for service member affairs at the Consumer Financial Protection Bureau, makes veterans "nothing more than dollar signs in uniform," a "lucrative target for exploitation."[4]

Stories emerged of the schools using aggressive marketing procedures to recruit veterans just as they had for civilians, often misleading them about the costs and debt they would incur. A combat veteran with posttraumatic stress disorder described his experience with ITT: "The ITT representative I met with told me that the military would pay for my schooling. Then a few months letter [sic], I got bills from Sallie Mae saying I owe money for two loans! A federal and a private loan! What!? I was told I would never see a bill."[5] A veteran who attended Ashford University, owned by Bridgepoint, found that contrary to what recruiters promised him, the Post-9/11 GI Bill did not cover all expenses and he would owe $11,000. "I was extremely disappointed, confused and angry. I felt that I have been misled, deceived, or even outright lied to in an effort to gain my contractual agreement."[6]

The for-profits continued to yield a poor outcome for many of their students and for the American public. In the group of universities with the highest veteran enrollments in bachelor's degree programs, 53 percent of the veterans enrolled in the for-profits withdrew from school within two years, compared to only 20 percent of those who attended public institutions. The average cost to taxpayers was more than twice as high for veterans enrolled at for-profits as at public colleges, $10,441 compared to $4,642, and the for-profits devoted as much of half of these public funds to marketing and profits.[7] Veterans who decided to transfer to nonprofit and public schools often found that their credits were not accepted elsewhere, and those who earned diplomas and sought jobs discovered that employers deemed their degrees to be of little value.[8] An Air Force veteran, Christopher Ford, used the GI Bill to take an online engineering course at a for-profit, but no employer would accept his training. Ford said, "It was heavily marketed so I took it. It sounded pretty good, but it turned out to be pretty predatory."[9]

It wasn't just veterans who brought their federal dollars to the for-profits in recent years; civilian students also swelled the ranks and helped the schools pocket 24 percent of the student aid dollars doled out under the Higher Education Act.[10] Overall, enrollments at the for-profits increased by 89 percent between 2006 and 2010, from over 1 million to over 2 million students.[11] The sector benefited richly from expanded Pell grant funding: its earnings from the program grew by 300 percent in just three years, from $2.5 billion in 2006–2007 to $7.5 billion in 2009–2010.[12] The for-profits' ability to capitalize on opportunities to benefit from federal student aid was nothing new, but now the benefits to the sector—and the costs to students and taxpayers—were greater than ever before.

In an era when reformers succeeded in ousting the banks from student lending, the for-profit industry managed to maintain its ability to exploit federal student aid for its own gain. But it did not prevail without a major fight. As soon as Barack Obama became president, the sector perceived that his administration would not support business as usual. Even more than the Bush administration before it, the Obama administration pursued its policy objectives for the for-profits by using its bureaucratic powers, through rule making in the US Department of Education, not through legislation in Congress. But unlike Bush appointees whose aim was to relax restrictions on the industry, Obama officials intended to strengthen such rules. In what turned out to be their most controversial proposal, the so-called gainful employment rule, they set out to limit federal student aid to schools that failed to establish a record of positive outcomes for their students, as indicated by measures of their subsequent earnings relative to their student loan debt and by their loan repayment rates.

A political firestorm ensued, beyond the scrutiny of much media attention and largely unknown to the general public, as the for-profits used all the leverage they could muster to protect their industry. Their lobbyists swarmed the capital; proponents of reform explained that the fight brought ten times as much lobbying to the White House as had the struggle over bank-based lending and made that controversy look like "a picnic" in comparison.[13] The for-profit lobby would spend over $11 million in the process. As described earlier, they gained the support of a strong and diverse phalanx of congressional politicians, including all Republicans and many House Democrats—among them some liberals and members of the Black Caucus—who fiercely opposed the Obama administration's efforts to regulate the sector. In the end, the administration was forced to water down its proposed rules, for example, by reducing, as a criterion for a school's student aid receipt, the percentage of students who must be successfully repaying their loans within three years of graduation from 45 percent to just 35 percent. At the outset the administration proposed standards that would have forced more than half of the for-profits to improve their outcomes or lose access to federal funding; the final standards were so low that only one in twenty schools would be affected.

How did the for-profit college industry manage to beat back reformers, and how, in an age of sharp polarization, did it enlist so many ardent supporters on both sides of the political aisle? The sector gained nearly unanimous support among congressional Republicans and strong advocacy by a large number of House Democrats, and it successfully intimidated the Obama White House. These developments raise the question of how political influence operates—how money yields power in American politics. To most Americans, it's a given that money influences politics, and in the many interviews I conducted with advocates of reform I heard the same refrain: "follow the money"; "it's all about money"; and "this is a lesson in how money talks."[14] But there's strong research suggesting that the connection between money and political influence is not as straightforward as it might appear.

Certainly policies abound that favor powerful industries and organizations, but the mechanisms those interests use to exert their will on lawmakers is less than clear. Scholars fail to find evidence of a quid pro quo between lobbyists and elected officials; what is apparent is that money does not simply "buy votes."[15] The dollar amounts that even the biggest industries invest in politicians' campaigns still end up being a small sum relative to the size of candidates' war chests; they are hardly large enough to explain why recipients might become beholden to the contributors once in office. Scholars have argued that given what's at stake in the policy process, what is actually remarkable is how *little* industries spend in their efforts to influence outcomes.[16]

The for-profits' ability to gain bipartisan support in a polarized age and to severely weaken the restraints reformers would place on them illustrates the mechanisms through which money matters and political influence operates in contemporary politics. Money certainly plays a role, but it does not operate independently as a silver bullet of political influence. Rather, money acts as a crucial lubricant that facilitates political relationships. It does so in three important ways: (1) by mobilizing partisanship among already polarized public officials, (2) by building bipartisan support through strategic exploitation of personal and professional networks, and (3) by fueling supporters' ability to rally on its behalf, outdoing the opposition. By using money effectively in each of these ways, the for-profit industry marshaled bipartisan support and fought back against reformers who challenged its claim on federal student aid.

This story illustrates how the US political system today has become a *polarized plutocracy*, with a government that is fiercely divided and ineffective, with rare exceptions—aside from those instances in which powerful, wealthy industries manage to unite lawmakers across the aisle in bipartisan support of government largesse directed toward them. In an age of rising economic inequality, American government has grown so polarized that most efforts to respond to public needs end in stalemate. Yet big money interests with political savvy yield the power to generate bipartisan support from political elites. In the case of the for-profits, such success has enabled them to divert funds intended for educational opportunity, using them instead to improve their bottom lines.

Putting the For-Profits in Perspective

Defenders of for-profit universities champion them as belonging to the private sector, but in recent years as in the past, they receive nearly all of their revenues from the US federal government. Table 6.1 shows the percentage of their revenues the largest ones, those now owned by individual shareholders and publicly traded on Wall Street, obtained from specific policies. Notably, these institutions, with only one exception, earned between 60.8 and 85.9 percent of their total revenues in 2010 from Title IV of the Higher Education Act, meaning predominantly student loans and Pell grants. The Apollo Group, owner of the University of Phoenix, gained between 85 and 88 percent of its income from these sources in each of the past three years. Most received an additional 2 to 5 percent from military educational programs, including the Post-9/11 GI Bill. The sum of these federal government funds added up, as a portion of all revenues collected, to a minimum of 65.8 percent for ITT and a maximum of 93.7 percent for Bridgepoint. In short, the for-profit schools are almost entirely subsidized by government.

In recent years, the for-profits have proven hugely lucrative for their owners and investors. In 2008, even as the S&P 500 declined by 39 percent overall, the nine major for-profit companies enjoyed 4 percent growth in their stocks.[17] They boasted impressive profit margins relative to other major corporations: in 2010, ITT and Strayer achieved margins of 38 and 34 percent, respectively, higher than that of Apple at 28 percent or Coca-Cola at 24 percent, and the Apollo Group and Corinthian, at 21 and 14 percent, respectively, topped Raytheon, at 10 percent.[18] Individuals at the top of these companies reap the benefits: in 2009–2010, when the five highest paid chief executives of public universities were compensated an average of $860,000, and those of Ivy League universities, $1.3 million, those at the helm of the for-profits gained an average of $10.5 million.[19] For example, the chairman and CEO of Strayer University, Robert Silberman, received $41.9 million, twenty-six times more than the most highly compensated president of a traditional university. Numerous leaders of the publicly traded

TABLE 6.1. A PRIVATE INDUSTRY FUNDED BY THE PUBLIC SECTOR: ENROLLMENTS AND PERCENTAGE OF REVENUES RECEIVED FROM FEDERAL STUDENT AID POLICIES BY PUBLICLY TRADED FOR-PROFIT UNIVERSITIES

	Enrollment, 2010	Percentage Revenues from Title IV, HEA, 2010	Percentage Revenues from Military Ed programs (Post-9/11 GI Bill & others)	Total Percentage Revenues from Federal Gov't
Apollo Group	406,963	85.3%	3.4%	88.7%
Education Management Corporation	152,786	77.4	2.5	79.9
Corinthian Colleges	132,229	81.9	1.2	83.1
Kaplan	129,070	85.9	2.0	87.9
DeVry	128,676	77.5	3.4	80.9
Career Education Corporation	127,041	81.5	3.8	85.3
ITT	86,824	60.8	5.1	65.9
Bridgepoint	64,585	85.1	8.6	93.7
Strayer, Inc	58,916	77.7	7.1	84.8
Lincoln Educational Services	42,198	82.7	1.3	84.0
Capella Education Company	39,457	78.2	2.6	80.8
American Public Educ., Inc	39,296	26.0	51.4	77.4
Grand Canyon Educ., Inc	37,440	84.9	2.2	87.1
Universal Technical Institute	26,396	72.5	2.5	75.0
National American University	9,700	76.1	3.9	80.0

SOURCE: US Senate, Health, Education, Labor and Pensions Committee, *Benefiting Whom? For-Profit Education Companies and the Growth of Military Educational Benefits,* December 8, 2010, 19–20; US Senate, Health, Education, Labor, and Pensions Committee, *For Profit Higher Education: The Failure to Safeguard the Federal Investment and Ensure Student Success,* Majority Staff Report and Accompanying Minority Committee Staff Views, July 30, 2012, Appendix 10, p. A10-1.

for-profits collected billions from the sales of company stock. These include, among many others, John Sperling, Apollo's chairman, who received $263.5 million over seven years, and Robert Knutson, retired CEO and chairman of Education Management, who netted $132.4 million over the same period.[20] These torrential profits resulted almost entirely from public sector revenues channeled in the form of student aid.

THE OBAMA ADMINISTRATION TAKES ON THE FOR-PROFITS

During the 2008 campaign and well into President Obama's first year in office, for-profit leaders anticipated that the president would rely on their colleges to achieve his goal of improving college graduation rates. After all, they were known for reaching out to those who would likely not attend college otherwise and attracting such individuals to become students. Enrollment in for-profit schools had been exploding, even during the economic downturn. The president of the University of Phoenix, whose student body spiked by 22 percent in one year to 443,000 students enrolled in 2009, said, "There are plenty of students out there. There are tens of millions who don't have a college degree. If we are going to fulfill the president's vision, we need to present people with a set of options."[21]

Once Obama entered office, however, industry leaders grew alarmed. In the spring of 2009, rumors began to fly among the for-profits that deputy undersecretary Robert Shireman intended to lead an effort to crack down on them. Shireman had not spoken out publicly against the for-profits, but as one of the early instigators of the move to direct lending beginning in the late 1980s, he had gained the reputation of being a formidable opponent of one mind with consumer organizations that both opposed bank-based lending and favored restricting the for-profits.[22] Panic ensued when the department announced that it planned a negotiated rule-making process in which an executive agency appoints a diverse group of stakeholders to meet and attempt to create industry rules to which they can all agree; in instances where consensus fails, the bureaucrats themselves issue the rule. Specifically, education officials called for a review of the use of federal student aid under Title IV of the Higher

Education Act by schools offering career training.[23] They aimed for the process to devise new rules to ensure program integrity, meaning that students at schools using student aid would be protected from aggressive or misleading recruitment practices; they would be offered data about school outcomes that would enable them to make enrollment decisions as informed consumers; and taxpayers would be protected against use of federal funds by schools that failed to meet standards.[24]

Industry leaders worried about several of the matters raised for consideration in the process, including incentive compensation—pay for student recruiters that improved with the rate of students they enrolled—and the definition of credit hours.[25] Immediately stocks of some of the largest publicly traded companies plummeted by more than 20 percent, and angry callers flooded the phone lines of the Department of Education, demanding clarification of its intentions.[26] In response, Shireman took the unprecedented action of holding conference calls with stakeholders—nearly seven hundred individuals participated—to reassure them that he did not aim to single out a particular sector of higher education.[27] "Our overall goal at the Department of Education in postsecondary education is to make sure that students—potential students—whether young or old, have access to college, they have the information they need to make good choices, and that they have good quality postsecondary education that serves both them as students and taxpayers as well," Shireman said. "If that's not the case, if there is not quality, we want to know about it and if we can, we want to do something about it. Whether that involves a public institution, a nonprofit, a for-profit, a two-year, a four-year, a trade program, whatever type or sector of institution, we want to do all we can to make sure that we get good quality and the degrees and certificates that we need in this country."[28]

Industry fears spiked again later in the year when the Department of Education released a draft of proposed regulations. The new rules would eliminate twelve of the "safe harbors" the department had created under the Bush administration as a means to permit career training programs to avoid complying with the 1992 restrictions on recruitment procedures. As a result of those loopholes in the interpretation of the law, the schools had returned to recruitment practices as egregious as the ones Senator Sam Nunn's committee investigation had uncovered nearly two decades earlier.

The department also put forth new metrics for assessing whether such programs offered training that actually led to "gainful employment," the term used in law to define their function ever since they became eligible for Title IV funds in 1972. The department proposed both "preferred" standards as well as "minimal" standards. Schools with low loan repayment rates would lose eligibility for student aid. At a minimum, this would exclude those with fewer than 35 percent of their students repaying their loans; by the preferred standards, it would exclude all with fewer than 45 percent in repayment. It would also exclude those with high debt-to-income ratios among graduates.[29] Schools would be considered exempt from the rules only if both completion rates and job placement rates surpassed at least 70 percent.

These rules would apply not only to the for-profit sector but also to career training programs at nonprofit and public institutions. But the proposed rules clearly posed the greatest threat to the for-profit colleges given their records. During the previous four years, for example, only 26 percent of graduates of Corinthian Colleges, a publicly traded company founded in 1995 that by 2009 enrolled 86,000 students, had made any payments on their student loans; at Kaplan, the figure was only 27 percent. Other large for-profits squeaked by the 35 percent cutoff, but some of their member colleges did not.[30]

A $32 billion industry faced a dire threat, and the administration soon learned that it would fight back with all of the resources—and personal connections—at its disposal.[31] While the incentive compensation rules were adopted fairly readily, the proposed gainful employment regulations faced an uphill battle. The remainder of this chapter examines that fight, with a focus on how influence operated.

THE LONG JOURNEY OF NEGOTIATED RULE MAKING

The bureaucratic details and arcane procedures required for negotiated rule making could easily obscure the intense drama that unfolded around the proposed gainful employment rules. It began when, in keeping with standard practices, department officials appointed a committee of negotiators, a wide array of stakeholders who were not part of the federal government: representatives of public and nonprofit institutions, officials from student groups (US Public Interest Research Group and, as an alternate, the United States Student Association), leaders of consumer advocacy organizations, and many others. Officials in the for-profits felt that the sector was severely underrepresented and requested parity through the appointment of additional individuals who could speak on its behalf. Those appeals were denied and the composition of the committee remained as it was.[32]

The process that ensued, with meetings held over a three-month period, proved exasperating to all involved. The negotiators sat at a table in the middle of the room, but other members of organizations and the public could sit behind them. A critic of the for-profits commented that the "walls were lined with people in suits—Wall Street paid so much attention to it."[33] According to a representative of the for-profits, it was "hell," a "punching match," throughout.[34] Ultimately, while the committee reached consensus on many issues, it did not agree on all; the gainful employment rule proved most divisive, and it was left to Department of Education negotiators to devise the outcome.

From the start of the rule-making process, the for-profit industry lambasted as "aggressive" and "overbearing" the metrics the Department of Education had proposed to assess whether schools actually offered gainful employment. It launched a political mobilization to oppose them that would be stronger than the one in the early 1990s.[35] Over the next year and a half, advocates pressured the White House, the Department of Education, and Congress in multiple ways. They slowed down the process, which gave them time to exert pressure and generate concessions, ultimately resulting in a much weaker final outcome. By April 2010, four months into the process, the criteria for exemption to the rule had been relaxed to a 50 percent degree completion rate; schools at which at least half of the students graduated would face no additional scrutiny in maintaining their access to federal loans and grants.[36] Two months later, the Department of Education announced that it would postpone releasing the rule, probably until late summer. By September, the department had received a record number of public comments on the proposed rules, and in response it delayed their release once again.[37] Once the proposal was finally made public in late October, it incorporated eighty changes. Lanny Davis, former special counsel to President Bill Clinton who had become a key spokesperson for the industry, said, "The new language is a real step in the right direction."[38] The for-profits continued to make their case, and the department took another six months to release the penultimate version. When the department delivered the rules to the Office of Management and Budget in May, industry lobbying reached a fever pitch.

The final rules were released in June, set to go into effect on July 1, 2012. Gone entirely were the gold standards the Obama administration had originally proposed to assess how well schools served their students; only minimal standards for compliance remained intact.[39] Their impact on the industry would be minor: officials had expected the higher benchmarks to push 55 percent of the schools to reform or lose their aid; the rules that were actually adopted would affect only 5 percent.[40]

FOLLOWING THE MONEY . . . BUT WHERE?

Over the year and a half that the program integrity rules were under consideration, the for-profit sector invested more than ever in its efforts at political influence. Collectively, in 2010, the career colleges poured over $8 million into lobbying, compared to $3.5 million in 2008 and $3.3 million in 2009.[41] Companies doubled, tripled, or even quadrupled their spending on lobbying compared to the previous year; the Education Management Corporation surpassed it by eight times.[42] Besides the universities themselves, their trade associations also invested considerably, with the Coalition for Educational Success and Association for Private Sector Colleges and Universities (APSCU) spending $1.65 million and $1.45 million each between January 2010 and October 2011.[43] The sector's campaign contributions also soared in the 2010 midterm elections, with several universities and the APSCU greatly increasing their contributions compared to previous election cycles, the latter by nearly 200 percent.[44]

For all the money sloshing around, however, its actual impact was less than obvious, hardly explaining how the industry managed to marshal such strong bipartisan support in a polarized age or how it succeeded in forcing agency officials to water down the proposed rules. Considering that the sector's revenues topped $20 billion the year before the gainful employment fight, with the bulk of it coming from the federal government, the amount invested in politics was actually quite modest.[45] In the 2010 election, the average victorious House candidate collected $563,000 from all PAC contributions representing all industries and interests.[46] That year the APSCU PAC, the for-profits' major trade association, gave $10,000 to Buck McKeon; Nancy Pelosi and five other members received $5,000 or $6,000. The remaining sixty-two beneficiaries received much smaller amounts. Members of the Black Caucus who went out a limb to advocate for the sector collected meager amounts, with Alcee Hastings receiving $1,500 and Edolphus Towns, $1,000.[47] Furthermore, not all who received funds from the industry supported it, as exemplified by House Education and Labor Committee chairman George Miller (D-CA) and Patty Murray (D-WA), who remained critics despite being among the largest congressional recipients of the sector's contributions.[48] Harris Miller, past president of APSCU, made the point succinctly: "I know some people think there's this simplistic correlation between writing a check and getting a vote. I wish it were that easy."[49] Indeed, money did not simply buy votes from members of Congress or buy off Department of Education officials so that they would relax their stance toward the for-profits. In order to understand the sector's influence, we need to consider not just the role of money by itself, but rather how it was used strategically: (1) to build a strong base of support in combination with partisanship, (2) to build a network of bipartisan defenders through personal and professional relationships, and (3) to promote mobilization among supporters.

Money, Partisanship, and Polarization

At first blush, high levels of partisan polarization—with all of the rigidity and obstruction it entails—might seem to complicate efforts by interest groups to sway public officials. In fact, polarization, with its strong party discipline and voting patterns, merely presents a different set of challenges and opportunities—analogous to a differently arranged chess board—than a political setting with low polarization and weak parties. When parties are weak, each individual legislator is relatively independent and responds to an array of influences, such as industries and organizations in the geographic area he or she represents. Confronted with these multiple, competing demands, each public official personally decides how to prioritize them. Such arrangements complicate interest groups' jobs by requiring them to lobby every elected official they hope to influence. In effect, each legislator becomes what Sean D. Ehrlich calls an "access point" for the influence of interest groups.[50] Conversely, when parties are strong, members of Congress take their cues from the party leadership and act in unison. This simplifies the task for interest groups and reduces the amount of effort involved in exerting influence. As long as they can gain the support of the leadership in one party, the rest of the members in that party should fall in line.

Today's unified, cohesive political parties actually present advantages, therefore, to interest groups that approach them strategically, and the for-profit colleges have excelled at working these circumstances in their favor. Intense political polarization enabled the for-profits to line up all Republicans on their side—something that had not been possible as recently as the 1980s and early 1990s, when fiscal conservatives in the party took issue with the sector's reliance on public funds and its record in serving students. After 1994, when Republicans regained control of both chambers, the party coalesced in strong support of the for-profit colleges, just as they did for bank-based lenders. As we saw in Chapter 3, these efforts intensified when John Boehner emerged as a chief advocate for the industry and rose in the leadership ranks in Congress, and after 2000, when President George W. Bush appointed former for-profit employees to leading roles in the US Department of Education. To be a Republican in Congress came to mean supporting the for-profit colleges unquestioningly and opposing any efforts to tie their access to aid to their performance. The industry slightly favored Republicans in its campaign contributions during this period, but it could count on the party's allegiance regardless of the size of contributions to any particular member. Within a short time period, it seemed inconceivable that in the 1980s it was education secretary William Bennett of the Reagan administration who lambasted the for-profits as "diploma mills designed to trick the poor into taking on federally backed debt" and that over the next several years, Republicans in Congress had put forward proposals for regulating the sector and worked together with Democrats such as Sam Nunn in those efforts.

Of course interest groups that play partisan politics risk alienating one party even as they gain staunch advocates in the other, and these dynamics help explain why Democrats in the Senate have become united in their opposition to the for-profits. Senator Tom Harkin (D-IA), chair of the HELP Committee, investigated the operations of the industry through hearings in 2011 that amounted to the most in-depth probe conducted since the Nunn hearings two decades earlier. But whereas Nunn's subcommittee involved bipartisan cooperation, Harkin's committee did not. From the start, ranking member Republican Mike Enzi objected to the hearings, saying they should focus more broadly on problems facing students in all types of institutions of higher education, not the for-profits alone. Once the hearings were under way, Senator John McCain walked out of one in protest after accusing Chairman Harkin of going on "ad nauseum" about the abuses of the for-profits.[51] Eventually all ten Republicans on the committee issued a letter to Harkin calling the hearings "prejudicial," and "most remarkable for a concerning lack of objectivity."[52] Whereas every member of Nunn's subcommittee, Democrat and Republican, put their name to their final report, the report issued by Harkin's committee was only a "majority committee staff report," and it included, at the end, a separate statement containing "minority staff views."[53] As the issue became increasingly partisan in the chamber,

Democratic senators joined Harkin's efforts and many emerged as out-spoken critics of the industry. They supported the rules being developed in the Department of Education and several of them—including Barbara Boxer, Patty Murray, Barbara Mikulski, and Jeff Merkeley, together with Harkin—introduced bills aimed at regulating the sector.[54] These developments, when viewed against the past, are as incongruous as changes in the Republican Party: not long ago, liberal Democratic leaders in Congress numbered among the sector's more stalwart defenders.

The GOP's transformation from the party of the industry's staunchest opponents to becoming its loyal and united ally makes sense only by recognizing that Congress is more sharply divided by partisanship than at any time since at least the early twentieth century. The contemporary Republican Party takes a very different approach toward governance, furthermore, than it did as recently as during the Reagan and George H. W. Bush administrations. The for-profit industry played these factors to its advantage, generating united support among Republicans.

STRATEGIC USE OF PERSONAL RELATIONSHIPS

Having used polarization effectively to win over one party, how could the for-profit colleges now manage to overcome polarization and gain a plurality of supporters? While the sector has lost this battle in the Senate, where Democrats have emerged as united critics, it has generated bipartisan support in the House. As described earlier, in February 2011, it managed to rally fifty-eight Democrats in the House along with nearly the entire Republican caucus to vote in a rebuke of the Obama administration's rule-making efforts. Then in April 2011, a bipartisan group of House members, including six Democrats and six Republicans, pushed to include in the budget a prohibition on further regulations of the for-profit sector. They wrote, "These burdensome and unnecessary regulations unfairly single out the private sector of postsecondary education and will negatively affect the landscape of our nation's higher education system."[55] Although the Senate later eliminated the provision, the House adopted it, showing that many Democrats disapproved of the

Obama administration's efforts to regulate the sector. It conveyed a powerful message to the White House to back off. One year later, sixty-nine House Democrats joined all Republicans in a vote to rescind a Department of Education rule requiring that colleges such as the University of Phoenix, with multiple campuses across states, receive state authorization in each state in which they operate—not just in the state of their home campus.[56]

Knowing that they could count on all Republicans—united in partisan loyalty—to support them, the for-profits devised a different strategy to court Democrats. They embarked on a charm offensive, using personal and professional relationships to build a network of Democratic supporters for the industry. Money served as a lubricant in this process.

Perhaps most importantly, the industry hired respected Democrats as lobbyists. In addition to Lanny Davis, their ranks included several former members of Congress, including Alan Wheat and former House majority leader Dick Gephardt, and former staffers such as an aide to Maryland senator Barbara Mikulski. Several for-profit companies also hired the lobbying firm of Heather Podesta, a major Democratic fundraiser and wife of Tony Podesta, who has worked on the campaigns of several Democratic presidential candidates. She is the sister-in-law of John Podesta, former chief of staff for President Bill Clinton who has since founded the Center for American Progress.[57]

The industry also hired organizational staff that helped it reach out to Democrats. Penny Lee, former aide to Senate majority leader Harry Reid of Nevada, became the director of Coalition for Educational Success, the new group representing over seventy career colleges that had also hired Lanny Davis.[58] APSCU, the major trade organization, hired as its chief lobbyist Brian Moran, brother of Democratic congressman Jim Moran of Virginia.[59]

By recruiting respected Democrats to speak on its behalf, the for-profit industry managed to make support for their schools "a Democratic issue," as one interview subject explained to me. "They made it hard" for Democrats "to say no to them."[60] Of course hiring lobbyists and organizational staff required money, but what advantaged the industry was its ability to spend those funds strategically, employing individuals well placed to elicit support for it among those who might otherwise have turned into opponents. In short, they used the bonds of partisanship to line up allies but managed to do so in both parties—a remarkable feat in such a polarized age.

The for-profits expanded their base further by cultivating supporters among the black and Hispanic communities, traditional Democratic strongholds. Mario Lopez, president of the Hispanic Leadership Fund, and Jesse Jackson of the Rainbow PUSH Coalition united with Harry Alford, president of the National Black Chamber of Commerce. Together they spoke out against the gainful employment rule, claiming that it "unfairly targets low-income and minority students who are often considered the most 'at-risk' for receiving a college education."[61] The Mexican American National Association and National Hispanic Caucus of State Legislators also expressed concerns.[62] In fact, the major civil rights groups—NAACP and National Council of La Raza—each supported the gainful employment provisions.[63] The minority opponents, however, received substantial media attention and their stance helped legitimize supporting the for-profits in the eyes of many Democrats.

Many in Congress who belonged to the Black Caucus, Hispanic Caucus, or Asian Pacific American Caucus vociferously criticized the industry. Maxine Waters remained a stalwart advocate for reform, characterizing many for-profits as "rip-off schools" that take advantage of vulnerable people.[64] And many worried about the schools because, as articulated by an aide to a Hispanic lawmaker, "We agree that the [for-profit] colleges provide the access. Our concern is that the quality of the education is not what it needs to be."[65] But with some prominent individuals in minority communities speaking out on behalf of the sector, members grew divided. Some, such as Alcee Hasting, became outspoken defenders of the industry.

Ultimately the for-profit industry managed to establish a diverse and prominent array of Democratic supporters. Developing that network cost money—in the form of hiring lobbyists and organizational staff—but in time it snowballed on its own. The listing of Democratic ties to the for-profits resembles a Who's Who of Washington insiders. Nancy Pelosi is reported to be a longtime friend of Apollo CEO John Sperling, who owns a home in her congressional district. She met with him in 2003 to plan how Democrats could reclaim the majority in the House and how she might become the Speaker.[66] Michael J. Wilson, president of Americans for Democratic Action, a liberal group, broke with recent tradition among the group's leaders and came out in support of the for-profits.[67] And so on. The industry actively cultivated—at a price—many of the prominent relationships between itself and Democrats in Congress, and others emerged by happenstance. And once established, these relationships worked powerfully to defend the for-profits' interests.

The for-profit industry surveyed the political landscape, planned strategically, and used its resources effectively to marshal political support. Money was an essential but not a sufficient ingredient in the sector's success. In combination with strategic use of personal ties, however, it proved remarkably effective.

OUT-MOBILIZING THE CRITICS

Besides playing polarization to its advantage to line up Republicans on its side and in addition to strategically cultivating ties across the aisle among Democrats, the for-profit sector exerted its influence effectively by out-mobilizing the advocates of regulation. Throughout the rule-making process, policymakers in Congress, the White House, and the Department of Education heard much more from the industry than from its critics. This is an expected outcome whenever benefits are limited to a small number of actors—in this case the for-profit colleges—and costs are diffuse, spread out widely among students and American taxpayers.[68] In the United States, business interests possess the greatest number of interest groups, while the public at large and less privileged groups in particular are much less well represented.[69] We saw this disparity in the fights over student lending, but the imbalance is even more pronounced when it comes to regulating the for-profit schools, where no major organization represents the interests of the American public at large, not to mention the sector's students. The major student associations that lobby Congress—US Public Interest Research Group (US PIRG) and the United States Student Association (USSA)—represent students at private nonprofit and public sector colleges, but not at for-profits. It is hardly surprising that no organization has emerged to represent the students of for-profits, aside from one instigated by the industry itself. Most such students share characteristics that make organizational involvement less likely, being predominantly from lower socioeconomic backgrounds and being burdened with work and family obligations. Meanwhile the industry's resources enable it to articulate its voice loudly, frequently, and at key junctures.

As a standard component of the negotiated rule-making process, the Department of Education granted the public sixty days to weigh in and register comments. Higher education rule-making processes had generated 1,832 comments in 2008 and under 400 in 2007 and 2009, but the proposed rules for the for-profits yielded 83,000 comments—most voicing opposition to the rules.[70] The overwhelming response appeared to have been mobilized by several sources. One of the largest for-profits, Education Management Corporation, hired a public relations firm to contact company employees and assist them in registering comments.[71] Students for Academic Choice, the organization formed with financial and technical support from the Career College Association during its annual Hill Day for lobbying in March 2010, also generated opposition. The group collected some 32,000 signatures on a petition opposing the proposed rules and encouraged students to register comments with the Department of Education.[72]

The industry and its supporters ran advertisements disparaging the proposed rules in newspapers throughout the nation. They placed colorful multipage ads in the *New York Times* and *Wall Street Journal,* and others in Politico, The Hill, and Roll Call, as well as in many regional newspapers. Frequent funders included the University of Phoenix, Corinthian Colleges, and the National Black Chamber of Commerce.[73]

The US Chamber of Commerce also opposed the gainful employment rule. Chamber president Thomas Donohue wrote to the Department of Education, saying, "This ill-conceived regulation will work against job creation, only resulting in jobs lost and fewer Americans getting the post-secondary education and training they need to secure work in today's economy."[74]

Lobbyists for the for-profits also barraged the White House. Records of the Office of Management and Budget (OMB) confirmed that during a nine-day period in May 2011, just before the release of the final rules, Obama administration officials conducted sixteen meetings with representatives of the for-profit industry and their lobbyists. The visitors included chief executives and other leaders of nineteen different schools or trade groups, as well as their lobbyists from some of the most prominent lobbying and law firms in the nation's capital. Democratic insiders helped facilitate the access: Anita Dunn, a friend of Obama's who had worked in his administration, assisted Kaplan University, and Jamie Rubin, a fund-raising bundler for Obama's reelection, made efforts for ATI, a Dallas-based group of colleges.[75] By contrast, advocates of the proposed rules, those representing consumer and student groups such as the National Consumer Law Center, US PIRG, and the USSA, were crowded into one single meeting with OMB.[76] The voices of students who had attended for-profits only to find themselves worse off later on, and the American public, which invests so much in schools with poor records, remained inaudible.

THE RULE THAT EMERGED

At last, in early June 2011—after three rounds of hearings and discussions and almost one hundred meetings with lobbyists and others, the Department of Education released the final version of the gainful employment rule. The essence of the rule was that for students of any particular school to use Title IV funds, programs had to meet at least one of three criteria indicating that the training they provide genuinely leads to gainful employment. First, at least 35 percent of a school's former students, roughly one out of three, must be successfully repaying their loans. As education secretary Arne Duncan put it, "We're asking companies that get up to 90 percent of their profits from taxpayer dollars to be at least 35 percent effective."[77] Second, as a measure of debt-to-income ratio, the estimated annual payment of the typical former students could not surpass 30 percent of his or her average discretionary income. Third, as an alternate measure of debt-to-income ratio, the annual payment from such borrowers must not be greater than 12 percent of their total earnings. Regulated institutions were required to disclose such information to prospective students, enabling them to make informed choices about attendance. Also, the final rules dictated that programs would not lose eligibility unless they failed to meet these criteria in three out of four years, rather than in one single year. The penalty for schools violating these principles would be the loss of eligibility for federal student aid programs for at least three years.[78]

The outcome sorely disappointed those who had long advocated for reform. Stephen Burd of the New America Foundation noted that the slow timetable adopted for implementation and the conciliatory "three strikes" approach undercut the possibilities for terminating federal aid to programs with egregious records.[79] One individual identified the announcement of the final rules as the "end of the idealistic phase of the Obama presidency."[80]

Others emphasized what had actually been accomplished. Kevin Carey, policy director of the group Education Sector, proclaimed it "historic change . . . a major step . . . that will have important benefits for students attending colleges of all kinds." He explained, "The important thing is to establish the principle and build the underlying structure of regulation and data collection on which the parameters are based," and he predicted that once the Department of Education established means of collecting such data, the procedures would acquire staying power.[81] Another proponent said that despite the extent to which the administration, under pressure from the for-profits, had weakened the outcome, nonetheless the new rules would make the sector subject to much greater accountability than in the past.[82]

Even with the reduced standards in the rules, the for-profit industry and its defenders complained loudly. Harris Miller of APSCU termed the outcome "basically a back-door way of price fixing."[83] Congressman John Kline, a Minnesota Republican who chairs the House Education and the Workforce Committee, said, "I remain concerned this regulation could undermine an entire sector of colleges in the name of rooting out a few bad actors."[84] Yet the rules announcement prompted a stock market rally for the publicly traded for-profit companies, as all of their shares rose in value on the day it was announced; shares of Education Management Corp and ITT soared by over 20 percent.[85] Investors' reactions belied the grim assessments of the industry spokesmen and advocates.

In June 2012, reformers' hopes for and industry's fears of the new gainful employment rules vanished in tandem when a federal judge in Washington, DC, Rudolph Contreras, struck down most of them on the grounds that they were based on an arbitrary standard. Some reform advocates took comfort in the fact that his decision accepted the department's authority to issue such a rule and to draw on the gainful employment criteria to do so. But the court's ruling also rejected the debt-repayment measure because it deemed the standard—that 35 percent of graduates who borrowed loans had to be repaying them for a school to qualify for additional Title IV funds—to lack a clear basis in reasoned decision making from research or industry standards. Contreras determined the other metrics to be soundly justified, but he rejected them also because their implementation would be entwined with the debt-repayment measure. Only the disclosure rule remained intact, dictating that colleges must reveal to prospective students information such as costs, graduation rates, placement rates, and debt levels.[86]

The creation of even the weak rules handed down in 2011 had required a Herculean effort. The officials in the Department of Education who provided the leadership for that round had long since departed. In August 2013, the department initiated another rulemaking process to create a new gainful employment rule.[87] Given the outcome of the process two years earlier, it remained unlikely that a new round of negotiations could lead to regulations that would be worth the inevitable struggle their creation would require.

Consistency and Change

Their names have changed over time—from proprietary or trade schools to career colleges, and then to for-profit universities—but these schools have, consistently, emerged and grown in pursuit of student aid funds from the federal government. Critics of federal student aid have long suggested that its very existence may cause colleges to raise tuition, but little evidence has been found that this occurs. In the case of the for-profits, however, the evidence is quite clear. A recent study by economists Stephanie Riegg Cellini and Claudia Goldin confirmed that for-profit institutions that were eligible for Title IV funds charged significantly more in tuition—on average 75 percent more—than those that offered similar programs but were not eligible.[88] There is no other conclusion to draw than that these schools, now as in the past, exist primarily to take advantage of opportunities to milk the system.

Yet the stakes have grown much higher, even compared to a decade ago. The number of students who attend for-profits has skyrocketed, as has the amount of debt they incur in the process, a large share of which they are likely to be unable to pay. For the American public, the cost of supporting these schools has ballooned—both in terms of student aid dollars and unpaid loans for which it remains on the hook. It is an investment with a disastrous return. Meanwhile, for-profit executives and shareholders benefit richly, numbering among the major winners of the contemporary economy—almost entirely at government expense.

The changing fortunes of the for-profits highlight transformations in American politics over time. The fiscal conservatism that infused yesteryear's Republican Party, a spirit that led several of its leaders to disdain the for-profits' use of public money, has been replaced by an ardent support for them. Despite contemporary conservatives' rhetoric in support of scaling back the size of government, that is not their goal in this domain. Rather, they seek to exploit opportunities provided by existing policies to channel government resources to favored constit-uencies in the private sector. By contrast to the past, the few clarion calls for reform in this area today come from Democratic senators, pre-dominantly liberals, many of whom would likely have been the indus-try's chief defenders just a quarter century ago. And yet contrary to the stark partisan polarization on most issues today, the high degree of bipartisanship around for-profits, particularly in the US House, il-lustrates that another dynamic—plutocracy—has the capacity to bring elected officials together across the aisle. Money greases the wheels of this polarized plutocracy. Not only has the number of dollars invested in campaigns and lobbying escalated sharply, but also—in the case of the for-profits—industry leaders have learned how to use money stra-tegically to construct winning coalitions. They have worked polariza-tion in their favor, gaining solid support from the GOP. They have built personal relationships with Democrats, bringing many of them on board to support the industry. Finally, they have out-mobilized the op-position, using money to encourage their own employees and students to defend them. Ordinary Americans—barely organized around the issues—never had a chance to have their voices heard.

For disadvantaged Americans who dared to imagine that they could improve their lives if they pursued an education, public funding of the for-profits in the absence of rigorous regulation is at the very least a cynical response and more likely an egregious affront to a legacy of expanding opportunity.

CHAPTER SEVEN

RESTORING THE PUBLIC
PURPOSES OF HIGHER EDUCATION

THE AMERICAN SYSTEM OF HIGHER EDUCATION IS IN CRISIS. WE TALK about it, though, in ways that mischaracterize the problem, focusing exclusively on high tuition, high student loan debt, and weak employment prospects for graduates and treating them as characteristics that permeate the system. In fact, few students who attend elite private nonprofit schools and flagship publics—which advertise high "sticker prices"—pay full fare and even if they do, what they pay and borrow in student loans usually amounts to a valuable investment, given high graduation rates and typical earnings of graduates. Despite considerably lower price tags at the public universities and colleges that three out of four Americans students attend, there soaring tuition *is* a dire problem, consuming substantially more of the average family's income than in the past and making enrollment unaffordable for many. As resources have become stretched thin at these institutions, class sizes have swelled, more classes are being taught online by adjuncts rather than in person by full-time professors, colleges offer less support for students—and all of these factors are lowering graduation rates. The worst problems of tuition and student loan debt occur at for-profit colleges, which charge far more than the publics and at which nearly all students borrow and, on average, borrow far higher amounts than those in other sectors. Yet they are the least likely to find jobs later on that enable them to repay their debts; going to college leaves many of them worse off than if they had never attended. All told, higher education today is becoming a caste system in which students from different socioeconomic backgrounds occupy distinct strata, and their experiences within those tiers end up making them increasingly unequal.

Misunderstanding the crisis leads us to overlook its predominant sources and to focus only on institutions and individuals. Certainly colleges and universities themselves deserve some of the blame, for instance, as spiraling administrative costs account for a large share of tuition increases. So too, individual students sometimes make poor choices, for example, by borrowing more than might be warranted given their major program of study. But the crisis is also fundamentally *political*. We have plenty of higher education policies created in the past but they function less well than they once did, generating unintended consequences or deteriorating due to their own design features or the impact of other policies on them. In short, they require updating and maintenance. Public officials should be fully capable of these tasks. The problem is that the political system today has grown dysfunctional. It is paralyzed by polarization that inhibits even these routine activities. In the rare instances when government functions, it takes on the character of a plutocracy, as lawmakers join forces across party lines to represent the advantaged and neglect the needs of ordinary Americans.

We are squandering one of the finest US accomplishments and historic legacies, a system of higher education that was long characterized by excellence and wide accessibility to what seemed to be an ever wider and more diverse group of citizens. This inheritance is vanishing as state governments divest in public universities and colleges such that they disintegrate in value and more of the burden of affording them is placed on students and their families. It diminishes as the federal government subsidizes the for-profits, permitting their owners to serve low income students poorly while benefiting at public expense. It withers as many nonprofit private universities and colleges, despite the ample public benefits that assist them, do too little either to recruit less advantaged students or to lower tuition costs for those who enroll. As a result of these trends, we are producing too few highly educated workers to provide the innovation and creativity the economy requires; our international competitiveness is fading; the ranks of those who participate intensely in the political process is growing more unequal; and the American dream is increasingly out of reach for most citizens. With our system of higher education in crisis, the core values and identity of the United States are at stake.

WHY IT MATTERS

Today we see college degrees as investments that only yield benefits to the individuals who acquire them, enabling them to get ahead and have a wider set of opportunities. But when the United States was founded, public officials promoted higher education because it mattered for the broader public. They strongly believed that by encouraging and subsidizing advanced learning, the nation would foster the knowledge, creativity, dynamism, leadership, and skills that would spur economic growth, technological innovation, and social advances. As Benjamin Franklin remarked in a proposal that led to the creation of the University of Pennsylvania: "The good Education of Youth has been esteemed by wise Men in all Ages, as the surest Foundation of the Happiness both of private families and of Commonwealth [nations]. Almost all Governments have therefore made it a principal Object of their Attention . . . [to] supply the succeeding Age with Men qualified to serve the Publick with Honour to themselves, and to their Country."[1]

In 1947 a commission appointed by President Harry Truman to examine the state of American higher education—just before landmark federal policies and state investment prompted massive expansions—lamented, "It is especially serious than not more of our most talented young people continue their schooling beyond high school in this day when the complexity of life and of our social problems means that we need every bit of trained intelligence we can assemble. The present state of affairs is resulting in far too great a loss of talent—our most precious natural resource."[2]

As Americans worry about declining competitiveness and the nation's position in the world economy, we need to promote higher education for these same kinds of reasons.[3] American businesses struggle to find highly skilled employees in numerous fields.[4] We need more minds to focus on countless problems, ranging from the need for sustainable energy to cures for diseases. Higher education is more necessary than ever to foster economic progress and growth, as well as innovations that benefit society as a whole.

The national drive to promote higher education has always emanated from broad public purposes inextricably entwined with deeply cherished ideals. Thomas Jefferson believed strongly that education provided the training for self-government: "No one more sincerely wishes the spread of information among mankind than I do, and none has greater confidence in its effect towards supporting free and good government."[5] Indeed, scholars who study citizen political involvement find that educational attainment comes closer than any other life experience in explaining individual participation, making education crucial to the health of democracy. In the twentieth century, access to higher education became widely associated with the pursuit of the American dream. The Truman Commission in 1947 articulated a version of this view when it detailed numerous obstacles to college enrollment and lambasted them for "denying to millions of young people what the democratic creed assumes to be their birth-right: an equal chance with all others to make the most of their native abilities."[6] Lyndon Johnson echoed these sentiments when he predicted that the Higher Education Act would open doors to college for many more Americans. Expanding college graduation rates promises to reduce income disparities.[7]

Economic inequality has been soaring for decades, and major studies find that government today is responsive primarily to the most privileged.[8] These developments threaten to transform the United States into a nation very different than American ideals would warrant. Consequently it is imperative for us to find ways for our system of higher education to mitigate such divisions and spur broader involvement.

POLICIES DON'T MAINTAIN THEMSELVES

The question is, then: How can the United States effectively expand opportunity to low and middle income Americans, enabling them to enroll in college, gain a quality education and graduate, while not taking on an unreasonable amount of debt? To do this, we must redirect resources and invest in institutions and policies that promise to be most effective. Several principles should guide us. We need to eliminate ineffective forms of student aid in order to make better use of available resources. We also need to terminate aid to institutions that serve students poorly. We must revitalize the historic partnership between the federal government and state governments and private nonprofit institutions to ensure that all parties do their part. In pursuing these goals, we should go by the maxim "first, do no harm," and maintain excellence where it exists. We should avoid approaches that subject institutions to a rigid set of performance standards, as learning outcomes defy precise measurement and, designed incorrectly, will yield unintended ill effects. Still, universities and colleges need to find means of assessing their impact on students.

We need to make a top priority of enabling the least advantaged Americans who wish to attend college and are qualified applicants to enroll and emerge better off as a result. The for-profit schools are the obvious place to start. We now spend one in four of our higher education dollars sending students to these colleges, and for that we reap a new underclass of highly indebted individuals, most of whom do not manage to complete their degrees. Those who do finish face job prospects that are dismal in light of the amount they have borrowed. Each of the players involved in perpetuating this system has the wrong incentives: the owners of the for-profits want to make more money; lawmakers want to cultivate friends in the business community, collect campaign contributions, and be able to say that they're promoting free market principles while helping the poor. Meanwhile, if for-profits continue to make the cost of student aid balloon, lawmakers may decide such programs are unsustainable and curtail them for all students, including the majority who study at universities and colleges with far better records.

At a minimum, lawmakers can build on past and existing regulatory efforts. They can scale back the amount of revenues that for-profits are allowed to receive from the federal government, specifically Title IV of the Higher Education Act, from 90 percent to a much lower rate, and remove the loophole that prevents funds from other programs, such as the GI Bill, from being included in that figure. They can prohibit aid to schools with default rates above a particular threshold. Although these kinds of proposals have encountered opposition in the past, the climate is changing in the Senate and could change in the House as well, given greater exposure to the issues. In addition, lawmakers should insist that the Department of Education implement the incentive compensation rules that it devised successfully during Obama's first term.

Lawmakers also need to consider more innovative approaches. They could limit the amount of federal aid available for study at for-profits to that typically provided to students who attain comparable career training at public institutions. This would force for-profits to compete with colleges providing educational services at much lower prices. Some will object, saying that such policies unfairly single out one sector of higher education and subject it to special regulations. But schools in other sectors do not rely nearly as heavily on the federal government for their funds, they don't use those funds to profit themselves, and they don't leave such a high percentage of their students so heavily indebted and unable to pay their loans. Government must intervene to protect the public's interests.

At the same time, we need to strengthen community colleges. These schools have accommodated less advantaged students without the intensive recruiting efforts used by the for-profits, and at a much lower cost. In the hierarchy of trade associations representing institutions of higher education in Washington, DC, those advocating for the community colleges are the least powerful. The sector found a ready advocate in President Barack Obama, only to have congressional leaders strike the major provision promised to them when the student aid package was combined with the health care reform law in a reconciliation bill. Because Republicans value the assistance community colleges can give local businesses, new legislation tailored specifically to aid these institutions should enjoy bipartisan support more easily than policies geared to the four-year institutions. One overarching goal should be to establish best practices to ensure that students who wish to continue on to a four-year degree receive the support and guidance they need to do so.[9] In addition, such policies should encourage colleges to work with local employers to identify types of job training that are most in demand and also to find ways to recruit and accommodate students whose personal schedules include work and family obligations.

Next we need to revitalize the partnership between the federal and state governments that long promoted higher education. In recent years, the federal government has increased its commitment to students, but the vast majority of states have declined to uphold their end of the bargain. In fact, the availability of federal student aid inadvertently rewards states that do less to offset the costs of tuition at public universities and colleges because more federal money will flow into their states if tuition costs are higher. In effect, states that game the system in this way rely on taxpayers elsewhere in the nation to fund what they are unwilling to support for their own citizens. Federal policymakers must seek means to pressure and induce the states to restore their commitment. One small program, the College Access Challenge grants, did tie states' eligibility to evidence that they exhibited "maintenance of effort" in funding their public university system. Congress should explore additional ways of extending this principle to funds appropriated under the Higher Education Act's Title IV, such that it rewards states that maintain their financial commitment to higher education, rather than those that fail to do so.[10] In addition, one of the most promising ways federal lawmakers could help states afford higher education spending would be to reduce competing demands for state revenues by encouraging implementation of health care reform and additional means of reducing health care costs.

In a parallel way, federal lawmakers should explore how to reward private nonprofit colleges and universities that enroll and graduate high percentages of low income students and penalize those that make limited efforts to do so. Some private colleges have distinguished themselves by actively recruiting low income students, providing them with ample student aid, and supporting them in ways that help ensure high graduation rates. Amherst College in Massachusetts provides a shining

example: there President Anthony Marx set a goal of increasing the percentage of Pell grant recipients in the student body and raising the funds
to help make tuition affordable for them. Today, such students compose
22 percent of Amherst's student body, and pay, on average, only $448
in tuition.[11] Other nonprofit colleges, however, either recruit few such
students or do little to supplement the Pell grants of those they do admit. Instead, they use funds from their endowments either to offer merit
aid to students with higher test scores, a strategy that may well boost
their rankings in *U.S. News & World Report* but tends to favor the well-
off, or to recruit less meritorious but high income students who will pay
close to full fare.[12] It is appropriate for national political leaders to expose
these schools, which benefit not only from Title IV funds but also from
other federal policies such as the tax-free status of charitable contributions, while using funding mechanisms to reward schools that expand
opportunity. By accepting federal funds, particularly from Title IV, colleges make themselves partners in the quest to broaden access to higher
education: they cannot leave it to the federal government alone to carry
the financial burden of this task. Congress should consider offering Pell
bonuses to colleges that operate on a tight financial margin, enroll high
rates of Pell grant recipients, and have high graduation rates; this would
enable such schools to offer more generous financial packages to needy
students. Conversely, wealthy colleges that offer little extra aid to Pell recipients while giving aid to affluent students should be required to pay a
matching contribution toward the support of the Pell recipients.[13]

Once the changes outlined above are under way, lawmakers should
make federal student aid more generous and effective. They can begin
by enlarging Pell grants so that they will go further in making college affordable, as they did at their inception in the 1970s. Increasing grant aid
will permit low income students to reduce the amount they borrow and
permit more students to stay enrolled full-time and graduate in a timely
manner. This goal cannot be sanctioned—and will not be sustainable—
unless federal lawmakers can induce states and the private sector to act
as responsible partners in higher education financing, and if they re-
strain the for-profits from abusing its availability.

At the same time, lawmakers should eliminate wasteful, ineffective student aid, namely, tuition tax breaks. These policies fail to raise college enrollment and they limit federal revenues. They have also become tilted over time toward well-off families.[14] By terminating these policies, lawmakers will have additional funds to commit to more effective forms of student aid.

Student loans, the topic that typically gets more media attention than any of the issues discussed above, may seem conspicuous by their absence on this list. Yet the extent of student loan indebtedness from undergraduate education varies dramatically by sector: among those with a bachelor's degree from a public university, 38 percent graduate debt-free and only 4 percent owe more than $40,000; by contrast, among those who attended for-profits, only 4 percent owe nothing and 24 percent owe more than $40,000.[15] Graduate students usually acquire greater debts—7 percent borrowed $80,000 or more—but typically those who take on such high amounts enter professions with high salaries and can readily pay off their loans.[16] For undergraduate students, if all of the other initiatives listed above are adopted, student loan indebtedness should become restrained and default rates curtailed. Income-based repayment and public service loan forgiveness policies have already been enacted, and these could be effectively utilized by many more borrowers who are eligible for them.[17] Still, some individuals, deeply indebted by their education, will encounter personal tragedies and hardships that leave them underwater. Therefore, Congress should eliminate the bankruptcy rule adopted in 1998 that prevents student loans from being discharged in bankruptcy. While we need to encourage responsible borrowing, individuals should not face financial ruin because they attempted to better their life through education.

PREPARING THE WAY FOR REFORM

Perhaps the most sobering message in this book is that the severely dysfunctional state of American politics today has real impacts, in this case undermining what has always been one of the nation's strongest policy legacies. It is hardly news that the political system has become deeply polarized and primarily responsive to the needs of vested interests, but what this study has made evident is the deleterious effects of such dynamics on higher education policy. These same patterns are repeated across numerous other policy areas, as well, leaving the United States unable to address many of its most pressing problems, whether pertaining to updating Social Security, immigration reform, tax reform, carbon emissions, and so forth.

Addressing major issues in any of these areas or creating the changes in higher education policy described above cannot occur unless we find ways to make elected officials more responsive to ordinary Americans and diffuse the forces of polarization and plutocracy. Partisan polarization produces stalemate, as policymakers form into teams and block each other's policy initiatives. But polarization also undermines the basic maintenance of existing policies by prompting lawmakers to ignore policy effects that occur automatically, to neglect implementation problems, to be too willing to forge agreement over what can be senseless policy "solutions," and on the rare occasions when majorities manage to enact major policies, to do so without sufficient attention to the feasibility of plans for administration and financing. The nation depends on constructive engagement by representatives of both parties to realize the benefits that result from greater deliberation over policymaking and oversight. Ironically, plutocracy can prompt even those who despise government spending to support plenty of it—when it goes to interests that they have chosen to defend. The same dynamics that hinder policy effectiveness in higher education perform in similar ways in numerous other issue areas, now interfering with governing responsibilities as basic as confirming political appointments, enacting a farm bill, and so forth.

How are we to proceed? Certainly many scholars have suggested institutional reforms that could help weaken partisanship and make politics safe once again for moderate Republicans. An obvious way to do this would be to alter the Senate's filibuster rule, such as by putting the burden back on the minority to sustain it, so that bills once again

can be routinely enacted by a majority rather than requiring a large supermajority of supporters.[18]

We also need reforms to limit the advantage that powerful interests
have over ordinary Americans. One way to level the playing field would
be to prohibit lawmakers from accepting campaign contributions from
lobbyists and their organizations.[19] We could also slow down the "re-
volving door"—introducing longer waiting periods and more comprehensive prohibitions on the extent to which individuals circulate back
and forth between positions in Congress, in industries subject to regulation, and in executive agencies that are charged with regulating those
industries.

Most importantly, we need to find ways to amplify the voice of ordinary Americans in the policymaking process and bring it to the attention of lawmakers. Over and over again in this book, we have seen
policy developments in which vested interests got most of what they
were after, but citizens generally were left out of the loop. One exception shows how much civic activism matters: once young people became more active in elections in 2006 and 2008, lawmakers responded
to them by improving federal student aid policies. Easing restrictions
on voting, making it easier to register and vote on the same day or in
advance of Election Day, and related reforms could go far to boost voter
turnout.[20] In addition, we need to seek ways to create, for a new era,
civic organizational forms that will allow citizen voices to be heard in
between elections. The best of nineteenth-century federated organizing
techniques can be combined with twenty-first-century technology to
facilitate this.[21]

In 1947 the Truman Commission warned, "If the ladder of educational opportunity rises high at the doors of some youth and scarcely
rises at all at the doors of others, while at the same time formal education is made a prerequisite to occupational and social advance, then
education may become the means, not of eliminating race and class
distinctions, but of deepening and solidifying them."[22] Afterward,
American lawmakers engaged in decades of successful policymaking
that led the United States to become the world leader in educational

attainment. But today this description offers a strikingly prescient depiction of higher education in our times.

From the Northwest Ordinance up through the enactment of Pell grants, the United States found innovative ways to promote higher education so that it would serve crucial and ambitious public purposes. It is now up to us to find ways to do so again, for our own time.

ACKNOWLEDGMENTS

I HAVE SPENT MUCH OF THE PAST EIGHT YEARS RESEARCHING AND WRITING this book, and throughout the journey I have been helped by a vast number of individuals in multiple ways. I am tremendously grateful to each one of them.

My understanding of higher education politics has been enhanced immeasurably by the thirty-one individuals I interviewed for this project, some of them two or three times. These individuals work as congressional staffers on Capitol Hill, employees of the US Department of Education, or lobbyists or higher education advocates for trade associations, student associations, consumer groups, and other groups involved in the policymaking process. Their identities are protected and therefore I cannot thank each one by name, but their willingness to give of their time and to share their knowledge, insights, and reflections candidly with me proved indispensable for this project.

A couple of generations of students have worked as research assistants on this project. The book's illustrations owe particularly to the marvelous expertise of Julianna Koch. In addition, I received excellent help from Matt Guardino and Sarah Byrnes at the Maxwell School at Syracuse University; and at Cornell University, from Dennis Hui, Mike Miller, Deondra Rose, Mallory SoRelle, Danielle Thomsen, Keith Tonsager, and Alexis Walker. Each one of them has made a mark on this book. Deondra's own scholarship on higher education policy has gone far to deepen my understanding, and our work on a joint conference paper influenced my analysis in Chapter 2.

Over the years, I have presented numerous papers drawn from this project: at academic conferences; at the Russell Sage Foundation; and at several universities, including the University of California at Berkeley, Cornell, MIT, Minnesota, Northwestern, and Oxford. I cannot begin to thank all of the individuals who raised useful questions and provided insightful comments on these occasions; suffice to say they have shaped what this book evolved into. Throughout the research process, several wonderful scholars offered incisive comments and raised probing questions, including Dan Carpenter, Luciana Dar, Alisa Hicklin Fryar, Jacob Hacker, Christopher Howard, Larry Jacobs, Desmond King, Steven Teles, and Theda Skocpol.

Two colleagues, Jeff Stonecash of Syracuse University and Richard Valelly of Swarthmore, exhibited incredible generosity by taking time out of their own busy schedules of research and writing to read the entire book manuscript. They offered trenchant—and indispensable— feedback and suggestions that greatly aided me in making revisions. The book has come to fruition thanks to my astute and gracious agent, Lisa Adams, and all of the talented, helpful staff at Basic Books, including Sandra Beris, Chrisona Schmidt, and Kaitlyn Zafonte. Anything I can write about the contribution of my editor, Tim Bartlett, risks severe understatement. He understood what I was trying to convey, perhaps better than I did, and how to help me accomplish it. He offered sage advice and raised penetrating questions on every single page of the manuscript. It has been an incredible privilege to work with him once again.

The project was funded primarily by a generous grant from the Spencer Foundation, as well as through leave time provided by Cornell University. Christina Leigh Deitz at Syracuse provided crucial help on grant writing, and Laurie Coon at Cornell expertly administered the grant. The research on developments during the Obama administration was supported by the Russell Sage Foundation, as part of a group convened to study policy developments in several issue areas in 2009–2011.

My greatest debts are to my family. My five siblings and I were fortunate to be raised by parents—John and Elinor Mettler—who were determined that each of us would go to college. They worked hard and sacrificed to ensure that we could. Later on, at my sisters' weddings and my own, my father would always stand up and make what amounted to a bold defense of higher education. He would announce to the guests, "I told each of my daughters that I wanted her to get a college degree so that she could support herself, and then she could marry any damn bum she wanted." I've been blessed a million times over—not least to have had incredible parents; for them to have supported me to attend Boston College, which opened up the world to me and set in motion a lifetime of intellectual engagement; and to have wound up with the (so-called) "damn bum" without whom this book would not exist, Wayne Grove. Wayne has discussed every facet of this book with me, time and again, throughout all of these years; he has read and commented on numerous chapter drafts; he has alerted me to countless reports and studies of higher education; he cooked one delicious meal after another with food grown in his abundant vegetable garden; and he and our daughters Sophie and Julia have made every day a joy.

It is my sister Jeanne Mettler who first ignited in me a zeal for higher education. Jeanne went off to college when I was just a kid, and when she came back home for visits, she was brimming over with excitement about the world of ideas, the liberal arts, and critical thinking. Through her, college professors became our dear family friends, especially Bill Darden and Diana Diaz, and the conversations were always invigorating. Jeanne—as a criminal defense attorney and as a teacher—has devoted several decades of her life to helping young people who grew up in far more difficult circumstances to have greater opportunities. She continues to be the most ardent defender of the value of higher education of anyone I know. This book is dedicated to her with admiration and love.

NOTES

INTRODUCTION

1. Dylan Matthews, "It's Official: The 112th Congress Was the Most Polarized Ever," Wonkblog, *Washington Post*, January 17, 2013, http://www.washington post.com/blogs/wonkblog/wp/2013/01/17/its-official-the-112th-congress-was-the -most-polarized-ever.

2. Vote Results on Full-Year Continuing Appropriations Act of 2011, H. Amendment 94: Roll Vote no. 92, February 18, 2011, http://clerk.house.gov/evs /2011/roll092.xml.

3. National Center for Education Statistics, *2010 Digest of Education Statistics*, Tables 197, 198, 201, http://nces.ed.gov/programs/digest/d10/tables/dt10_197 .asp; http://nces.ed.gov/programs/digest/d10/tables/dt10_198.asp; http://nces.ed .gov/programs/digest/d10/tables/dt10_201.asp.

4. *Trends in Higher Education* (New York: College Board, 2012), fig. 1A, http://trends.collegeboard.org/college-pricing/figures-tables/average-published -undergraduate-charges-sector-2012-13; David Glenn, "Annual Portrait of Education Documents Swift Rise of For-Profit Colleges," *Chronicle of Higher Education*, May 26, 2011.

5. Patricia Steele and Sandy Baum, *How Much Are College Students Borrowing?* Policy Brief (New York: College Board, 2009), 2–3, http://professionals.col-legeboard.com/profdownload/cb-policy-brief-college-stu-borrowing-aug-2009. pdf. See also Sandy Baum and Patricia Steele, *Who Borrows Most? Bachelor's Degree Recipients with High Levels of Student Debt*, Trends in Higher Education Series (New York: College Board, 2010), 1, http://advocacy.collegeboard.org/sites /default/files/Trends-Who-Borrows-Most-Brief.pdf.

6. David Glenn, "Annual Portrait of Education Documents Swift Rise of For-Profit Colleges," *Chronicle of Higher Education*, May 26, 2011; Sandy Baum and Kathleen Payea, *Trends in For-Profit Postsecondary Education: Enrollment, Prices, Student Aid, and Outcomes,* Trends in Higher Education Series (New York:

College Board, 2011), http://advocacy.collegeboard.org/sites/default/files/11b_3376_Trends_Brief_4Pass_110414.pdf.

7. David J. Deming, Claudia Goldin, and Lawrence F. Katz, "The For-Profit Postsecondary School Sector: Nimble Critters or Agile Predators?" *Journal of Economic Perspectives* 26, no. 1 (Winter 2012): 159–160; US General Accountability Office, *Postsecondary Education: Student Outcomes Vary at For-Profit, Nonprofit, and Public Schools*, GAO-12-143 (Washington, DC: General Accountability Office, 2011), http://www.gao.gov/new.items/d12143.pdf.

8. College Board, *Two-Year and Three-Year Cohort Default Rate by Sector*, Trends in Higher Education, http://trends.collegeboard.org/student-aid/figures-tables/federal-student-loan-default-rates-sector.

9. US Senate, Committee on Health, Education, Labor, and Pensions, *For-Profit Higher Education: The Failure to Safeguard the Federal Investment and Ensure Student Success*, 112th Cong., 2nd sess., vol. 1 of 4, July 30, 2012, 19.

10. Ibid., 4.

11. Ibid., 1, 3.

12. Office of the Clerk, US House, Final Vote Results for Roll Call 719, H.R. 3221, http://clerk.house.gov/evs/2009/roll719.xml.

13. This will be demonstrated in Chapter 2.

14. Christopher J. Lucas, *American Higher Education: A History*, 2nd ed. (New York, Macmillan Palgrae, 2006), 117.

15. Association of Public and Land-Grant Universities, *The Land Grant Tradition* (Washington, DC: Association of Public and Land-Grant Universities, 2012), 6, http://www.aplu.org/document.doc?id=780.

16. Suzanne Mettler, *Soldiers to Citizens: The G.I. Bill and the Making of the Greatest Generation* (New York: Oxford University Press, 2005), 7, 136.

17. Christopher P. Loss, *Between Citizens and the State: The Politics of American Higher Education in the Twentieth Century* (Princeton: Princeton University Press, 2012).

18. Deondra Eunique Rose, "The Development of U.S. Higher Education Policy and Its Impact on the Gender Dynamics of American Citizenship" (PhD diss., Cornell University, 2012).

19. Roger L. Geiger and Donald E. Heller, "Financial Trends in Higher Education: The United States" (Working Paper no. 6, Penn State, College of Education, Center for the Study of Higher Education), 3, http://www.ed.psu.edu/educ/cshe/working-papers/WP%236; Donald E. Heller, "Trends in the Affordability of Public Colleges and Universities: The Contradiction of Increasing Prices and Increasing Enrollment," in *The States and Public Higher Education Policy*, 2nd ed. (Baltimore: Johns Hopkins, 2011), 22.

20. Claudia Goldin and Lawrence Katz, *The Race Between Education and Technology* (Cambridge: Harvard University Press, 2008), chap. 6; US Census Bureau, *Educational Attainment in the United States: 2009, Current Population Reports*, February 2012, http://www.census.gov/prod/2012pubs/p20-566.pdf.

21. Mettler, *Soldiers to Citizens*, 95.

22. For example, Sidney Verba, Kay Lehman Schlozman, and Henry E. Brady, *Voice and Equality: Civic Voluntarism in American Politics* (Cambridge: Harvard University Press, 1995).

23. Ibid., chaps. 7–8.

24. Ibid., 105.

25. Rose, "Development of U.S. Higher Education Policy," 286.

26. OECD, *Education at a Glance 2012*, Table A1.3a, doi: 10.1787eag-2012 -table8-en.

27. Thomas Mortensen, "Family Income and Educational Attainment, 1970 to 2010," *Postsecondary Education Attainment*, January 2012, www.postsecondary .org, 1–9; Martha J. Bailey and Susan M. Dynarski, "Inequality in Postsecond-ary Education," in *Whither Opportunity?* eds. Greg Duncan and Richard Murane (New York: Russell Sage Foundation, 2011), 117–131.

28. Heller, "Trends in the Affordability of Public Colleges and Universities," 13–36.

29. Author's calculation, using tuition statistics from the *Digest of Educational Statistics: 2010*, Table 345, Average Undergraduate Tuition and Fees and Room and Board Rates Charged for Full-time Students in Degree-granting Institutions, by Type and Control of Institution: 1964–1965 through 2009–2010, http://nces .ed.gov/programs/digest/d10/tables/dt10_345.asp?referrer=report; US Census Bu-reau, "Income/Families F-6 Regions—Families (All Races) by Median and Mean Income," Income Historical Tables, http://www.census.gov/hhes/www/income /data/historical/families; US Department of Labor, Bureau of Labor Statistics, *Con-sumer Price Index: All Urban Consumers, U.S. City Average,* ftp://ftp.bls.gov/pub /special.requests/cpi/cpiai.txt.

30. Ronald Ehrenberg, *Tuition Rising: Why College Costs So Much* (Cambridge: Harvard University Press, 2002); Robert B. Archibald and David H. Feldman, "Are Plush Dorms and Fancy Food Plans Important Drivers of College Cost?" *Change,* January–February 2011, 31–37.

31. For an excellent treatment, see Robert B. Archibald and David H. Feldman, "Why Do Higher Education Costs Rise More Rapidly Than Prices in General?" *Change,* May–June 2008, 25–31.

32. College Board, *Maximum Pell Grant as Percentage of Tuition and Fees and Total Charges over Time* (New York: College Board, 2013), http://trends.college board.org/student-aid/figures-tables/fed-aid-maximum-pell-grant-percentage -total-charges-over-time; David S. Baime and Christopher M. Mullin, *Promoting Educational Opportunity: The Pell Grant Program at Community Colleges* (Wash-ington, DC: AACC Policy Brief 2011-03PBL, 2011), http://www.aacc.nche.edu/ Publications/Briefs/Documents/PolicyBrief_Pell%20Grant.pdf; Shannon M. Ma-han, "Federal Pell Grant Program of the Higher Education Act: Background, Recent Changes, and Current Legislative Issues," Congressional Research Service, May 12, 2011, 25.

33. Stephen Burd, "Moving On Up: How Tuition Tax Breaks Increasingly Favor the Upper-Middle Class," *Education Sector,* April 2012, http://www.education sector.org/sites/default/files/publications/TaxCredit_CYCT_RELEASED.pdf, 8.

34. Geiger and Heller, "Financial Trends in Higher Education," 3.

35. John Quinterno, *The Great Cost Shift: How Higher Education Cuts Undermine the Middle Class* (New York: Demos, 2012), 8–11, http://www.demos.org/sites/default/files/publications/TheGreatCostShift_Demos.pdf.

36. Ronald G. Ehrenberg, "The Perfect Storm and the Privatization of Public Higher Education," *Change,* January–February 2006, 47–53.

37. National Center of Education Statistics, *Digest of Education Statistics,* Table 349: Average Undergraduate Tuition and Fees and Room and Board Rates Charged for Full-time Students in Degree-Granting Institutions by Level and Control of Institution: 1964–1965 through 2010–2011, http://nces.ed.gov/programs/digest/d11/tables/dt11_349.asp.

38. Norman Draper, "Back in the Day, It Was Easier to Pay: As Higher Education Costs Continue to Skyrocket, Sticker-Shocked Minnesota Families Scramble to Cope," *Star Tribune,* March 17, 2007.

39. John Bound, Michael Lovenheim, and Sarah Turner, *Increasing Time to Baccalaureate Degree in the United States,* Population Studies Center, University of Michigan, Research Report 10-698, April 2010, http://www.nber.org/papers/w15892.

40. The benefits that well-endowed universities gain from the tax code are vast but barely visible, like other benefits described in Suzanne Mettler, *The Submerged State* (Chicago: University of Chicago Press, 2011), Chap. 1.

41. Susan Dynarski, "Hope for Whom? Financial Aid for the Middle Class and Its Impact on College Attendance," *National Tax Journal* 53, no. 3, pt. 2 (2000): 629–662; Marian Wang, "Public Universities Ramp Up Aid for the Wealthy, Leaving the Poor Behind," *Chronicle of Higher Education,* September 11, 2013, http://chronicle.com/article/Public-Colleges-Quest-for/141541.

42. Stephen Burd, "Undermining Pell: How Colleges Compete for Wealthy Students and Leave the Low-Income Behind," *New America Foundation,* 2013, http://education.newamerica.net/sites/newamerica.net/files/policydocs/Merit_Aid%20Final.pdf.

43. These are abundant. To begin, see the annual *Trends in Student Aid* published by the College Board; Advisory Committee on Student Financial Assistance, *Rising Price of Inequality: How Inadequate Grant Aid Limits College Access and Persistence* (2010).

44. In addition to those described in the next sentences in the text, see Donald E. Heller, ed., *The States and Public Higher Education Policy,* 2nd ed. (Baltimore: Johns Hopkins University Press, 2011); William G. Bowen, Marvin A. Kurzweil, and Eugene M. Tobin, *Equity and Excellence in American Higher*

Education (Charlottesville: University of Virginia Press, 2005); Donald E. Heller, ed., *Condition of Access: Higher Education for Lower Income Students* (Westport, CT: Praeger, 2002); Michael S. McPherson and Morton Owen Schapiro, *College Access: Opportunity or Privilege?* (New York: College Board, 2006); Samuel Bowles, Herbert Gintis, and Melissa Osborne Groves, eds., *Unequal Chances: Family Background and Economic Success* (New York: Russell Sage Foundation, 2005).

45. Goldin and Katz, *Race Between Education and Technology.*

46. Greg Duncan and Richard Murane, eds., *Whither Opportunity?* (New York: Russell Sage Foundation, 2011); Richard D. Kahlenberg, *Rewarding Strivers: Helping Low-Income Students Succeed in College* (New York: Century Foundation Press, 2010). On trends in state-level support, see Ronald G. Ehrenberg, ed., *What's Happening to Public Higher Education? The Shifting Financial Burden* (Baltimore: Johns Hopkins University Press, 2006).

47. Hacker, "Privatizing Risk Without Privatizing the Welfare State," *American Political Science Review* 98, no. 2 (May 2004): 247.

48. Stephanie Riegg Cellini and Claudia Goldin, "Does Federal Student Aid Raise Tuition? New Evidence on For-Profit Colleges" (Working Paper no. 17827, National Bureau of Economic Research, February 2012), http://www.nber.org/papers/w17827.

49. Senator Nancy Kassebaum, telephone interview by author, March 19, 2013.

50. Nolan McCarty, Keith T. Poole, and Howard Rosenthal, *Polarized America: The Dance of Ideology and Unequal Riches* (Cambridge: MIT Press, 2006).

51. For an excellent treatment of how institutions of higher education influenced American citizenship throughout the twentieth century, see Loss, *Between Citizens and the State.*

52. US Congress, *Congressional Record: House,* February 17, 2011, H1154.

53. Goldie Blumenstyk, "Economic Downturn Brings Prosperity and Opportunities to For-Profit Colleges," *Chronicle of Higher Education,* December 19, 2008, 13.

Chapter One

1. Libby A. Nelson, "Occupy Protests Focusing Increasingly on Student Debt," *Inside Higher Ed,* November 15, 2011, http://www.insidehighered.com/news/2011/11/15/occupy-protests-focusing-increasingly-student-debt.

2. Ibid., 2.

3. Paul Fain, "Politicians and Pundits Ramp Up Questions About Value of Degrees," *Inside Higher Ed,* June 29, 2012, http://www.insidehighered.com/news/2012/06/29/politicians-and-pundits-ramp-questions-about-value-degrees.

4. Robert J. Samuelson, "It's Time to Drop the College-for-all Crusade," *Washington Post,* May 27, 2012, http://articles.washingtonpost.com/2012-05-27/opinions/35456501_1_college-students-josipa-roksa-private-colleges-and-universities.

5. Clive Crook, "A Matter of Degrees," *Atlantic Monthly*, November 2006, http://www.theatlantic.com/magazine/archive/2006/11/a-matter-of-degrees /305269.

6. Alex Williams, "Saying No to College," *New York Times*, November 30, 2012, http://www.nytimes.com/2012/12/02/fashion/saying-no-to-college.html ?pagewanted=all&_r=0.

7. Amanda M. Fairbanks, "Peter Thiel Awards $100,000 to Entrepreneurs Under 20," Huffington Post, May 25, 2011, http://www.huffingtonpost .com/2011/05/25/peter-thiel-fellowship_n_867134.html.

8. US Census Bureau, Table A-2, *CPS Historical Time Series Tables*, http:// www.census.gov/hhes/socdemo/education/data/cps/historical/index.html.

9. Tamar Lewin, "Record Number Complete High School and College," *New York Times*, November 6, 2012, A17; Tamar Lewin, "Once a Leader, US Lags in College Degrees," *New York Times,* July 23, 2010, http://www.nytimes.com /2010/07/23/education/23college.html?_r=0.

10. Scott Jaschik, "A Degree Still Matters," *Inside Higher Ed*, August 15, 2012, http://www.insidehighered.com/news/2012/08/15/study-documents-value -college-degree-even-recession.

11. National Center for Education Statistics, "Fast Facts: What Is the Average Income for Young Adults?" Institute for Education Statistics, http://nces.ed.gov/ fastfacts/display.asp?id=77.

12. Michael Greenstone and Adam Looney, "Where Is the Best Place to Invest $102,000—In Stocks, Bonds, or a College Degree?" *Brookings Institution*, June 25, 2011, http://www.brookings.edu/research/papers/2011/06/25-education -greenstone-looney.

13. Robert Wood Johnson Foundation, "Why Does Education Matter So Much to Health?" *Health Policy Snapshot: Public Health and Prevention,* Issue Brief, March 2013, http://www.rwjf.org/content/dam/farm/reports/issue_briefs/2012 /rwjf403347.

14. Sidney Verba, Kay Lehman Schlozman, and Henry Brady, *Voice and Equality: Civic Voluntarism and American Politics* (Cambridge: Harvard University Press, 1995).

15. Susan Dynarski, testimony before the Committee on Finance, US Senate, 112th Cong., July 25, 2012, http://www.finance.senate.gov/imo/media/doc /Dynarski%20Testimony.pdf.

16. This paragraph is based on analysis conducted by Thomas G. Mortensen, "Family Income and Unequal Educational Opportunity, 1970 to 2011," *Postsecondary Education Attainment,* November 2012, www.postsecondary.org, 1. Comparable analysis, results, and conclusions appear in Martha J. Bailey and Susan M. Dynarski, "Inequality in Postsecondary Education," in *Whither Opportunity?* eds. Greg Duncan and Richard Murane (New York: Russell Sage Foundation, 2011), 117–131.

17. Thomas Mortensen, "Family Income and Educational Attainment, 1970 to 2010," *Postsecondary Education Attainment*, January 2012, www.postsecondary .org, 1–9. Also see Bailey and Dynarski, "Inequality in Postsecondary Education," 128; Tamar Lewin, "College Graduation Rates Are Stagnant Even as Enrollment Rises, A Study Finds," *New York Times*, September 27, 2011, A15.

18. These unequal college completion patterns emerge when we consider trends in terms of race and ethnicity as well. Among those who enroll in college, 60 percent of white students have earned a bachelor's degree four years later, but only 49 percent of Hispanic students and 40 percent of black students. Jennifer Gonzalez, "Reports Highlight Disparities in Graduation Rates Among White and Minority Students," *Chronicle of Higher Education*, August 9, 2010.

19. James E. Rosenbaum, *Beyond College for All: Career Paths for the Forgotten Half* (New York: Russell Sage Foundation, 2001).

20. Samuelson, "It's Time to Drop the College-for-all Crusade."

21. Richard Vedder, interview by Lauren Weber, in "Do Too Many Young People Go to College?" *Wall Street Journal*, June 21, 2012, http://online.wsj.com /article/SB10001424052970203960804577239253121093694.html.

22. A voluminous literature examines this relationship. It is well synthesized and summarized in William G. Bowen, Martin A. Kurzweil, and Eugene M. To-bin, *Equity and Excellence in American Higher Education* (Charlottesville: University of Virginia Press, 2005), chap. 4.

23. Greg J. Duncan and Richard J. Murnane, "Introduction: The American Dream, Then and Now," in *Whither Opportunity?* (New York: Russell Sage Foundation, 2011), 11.

24. Thomas J. Kane, "College-going and Inequality," in *Social Inequality*, ed. Kathryn M. Neckerman (New York: Russell Sage Foundation, 2004), 332–335.

25. Alan Seidman, ed., *College Student Retention: Formula for Student Success* (Westport, CT: Praeger, 2005); Vincent Tinto, "Student Retention and Graduation: Facing the Truth, Living with the Consequences," Occasional Paper 1, Pell Institute for the Study of Opportunity in Higher Education, Washington, DC, July 2004, http://www.pellinstitute.org; Melanie E. Corrigan, "Beyond Access: Persistence Challenges and the Diversity of Low-income Students," in *Changing Student Attendance Patterns: Challenges for Policy and Practice: New Directions for Higher Education*, no. 121, eds. J. King, E. Anderson, and M. Corrigan (San Francisco: Jossey Bass, 2003), 25–34.

26. For a thorough discussion of findings in the relevant literature, see Anthony P. Carnevale and Jeff Strohl, "How Increasing College Access Is Increasing Inequality, and What to Do About It," in Richard D. Kahlenberg, ed., *Rewarding Strivers: Helping Low-Income Students Succeed in College* (New York: Century Foundation Press, 2010), 71–190.

27. John Bound, Michael Lovenheim, and Sarah Turner, *Increasing Time to Baccalaureate Degree in the United States*, University of Michigan Research

Report 10-698, April 2010, http://www.psc.isr.umich.edu/pubs/pdf/rr10-698
.pdf.

28. Jenny Wilson, "Rally for Action: Students Say Proposed Tuition Increase
Symptom of Broken System; Central Connecticut State University," *Hartford
Courant,* March 12, 2013.

29. Edward B. Fiske, "The Carolina Covenant," in Richard D. Kahlenberg, ed.,
Rewarding Strivers: Helping Low-Income Students Succeed in College (New York:
Century Foundation Press, 2010), 17–70.

30. Neil Fligstein, "The G.I. Bill: Its Effects on the Educational and Occupational Attainment of U.S. Males: 1940–1973" (CDE Working Paper 76-9, Center
for Demography and Ecology, University of Wisconsin–Madison, 1976); Jere R.
Behrman, Robert A. Pollack, and Paul Taubman, "Family Resources, Family Size,
and Access to Financing for College Education," *Journal of Political Economy* 97,
no. 2 (1989); Deondra Eunique Rose, "The Development of U.S. Higher Education Policy and Its Impact on the Gender Dynamics of American Citizenship"
(PhD diss., Cornell University, 2012).

31. David L. Featherman and Robert M. Hauser, *Opportunity and Change*
(New York: Academic Press, 1978).

32. Pew Charitable Trusts, "Does America Promote Mobility As Well As Other
Nations?" Economic Mobility Project, November 2011, 2, 4, https://www.russell
sage.org/sites/all/files/does-america-promote-economic-mobility.pdf.

33. John Ermisch et al., "Advantage in Comparative Perspective," in *From
Parents to Children: The Intergenerational Transmission of Advantage,* eds. John
Ermisch, Markus Jantti, and Timothy M. Smeeding (New York: Russell Sage
Foundation, 2012), 18.

34. Economic Policy Institute, "College Wage Premium by Gender," in *The
State of Working America,* eds. Lawrence Mishel et al., 12th ed. (Ithaca, NY: Cornell University Press, 2012), http://stateofworkingamerica.org/chart/swa-wages
-figure-4n-college-wage-premium.

35. Carnevale and Strohl, "How Increasing College Access Is Increasing Inequality," 135–136.

36. Ibid., 135–138.

37. Ibid., 131–133.

38. Peter Jacobs, "America's Real Most Expensive Colleges," *Business Insider,* July
10, 2013, http://www.businessinsider.com/most-expensive-colleges-in-america
-2013-7?op=1.

39. College Board, *Trends in College Pricing 2012,* Trends in Higher Education
Series (New York: College Board, 2012), 20.

40. Janet Lorin, "Colleges in U.S. Offer Highest-Ever Discount to Entice Students," Bloomberg.com, May 6, 2013, http://www.bloomberg.com/news/print
/2013-05-06/colleges-in-u-s-offer-highest-ever-discount-to-entice-students
.html.

41. Carnevale and Strohl, "How Increasing College Access Is Increasing Inequality," 112, 97.

42. Ibid., 79, 97.

43. Richard D. Kahlenberg, "Introduction," *Rewarding Strivers: Helping Low-Income Students Succeed in College* (New York: Century Foundation Press, 2010), 11–12.

44. Stephen Burd, *Undermining Pell: How Colleges Compete for Wealthy Students and Leave the Low-Income Behind* (Washington, DC: New America Foundation, May 2013), http://newamerica.net/sites/newamerica.net/files/policydocs/Merit_Aid%20Final.pdf.

45. Ben Miller and Phuong Ly, "College Dropout Factories," *Washington Monthly*, August 22, 2010, http://www.washingtonmonthly.com/college_guide/feature/college_dropout_factories.php; "2010 Dropout Factories," *Washington Monthly*, 2010, http://www.washingtonmonthly.com/college_guide/rankings_2010/dropout_factories.php.

46. National Center for Education Statistics, *Digest of Education Statistics*, Table 328, http://nces.ed.gov/programs/digest/d95/dtab328.asp; Table 412, http://nces.ed.gov/programs/digest/d12/tables/dt12_412.asp; Table 415, http://nces.ed.gov/programs/digest/d12/tables/dt12_415.asp.

47. Bound, Lovenheim, and Turner, "Increasing Time to Baccalaureate Degrees," Table 3.

48. Tamar Lewin, "Colleges Adapt Online Courses to Ease Burden," *New York Times*, April 29, 2013; Lewin, "Universities Team with Online Course Provider," *New York Times*, May 30, 2013.

49. Pew Internet, "The Digital Revolution and Higher Education," August 28, 2011, http://www.pewinternet.org/~/media//Files/Reports/2011/PIP-Online-Learning.pdf.

50. Thomas L. Friedman, "Revolution Hits the Universities," *New York Times*, January 26, 2013.

51. Di Xu and Shanna Smith Jaggars, *Adaptability to Online Learning: Differences Across Types of Students and Academic Subject Areas*, Community College Research Center, Columbia University Teachers College, February 2013, http://ccrc.tc.columbia.edu/publications/adaptability-to-online-learning.html.

52. Mark Kantrowitz, "Characteristics of Students Enrolling at For-Profit Colleges," December 22, 2009, http://www.finaid.org/educators/20091222for-profit-colleges.pdf.

53. David J. Deming, Claudia Goldin, and Lawrence F. Katz, "The For-Profit Postsecondary School Sector: Nimble Critters or Agile Predators?" *Journal of Economic Perspectives* 26, no. 1 (Winter 2012): 140; National Center for Education Statistics, *2010 Digest of Education Statistics*, Tables 197, 198, 201, http://nces.ed.gov/programs/digest/d10/tables/dt10_197.asp, http://nces.ed.gov/programs/digest/d10/tables/dt10_198.asp, http://nces.ed.gov/programs/digest/d10/tables/dt10_201.asp.

54. National Center for Education Statistics, *2011 Digest of Education Statistics* Table 279, Degree-granting Institutions, by Control and Level of Institution: Selected Years, 1949–50 through 2010–11, http://nces.ed.gov/programs/digest/d11/tables/dt11_279.asp.

55. Daniel L. Bennett, Adam R. Lucchesi, and Richard K. Vedder, *For-Profit Higher Education: Growth, Innovation and Regulation,* Center for College Affordability and Productivity, no. 15, July 2010, http://heartland.org/sites/all/modules/custom/heartland_migration/files/pdfs/29010.pdf; Barbara Mantel, "Career Colleges: Do They Take Advantage of Low-Income Students?" *CQ Researcher* 21 (2011): 1–24.

56. Andrew S. Rosen, *Change.edu: Rebooting for the New Talent Economy* (New York: Kaplan Publishing, 2011), 198.

57. Laurel Rosenhall and Phillip Reese, "Students Pile Up Trade School Debt: Many Attending Private Career Colleges Can't Get Jobs in Their Fields," *Sacramento Bee,* November 7, 2010.

58. David Glenn, "Annual Portrait of Education Documents Swift Rise of For-Profit Colleges," *Chronicle of Higher Education,* May 26, 2011.

59. Gregory D. Kutz, *For-Profit Colleges: Undercover Testing Finds Colleges Encouraged Fraud and Engaged in Deceptive and Questionable Marketing Practices,* testimony before the Committee on Health, Education, Labor, and Pensions, US Senate, 11th Cong., August 4, 2010; Tamar Lewin, "Questions Follow Leader of For-Profit Colleges," *New York Times,* May 26, 2011, http://www.nytimes.com/2011/05/27/education/27edmc.html?pagewanted=all; Kelly Field, "Career Colleges Are Accused of Job-Placement Fraud," *Chronicle of Higher Education,* November 13, 2011, http://chronicle.com/article/Career-Colleges-Are-Accused-of/129754.

60. Kutz, *For-Profit Colleges.*

61. Project on Student Debt, "Quick Facts About Student Debt," January 2010, http://projectonstudentdebt.org/files/File/Debt_Facts_and_Sources.pdf.

62. Deming, Goldin, and Katz, "The For-Profit Postsecondary School Sector: Nimble Critters or Agile Predators?" 159–160; US General Accountability Office, *Postsecondary Education: Student Outcomes Vary at For-Profit, Nonprofit, and Public Schools,* GAO-12-143 (Washington, DC: General Accountability Office, December 2011), http://www.gao.gov/new.items/d12143.pdf.

63. Kevin Lang and Russell Weinstein, "Evaluating Student Outcomes at For-Profit Colleges" (NBER Working Paper Series, 18201, June 2012), http://www.nber.org/papers/w18201.

64. Stephanie Riegg Cellini and Latika Chaudhary, "The Labor Market Returns to a For-Profit College Education" (NBER Working Paper Series, 18343, August 2012), http://www.nber.org/papers/w18343.pdf.

65. See Table 1.1; also Goldie Blumenstyk, "Default Rate on Federal Student Loans Jumps to 8.9%, a Nearly 2-Point Rise," *Chronicle of Higher Education,* May 20, 2011, http://chronicle.com/article/Default-Rate-on-Federal/127602.

66. Sandy Baum, *Drowning in Debt: Financial Outcomes of Students at For-Profit Colleges, Testimony to the Senate Health, Education, Labor, and Pensions Committee,* June 7, 2011, 6, http://www.help.senate.gov/imo/media/doc/Baum.pdf.

67. Ralph Kelchen, "America's Best-Bang-for-the-Buck Colleges," *Washington Monthly,* September–October 2013, http://www.washingtonmonthly.com /magazine/september_october_2013/features/americas_bestbangforthebuck_co _1046447.php.

68. Carnevale and Strohl, "How Increasing College Access Is Increasing Inequality," 133–134.

69. FTI Consulting, "Northeastern University: Innovation in Higher Education Survey Toplines," 9, http://www.northeastern.edu/innovationsurvey/pdfs /survey-results.pdf; "Americans Believe Higher Education Must Innovate," *Northeastern News,* November 27, 2012, http://www.northeastern.edu/news/2012/11 /innovation-summit.

70. American National Election Studies, Cumulative File, 1948–2008, 1986 and 1996, http://www.electionstudies.org.

71. Benjamin I. Page and Lawrence R. Jacobs, *Class War? What Americans Really Think About Economic Inequality* (Chicago: University of Chicago Press, 2009), 59.

72. FTI Consulting, "Northeastern University: Innovation in Higher Education Survey Toplines," 4.

73. Kay Lehman Schlozman et al., "Inequalities of Political Voice," in *Inequality and American Democracy,* eds. Lawrence R. Jacobs and Theda Skocpol (New York: Russell Sage Foundation, 2005), 23–25, 28.

74. American National Election Studies, Cumulative File, 1948–2008.

75. Benjamin I. Page and Robert Y. Shapiro, *The Rational Public: Fifty Years of Trends in Americans' Policy Preferences* (Chicago: University of Chicago Press, 1992), 132–133.

76. The importance of college graduation to the American dream was ranked similarly to "owning your own home," "retiring comfortably in the way and at the time you expect," and "raising a family and making sure they have more opportunity than you did." Interestingly, only 42 percent of respondents gave "becoming wealthy" comparable rankings. Survey by Allstate, National Journal, conducted by FD America, March 4–8, 2011; 1,000 telephone surveys.

77. Pew Research Center for the People and the Press, Survey conducted by Princeton Survey Research Associates International, February 2–7, 2011; based on 1,385 telephone surveys.

78. For exceptions that examine how policies develop over time, see Paul Pierson, *Politics in Time: History, Institutions, and Social Analysis* (Princeton: Princeton University Press, 2004); Paul Pierson, "The Study of Policy Development," *Journal of Policy History* 17, no. 1 (2005): 34–51; Eric M. Patashnik, *Reforms at Risk: What Happens After Major Policy Changes Are Enacted* (Princeton:

Princeton University Press, 2008); Jeffery A. Jenkins and Eric M. Patashnik, eds., *Living Legislation: Durability, Change and the Politics of American Lawmaking* (Chicago: University of Chicago Press, 2012); Kathleen Thelen and Wolfgang Streeck, eds., *Beyond Continuity: Institutional Change in Advanced Political Economies* (New York: Oxford University Press, 2005).

79. Hacker, "Privatizing Risk Without Privatizing the Welfare State."

80. Excellent summaries of the literature appear in Geoffrey C. Layman, Thomas M. Carsey, and Juliana Menasce Horowitz, "Party Polarization in American Politics: Characteristics, Causes, and Consequences," *Annual Review of Political Science* 9 (2006): 83–110; Barbara Sinclair, *Party Wars: Polarization and the Politics of National Policy Making* (Norman: University of Oklahoma, 2005), chaps. 1–2; Thomas E. Mann and Norman Ornstein, *It's Even Worse Than It Looks: How the American Constitutional System Collided with the New Politics of Extremism* (New York: Basic, 2012), 44–58; Danielle Thomsen, "Party Fit Theory: A Candidate-Level Explanation for Partisan Polarization in Congress," unpublished paper, http://daniellethomsen.files.wordpress.com/2012/10/thomsen_polarization_5-30.pdf.

81. Nolan N. McCarty, Keith T. Poole, and Howard Rosenthal, *Polarized America: The Dance of Ideology and Unequal Riches* (Cambridge: MIT Press, 2006); also see voteview.com.

82. Sinclair, *Party Wars.*

83. Barbara Sinclair, "The New World of U.S. Senators," in *Congress Reconsidered,* eds. Lawrence C. Dodd and Bruce I. Oppenheimer, 10th ed. (Washington, DC: CQ Press, 2013), 7–8. The use of cloture—moving on to avoid the threat of extended debate—is even more common and has increased "in tandem," as Sinclair explains.

84. Sinclair, *Party Wars,* chap. 6.

85. Molly Ball, "Even the Aide Who Coined the Hastert Rule Says the Hastert Rule Isn't Working," *The Atlantic.com,* July 21, 2013, http://www.theatlantic.com/politics/archive/2013/07/even-the-aide-who-coined-the-hastert-rule-says-the-hastert-rule-isnt-working/277961.

86. Jacob Hacker and Paul Pierson, *Off Center: The Republican Revolution and the Erosion of American Democracy* (New Haven, CT: Yale University Press, 2005), 6–7; Adam Bonica, "The Punctuated Origins of Senate Polarization," *Legislative Studies Quarterly,* forthcoming, http://papers.ssrn.com/sol3/papers.cfm?abstract_id=2253028; Theda Skocpol and Vanessa Williamson, *The Tea Party and the Remaking of the Republican Party* (New York: Oxford University Press, 2012); Mann and Orenstein, *It's Even Worse Than It Looks.*

87. Kent B. Germany, "Lyndon B. Johnson and Civil Rights: Introduction to the Digital Edition," Presidential Recordings of Lyndon B. Johnson, University of Virginia, http://presidentialrecordings.rotunda.upress.virginia.edu/essays?series=CivilRights#fn3.

88. The end of the single-party South is only one of several factors that seem to underlie partisan polarization. For a treatment of a wider array of factors, see Layman, Carsey, and Horowitz, "Party Polarization in American Politics;" in *Class and Party in American Politics,* ed. Jeffrey M. Stonecash (Boulder: Westview, 2000); Mark D. Brewer and Jeffrey M. Stonecash, *Split: Class and Cultural Divides in American Politics* (Washington, DC: Congressional Quarterly Press, 2007).

89. Sinclair, *Party Wars,* chaps. 1–5; Mann and Ornstein, *It's Even Worse Than It Looks,* 31–50.

90. Lincoln Chafee, on *The Daily Show with Jon Stewart,* December 11, 2006, http://www.thedailyshow.com/watch/mon-december-11-2006/lincoln-chafee.

91. Glenn Kessler, "When Did McConnell Say He Wanted to Make Obama a One-Term President?" The Fact Checker, *Washington Post,* September 25, 2012, http://www.washingtonpost.com/blogs/fact-checker/post/when-did-mcconnell -say-he-wanted-to-make-obama-a-one-term-president/2012/09/24/79fd5cd8 -0696-11e2-afff-d6c7f20a83bf_blog.html.

92. Larry M. Bartels, *Unequal Democracy* (New York: Russell Sage, 2008), chap. 9; Martin Gilens, *Affluence and Influence* (New York: Russell Sage, 2012); Lawrence R. Jacobs and Benjamin I. Page, "Who Influences U.S. Foreign Policy?" *American Political Science Review* 99 (2005): 107–123.

93. Center for Responsive Politics, "Lobbying Database," http://www.opensecrets .org/lobby; Campaign Finance Institute, "Table 3.1: The Cost of Winning a House and Senate Seat, 1986–2012," http://www.cfinst.org/data/historicalstats.aspx.

94. Christopher Howard, *The Hidden Welfare State: Tax Expenditures and Social Policy in the United States* (Princeton: Princeton University Press, 1997), chaps. 2, 5.

95. For a nuanced recent treatment of this phenomena, see Daniel Carpenter and David A. Moss, eds., *Preventing Regulatory Capture: Special Interest Influence and How to Limit It* (New York: Cambridge University Press, 2013).

CHAPTER TWO

1. Lyndon B. Johnson, "Remarks at Southwest Texas State College upon Signing the Higher Education Act of 1965," November 8, 1965, in *Public Papers of the Presidents, 1965, Book II* (Washington, DC: Government Printing Office, 1965), 603.

2. Ibid.

3. US Department of Education, *2011–12 Federal Pell Grant End-of-Year Report, Table 1: Federal Pell Grant Program: Summary of Statistics for Cross-Year Reference,* http://www2.ed.gov/finaid/prof/resources/data/pell-data.html; *2000 Status Report on the Pell Grant Program* (Washington, DC: American Council on Education, Center for Policy Analysis, 2000), 32–33.

4. College Board, *Trends in Student Aid 2012,* Trends in Higher Education Series (New York: College Board, 2012), Figure 3, Excel spreadsheet, http://trends .collegeboard.org/student-aid.

5. Author's calculations using data displayed in Figure 2.1.

6. See sources in Figure 2.1. Data was not available for total student loan debt at graduation for the years preceding 1992.

7. The effect of increasing partisan polarization on higher education issues has been documented and analyzed by William R. Doyle, "U.S. Senator's Ideal Points for Higher Education: Documenting Partisanship, 1965–2004," *Journal of Higher Education* 81, no. 5 (2010): 619–644.

8. Suzanne Mettler, *Soldiers to Citizens: The GI Bill and the Making of the Greatest Generation* (New York: Oxford University Press, 2005), chap. 1.

9. Ibid., 41.

10. Neil Fligstein, "The GI Bill: Its Effects on the Educational and Occupational Attainments of U.S. Males: 1940–1973" (CDE Working Paper 76-9, Center for Demography and Ecology, University of Wisconsin–Madison, 1976); Jere Behrman, Robert A. Pollak, and Paul Taubman, "Family Resources, Family Size, and Access to Financing for College Education," *Journal of Political Economy* 97, no. 2 (1989).

11. John Brademas, *The Politics of Education: Conflict and Consensus on Capitol Hill* (Norman: University of Oklahoma Press, 1989), 9; Wayne J. Urban, *More Than Science and Sputnik: The National Defense Act of 1958* (Tuscaloosa: University of Alabama Press, 2010).

12. National Defense Education Act (NDEA), Pub. L. no. 85-864, September 2, 1958, *United States Statutes at Large*, vol. 72, 1581. Italics mine.

13. Deondra Rose, "The Development of U.S. Higher Education Policy and Its Impact on the Gender Dynamics of American Citizenship" (PhD diss., Cornell University, 2012), 84–85, 104; Pamela Ebert Flattau et al., "The National Defense Education Act of 1958: Selected Outcomes," Institute for Defense Analysis, Science and Technology Institute, March 2006, https://www.ida.org/upload/stpi/pdfs/ida-d-3306.pdf.

14. Hugh Davis Graham, *The Uncertain Triumph: Federal Education Policy in the Kennedy and Johnson Years* (Chapel Hill: University of North Carolina Press, 1984), 7–10, 19.

15. Lawrence E. Gladieux and Thomas R. Wolanin, *Congress and the Colleges: The National Politics of Higher Education* (Lexington, MA: Lexington Books, 1976); Sally A. Davenport, "Smuggling-in Reform: Equal Opportunity and the Higher Education Act, 1965–80" (PhD diss., Johns Hopkins University, 1982), 181.

16. Graham, *Uncertain Triumph*, 19–29.

17. Rose, "Development of U.S. Higher Education Policy," 83, 89–90, 97.

18. For more on this subject, see Ira Katznelson and Suzanne Mettler, "On Race and Policy History: A Dialogue about the GI Bill," *Perspectives on Politics* 6, no. 3 (September 2008): 519–537. Also see Rose, "Development of U.S. Higher Education Policy."

19. José Chávez, "Presidential Influence on the Politics of Higher Education: The Higher Education Act of 1965" (PhD diss., University of Texas, 1975), 48;

Muhammad Attaullah Chaudhry, "The Higher Education Act of 1965: An Historical Case Study," (EdD diss., Oklahoma State University, 1981), 73–78.

20. Robert C. Albright, "Education Tax Credits Defeated," *Washington Post*, February 5, 1964, A1.

21. "Scholarships Featured in College Aid Bill," in *Congressional Quarterly Almanac* (Washington, DC: CQ Press, 1965), 301; Chaudhry, "Higher Education Act of 1965," 108.

22. Chávez, "Presidential Influence on the Politics of Higher Education," 88–91.

23. Wayne Urban, *More Than Science and Sputnik* (Tuscaloosa: University of Alabama Press, 2010).

24. "President's Consumer Panel Studies High Interest Rates on Student Loans," *Washington Post*, February 29, 1964, A3.

25. Graham, *Uncertain Triumph*, 82.

26. Under the proposed legislation, policymakers would set low interest rates, and government would subsidize lenders by paying half of those rates, making borrowing feasible for many more students.

27. US Congress, House of Representatives, *Higher Education Act of 1965: Hearings Before the Special Subcommittee on Education of the Committee on Education and Labor, February 1–May 1, 1965*, 98th Cong., 1st sess., 1965, 681–701, 778–795; US Congress, Senate, *Higher Education Act of 1965: Hearings Before the Subcommittee on Education of the Committee on Labor and Public Welfare, March 16–June 11*, 98th Cong., 1st sess., 1965, 1008–1057, 1093–1112; Chávez, "Presidential Influence on the Politics of Higher Education," 95; "Scholarships Featured in College Aid Bill," in *CQ Almanac 1965*, 21st ed. (Washington, DC: Congressional Quarterly, 1966), http://library.cqpress.com.proxy.library.cornell.edu/cqalmanac/cqal65-1259145.

28. Chávez, "Presidential Influence on the Politics of Higher Education," 123; Chaudhry, "Higher Education Act of 1965," 97–99. The final bill included amendments that promoted private lending by requiring the allocation of federal funds to state or private nonprofit lending organizations. It mandated that the new federal guaranteed loans would be used only if the commissioner of education determined those provisions to be inadequate (Chávez, 121–123). In addition, student loan provisions would operate initially for a three-year trial period—less than the five years supported by the Senate, but more than the one-year limit imposed by Green in the House version (Chaudhry, 99).

29. Robert Dallek, *Flawed Giant: Lyndon B. Johnson, 1960–1973* (New York: Oxford University Press, 1998), 195–196.

30. Chaudhry, "Higher Education Act of 1965," 80.

31. The Senate passed the law by voice vote.

32. John R. Thelin, "Higher Education's Student Financial Aid Enterprise in Historical Perspective," in *Footing the Tuition Bill: The New Student Loan Sector*,

ed. Frederick M. Hess (Washington, DC: AEI Press, 2007), 31–32. One controversy surrounding the Education Amendments did not pertain to the core issues but rather to busing: Nixon was expected to veto due to antibusing language that Congress included. In the end, though, he signed it into law. Federal education programs, 1969–1972 legislative overview (1973). *Congress and the Nation, 1969–1972,* vol. 3 (Washington, DC: CQ Press, 1976), http://library.cqpress.com.proxy.library .cornell.edu/congress/catn69-0008167387.

33. William H. Honan, "Claiborne Pell, Ex-Senator, Dies at 90," *New York Times,* January 2, 2009, http://nyti.ms/13Bic6r.

34. Gladieux and Wolanin, *Congress and the Colleges,* 61–62, 71.

35. Thelin, "Higher Education's Student Financial Aid Enterprise in Historical Perspective," 33.

36. On this controversy, see Gladieux and Wolanin, *Congress and the Colleges.*

37. *Washington Post,* "A Breakthrough for Education," May 21, 1972, B6.

38. The 1978 passage of the Middle Income Student Assistance Act (MISAA) signaled the end of federal higher education policy that emphasized need-based grants to students: it effectively lifted income limitations on the availability of student aid. MISAA both widened eligibility for Pell grants and broadened access to subsidized student loans. Lawrence E. Gladieux and Arthur M. Hauptman, *The College Aid Quandary: Access, Quality, and the Federal Role* (Washington, DC: Brookings Institution, 1995), chap. 1.

39. For a superb treatment of the era, see Thomas Borstelmann, *The 1970s: A New Global History from Civil Rights to Economic Inequality* (Princeton: Princeton University Press, 2012).

40. Ronald Reagan, inaugural address, January 20, 1981, Ronald Reagan Library, http://www.reagan.utexas.edu/resource/speeches/1981/12081a.htm.

41. "College Student Aid," in *CQ Almanac 1980* (Washington, DC: CQ Press, 1981), 2. In addition, college students between eighteen and twenty-two who had a deceased or disabled parent lost the right to claim dependent benefits under Social Security. See Lawrence E. Gladieux, *The Crisis in Higher Education: The Issue of Equity in College Finance* (New York: Academy of Political Science, 1983); Susan Dynarski, "Does Aid Matter? Measuring the Effect of Student Aid on College Attendance and Completion," Harvard University, Kennedy School of Government, Faculty Research Working Paper Series, September 2001, 1–31.

42. *CQ Almanac 1982,* 485.

43. Janet Hook, "Hawkins Succeeded Perkins: A Change in Style, Not Goals, Expected at Education-Labor," *Congressional Quarterly Weekly,* September 29, 1984, 2357.

44. "Education Bills Advanced in Committees," in *CQ Almanac 1990* (Washington, DC: CQ Press, 1991), 367. Fellow Democrats were also unwilling to push Ford's plans in 1992. "Congress Expands College Loan Eligibility," in *CQ Almanac 1991* (Washington, DC: CQ Press, 1992), 440, 442.

45. James C. Hearn and Janet M. Holdsworth, "Federal Student Aid: The Shift from Grants to Loans," in *Public Funding of Higher Education: Changing Contexts and New Rationales,* eds. Edward P. St. John and Michael D. Parsons (Baltimore: Johns Hopkins University Press, 2004); Lawrence E. Gladieux and Laura Perna, *Borrowers Who Drop Out: A Neglected Aspect of the College Student Loan Trend,* National Center for Public Policy and Higher Education, National Center Report 05-2, 2005.

46. Jacob Hacker, "Privatizing Risk without Privatizing the Welfare State: The Hidden Politics of Social Policy Retrenchment in the United States," *American Political Science Review* 98, no. 2 (May 2004): 246.

47. Gladieux and Hauptman, *College Aid Quandary,* 19.

48. "Student Loan Changes," in *CQ Almanac 1985* (Washington, DC: CQ Press, 1986), 268.

49. Jill Zuckman, "Education: Nunn Blasts Loan System in Long-Awaited Critique," *CQ Weekly,* May 18, 1991, 1288; "Education Bills Advanced in Committees," 368.

50. Jill Zuckman, "Cherished Student Loan Program Plagued by a Tattered Image," *CQ Weekly,* March 16, 1991, 674–680, http://library.cqpress.com.proxy .library.cornell.edu/cqweekly/WR102402741.

51. "Education Bills Advanced in Committees," 368.

52. Zuckman, "Education: Nunn Blasts Loan System in Long-Awaited Critique," 1288.

53. "Education Bills Advanced in Committees," 368–370; "Congress Expands College Loan Eligibility," 441; Michael D. Parsons, *Power and Politics: Federal Higher Education Policymaking in the 1990s* (Albany: SUNY Press, 1991), 139.

54. Confidential source, telephone interviews by author, Washington, DC, March 5, 2013; G. V. "Sonny" Montgomery, *Across the Aisle: The Seven Year Journey of the Historic Montgomery GI Bill* (Jackson: University Press of Mississippi, 2010), 47.

55. Montgomery, *Across the Aisle,* 15.

56. Ibid., 39; confidential source, interview, March 5, 2013.

57. Kim Wincup, Committee on Armed Services, House of Representatives, quoted in Montgomery, *Across the Aisle,* 101.

58. Senator Nancy Kassebaum, interview by author, March 19, 2013.

59. Scott Jaschik, "Bankers Descend on Capitol Hill," *Chronicle of Higher Education,* March 10, 1993.

60. Jim Zook, "Stock Hits New Low: Sallie Mae Fights Direct Lending Plan," *Chronicle of Higher Education,* February 24, 1993.

61. Scott Jaschik, "Opponents of Loan Plan Are Said to Use Students as Fronts," *Chronicle of Higher Education,* June 2, 1993.

62. "The Direct Approach to Student Loans," in *CQ Almanac 1992* (Washington, DC: CQ Press, 1993), 410–411.

63. Barbara Sinclair, *Party Wars: Polarization and the Politics of National Policy Making* (Norman: University of Oklahoma, 2005), 122–130; Thomas E. Mann and Norman Ornstein, *It's Even Worse Than It Looks: How the American Constitutional System Collided with the New Politics of Extremism* (New York: Basic, 2012), 39–43.

64. Sinclair, *Party Wars.*

65. Burdett Loomis, "Does K Street Run Through Capitol Hill? Lobbying Congress in the Republican Era," in *Interest Group Politics,* eds. Allan J. Cigler and Burdett A. Loomis (Washington, DC: CQ Press, 2007); Nicholas Confessore, "Welcome to the Machine," *Washington Monthly,* July–August 2003.

66. Democrats achieved some of their priorities: lower interest rates on student loans, modest increases in Pell grants (though rates still lagged well behind even their real value in the 1970s), and various perks such as forgiveness of up to $5,000 in loans for borrowers who taught for five years in underserved areas.

67. "Higher Education Act Reduces Interest Rates, Increases Grants," in *CQ Almanac 1998* (Washington, DC: Congressional Quarterly, 1999), http://library .cqpress.com.proxy.library.cornell.edu/cqalmanac/cqal98-0000019992.

68. Ibid.

69. Ibid.

70. "President Signs Two Other Education-Related Bills; Sallie Mae, Connie Lee," in *CQ Almanac 1997* (Washington, DC: CQ Press, 1998), 20–21; Jim Zook, "Stock Hits New Low: Sallie Mae Fights Direct Lending Plan," *Chronicle of Higher Education,* March 24, 1993.

71. Some who testified at a hearing on this subject in 1995 promoted the adoption of substantial offset fees and exit fees. See US Senate, *Committee on Labor and Human Resources, Hearing on Privatization of Sallie Mae and Connie Lee,* June 20, 1995.

72. Confidential source, interview by author, Washington, DC, November 15, 2007.

73. "Sallie Mae Directors to Profit Handsomely," August 6, 2007, http://inside highered.com/news/2007/08/06/sallie.

74. Dawn Kopecki, "Sallie Mae Complete Privatization 4 Years Early," *Wall Street Journal,* December 10, 2004, http://online.wsj.com/article/SB1104335103 16112008.html.

75. Ibid.

76. Bethany McLean, "Sallie Mae: A Hot Stock, A Tough Lender," CNN Money, December 14, 2005, http://money.cnn.com/2005/12/14/news/fortune500/sallie _fortune_122605/index.htm.

77. "Top 100 Executives by Total Compensation," *Washington Post,* July 10, 2006.

78. Center for Responsive Politics, Lobbying Database, http://www.opensecrets .org/lobby/index.php.

79. Center for Responsive Politics, http://www.opensecrets.org, 2007.

80. Ibid.

81. Stephen Burd, "The Congressman and Sallie Mae," *Chronicle of Higher Education*, January 27, 2006; confidential source, interview by author, Washington, DC, October 26, 2007.

82. Albert B. Crenshaw, "Tax Credits of Dubious Value: Tuition Help for Middle Class Can Backfire, Study Says," *Washington Post*, May 20, 2001, H2.

83. Dick Morris, *Behind the Oval Office: Winning the Presidency in the Nineties* (New York: Random House, 1999), 223–224.

84. Ibid., 224.

85. Ibid., 225.

86. Pew Tax Expenditure Database, "Tax Credits for Tuition for Post-Secondary Education," http://subsidyscope.org/tax_expenditures/db; US Department of Education, "Education Department History Table FY1980–2012," http://www2.ed.gov/about/overview/budget/history/index.html.

87. Bridget Terry Long, "The Impact of Federal Tax Credits for Higher Education Expenses" (NBER Working Paper no. w9553.JEL no. I2, H2, 2003), 1–70; Michael S. McPherson and Morton Owen Schapiro, *The Student Aid Game: Meeting Need and Rewarding Talent in American Higher Education* (Princeton: Princeton University Press, 1998), 87.

88. Morris, *Behind the Oval Office*, 223–225; Jake Haselswerdt and Brandon Bartels, "Public Opinion, Policy Tools, and Policy Feedbacks: Evidence from a Survey Experiment," unpublished paper.

89. Christopher Howard, *The Hidden Welfare State: Tax Expenditures and Social Policy in the United States* (Princeton: Princeton University Press, 1997), 180.

90. Howard, *Hidden Welfare State*; Suzanne Mettler, *The Submerged State: How Invisible Government Policies Undermine American Democracy* (Chicago: University of Chicago Press, 2011).

91. Many states have comparable policies known as 529 plans for the section of the tax code through which they were created in 1996.

92. Susan Dynarski, "Who Benefits from the Education Saving Incentives? Income, Educational Expectations, and the Value of the 529 and Coverdell," Harvard University, Kennedy School of Government & National Bureau of Economic Research, April 5, 2004, 1–30.

93. Homer D. Babbidge and Robert M. Rosenzweig, *The Federal Interest in Higher Education* (New York: McGraw-Hill, 1962), 92–113; Constance Ewing Cook, *Lobbying for Higher Education: How Colleges and Universities Influence Federal Policy* (Nashville: Vanderbilt University Press, 1998), 28–31; Michael D. Parsons, *Power and Politics: Federal Higher Education Policymaking in the 1990s* (Albany: SUNY Press, 1997), 83–84.

94. Dan Morgan, "The Higher Education of Washington: Universities Step Up Lobbying to Protect Funding Interests," *Washington Post*, February 4, 2004, A21.

95. Several confidential sources, interviews by author, Washington, DC, October 26, 2007 and November 15–16, 2007.

96. Confidential source, interview by author, Washington, DC, October 26, 2007.

97. Ben Adler, "Inside Higher Education Policy: Welcome to One Dupont Circle, Where Good Education-Reform Ideas Go to Die," *Washington Monthly*, June 2007, http://www.washingtonmonthly.com/features/2007/0709.adler.html.

CHAPTER THREE

1. Rebecca Leung, "For Profit Colleges: Costly Lesson," CBS News, February 11, 2009, http://www.cbsnews.com/8301-18560_162-772913.html.

2. Maxine Waters, telephone interview by author, August 2, 2013.

3. Halimah Abdullah, "Are For-Profit Colleges Good for Black Students?" March 5, 2012, The Grio.com, http://thegrio.com/2012/03/05/are-for-profit-colleges -good-for-black-students.

4. National Center for Education Statistics, *2010 Digest of Education Statistics*, Tables 197, 198, 201, http://nces.ed.gov/programs/digest/d10/tables/dt10_197.asp; http://nces.ed.gov/programs/digest/d10/tables/dt10_198.asp; http://nces.ed.gov /programs/digest/d10/tables/dt10_201.asp.

5. US Department of Education, Student Financial Assistance, Program Review Report/PRCN 200340922254, University of Phoenix, Phoenix, Arizona, August 18–22, 2003, 5.

6. Suzanne Mettler, *Soldiers to Citizens: The GI Bill and the Making of the Greatest Generation* (New York: Oxford University Press, 2005), 7, 78–79.

7. Ibid., 94–100.

8. US Congress, Committee on Labor and Public Welfare, *Report on Education and Training Under the Servicemen's Readjustment Act, as Amended, from the Administrator of Veterans' Affairs* (Washington, DC: GPO, 1950), 9.

9. Hearings before the Special Subcommittee on Veterans' Education and Rehabilitation Benefits for the Committee on Labor and Public Welfare, United States Senate, 82nd Cong., 2nd sess., on H.R. 7656, June 10–13 and 17, 1952, 22–23.

10. President's Commission on Veterans' Pensions, *Readjustment Benefits: Education and Training*, staff report IX, Part B, September 12, 1956, 84th Cong., 2nd sess., House Committee print no. 291, 36.

11. "GI Schooling Programs," *CQ Almanac* Online Edition, cqal50-1374614. Originally published in *CQ Almanac 1950* (Washington, DC: Congressional Quarterly 1951).

12. Hearings before the Special Subcommittee on Veterans' Education, 22–23.

13. "GI Schooling Probe," in *CQ Almanac 1951* (Washington, DC: CQ Press, 1952), 210.

14. Hugh Heclo, *Modern Social Policies in Britain and Sweden: From Relief to Income Maintenance* (New Haven, CT: Yale University Press, 1974).

15. "GI Bill Extended to Korea Veterans," in *CQ Almanac 1952*, 8th ed. (Washington, DC: Congressional Quarterly, 1953), http://library.cqpress.com.proxy .library.cornell.edu/cqalmanac/cqal52-1378844.

16. Melinda Pash, "'A Veteran Does Not Have to Stay a Veteran Forever': Congress and the Korean GI Bill," in *Veterans' Policies, Veterans' Politics: New Perspectives on Veterans in the Modern United States*, ed. Stephen R. Ortiz (Gainesville: University Press of Florida, 2012), 222–240. Pash noted that some members voted "present," concerned that the rule would hinder historically black institutions in the South, 239, n. 63.

17. Senate Report 128, quoted in *Cleland v. National College of Business*, 435 U.S. 213 (1978). Decided March 20, 1978, http://caselaw.lp.findlaw.com/scripts /getcase.pl?court=us&vol=435&invol=213.

18. Quoted in Lawrence E. Gladieux and Thomas R. Wolanin, *Congress and the Colleges* (Lexington, MA: Lexington, 1976), 70.

19. Gladieux and Wolanin, *Congress and the Colleges*, 72–73.

20. "Major Aid-to-Education Bill Held Over Until 1972," in *CQ Almanac 1971*, 27th ed. (Washington, DC: Congressional Quarterly, 1972), http://library.cq press.com.proxy.library.cornell.edu/cqalmanac/cqal71-1253923.

21. Gladieux and Wolanin, *Congress and the Colleges*, 226. Also see David A. Trivett, *Proprietary Schools and Postsecondary Education*, ERIC Higher Education Research Report no. 2 (Washington, DC: American Association of Higher Education, 1974).

22. "A Breakthrough for Higher Education," *Washington Post*, May 21, 1972, B6.

23. Gladieux and Wolanin, *Congress and the Colleges*, passim; *CQ Almanac Online*, "Major Aid to Education Bill Held Over Until 1972."

24. US Department of Education, "Institutional Eligibility," in *Federal Student Aid Handbook*, April 2011, 2-2, http://www.ifap.ed.gov/fsahandbook/attachments /0910FSAHbkVol2Ch1School.pdf.

25. Kevin Kinser, *From Main Street to Wall Street: The Transformation of For-Profit Higher Education* (Hoboken, NJ: Jossey-Bass, 2006), 116.

26. David W. Breneman, Brian Pusser, and Sarah E. Turner, "The Contemporary Provision of For-Profit Higher Education," in *Earning from Learning: The Rise of For-Profit Universities* (Albany: State University of New York Press, 2006), 16, n. 2; Jason DeParle, "Report Cites Flaws in Regulation of Trade Schools," *New York Times*, September 12, 1990, sec. B, 7, col. 1.

27. Fred M. Hechinger, "About Education: Competing for Students," *New York Times*, March 31, 1987, sec. C, 8, col. 3; Joseph Berger, "Study Faults Trade Schools' Results," *New York Times*, February 28, 1989, sec. B, 2, col. 1.

28. Joseph Berger, "Changes in Welfare a Boon to Trade Schools," *New York Times*, August 6, 1988, sec. 1, 1, col. 2; Berger, "Study Faults Trade Schools' Results"; DeParle, "Report Cites Flaws."

29. Mettler, *Soldiers to Citizens*.

30. "Schools on List of those Losing Loan Eligibility," *New York Times*, July 29, 1982, sec. D, 18, col. 1.

31. "Congress Moves to Stem Student-Loan Losses," in *CQ Almanac 1988* (Washington, DC: CQ Press, 1989), 190.

32. "Action Postponed on Student-Loan Defaults," in *CQ Almanac 1988* (Washington, DC: CQ Press, 1989), 337.

33. "Action Postponed on Student-Loan Defaults," 340.

34. "Congress Moves to Stem Student Loan Losses," 190.

35. Ibid.

36. Ibid.

37. "Institutions with High Default Rates Denied Participation in Loan Program," in *CQ Almanac 1989* (Washington, DC: CQ Press, 1990), 626–627.

38. US Senate, Committee on Governmental Affairs, *Abuses in Federal Student Aid Programs*, 102nd Cong., Senate Report 102-58, 102 S. Rpt. 58, May 17, 1991.

39. Chris Kirkham, "Deregulation of Online Learning, Leading to Explosive Growth at For-Profit Colleges," Huffington Post, July 29, 2011, http://www.huffingtonpost.com/2011/07/29/john-boehner-for-profit-colleges_n_909589.html.

40. Ibid.

41. Ibid. Among Democrats, Sam Nunn had a DW-Nominate score in 1990 of -0.134, and Joseph Lieberman -0.273, both quite conservative scores; three others were more moderate, including John Glenn (OH), James Sasser (TN), Herbert Kohl (WI); only Carl Levin was strongly liberal, with a score of -.45. Republicans were strikingly moderate, by contemporary standards: William Cohen (ME), .04; Ted Stevens (AK), .187; Warren Rudman (NH), .244; William Roth (DE), .261; http://voteview.com.

42. Confidential source, interview by author, Washington, DC, March 7, 2012.

43. Jill Zuckman, "Education: Nunn Blasts Loan System in Long-Awaited Critique," *CQ Weekly*, May 18, 1991, 1288.

44. Jill Zuckman, "Cherished Student Loan Program Plagued by a Tattered Image," *CQ Weekly*, March 16, 1991, 674.

45. "Congress Expands College Loan Eligibility," in *CQ Almanac 1991* (Washington, DC: CQ Press, 1992), 443; Jason DeParle, "Trade Schools Near Success as They Lobby for Survival," *New York Times*, March 25, 1992, http://www.nytimes.com/1992/03/25/news/trade-schools-near-success-as-they-lobby-for-survival.html?pagewanted=all&src=pm.

46. The original rule established in the Korean War era referred to the percentage of enrollment rather than percentage of revenue. Rebecca R. Skinner, *Institutional Eligibility and the Higher Education Act: Legislative History of the 90/10 Rule and Its Current Status*, CRS Report for Congress, Congressional Research Service, Updated January 19, 2005, http://www.policyarchive.org/handle/10207/1904. Roukema offered an amendment prohibiting schools from participating in

the student loan program if they had default rates above 25 percent for three consecutive years, and Gordon followed with one that would disqualify those same schools from Pell grant receipt.

47. "Congress Expands College Loan Eligibility,"443, 450–451, 454.

48. Confidential interview by author, Washington, DC, March 7, 2012.

49. "Congress Moves to Stem Student Loan Losses"; Karen De Witt, "Education Lobby Getting Crowded," *New York Times*, January 6, 1991, sec. 4A, 38, col. 3; Jason de Parle, "Trade Schools Near Success as They Lobby for Survival," *New York Times*, March 25, 1992, sec. A, 1, col. 1.

50. Center for Responsive Politics, "PACs: Apollo Group Summary," http://www .opensecrets.org/pacs/lookup2.php?strID=C00309781; Association of Private Colleges and Universities, 2014 PAC Summary Data, http://www.opensecrets.org /pacs/lookup2.php?strID=C00213066.

51. John Sperling, *Rebel with a Cause: The Entrepreneur Who Created the University of Phoenix and the For-Profit Revolution in Higher Learning* (New York: John Wiley, 2000), 148.

52. Ibid., 183.

53. Ibid., 184.

54. Brian Pusser and David A. Wolcott, "A Crowded Lobby: Nonprofit and For-Profit Universities and the Emerging Politics of Higher Education," in *Earning from Learning: The Rise of For-Profit Universities,* eds. David W. Breneman, Brian Pusser, and Sarah E. Turner (Albany: State University of New York Press, 2006), 178; Stephen Burd, "Selling Out Higher Education Policy?" *Chronicle of Higher Education*, July 30, 2004, 16.

55. US Senate, HELP Committee, "Apollo Group, Inc.," 272, http://www.help .senate.gov/imo/media/for_profit_report/PartII/Apollo.pdf.

56. Michael Winerip, "Overhauling School Grants: Much Debate but Little Gain," *New York Times*, sec. A, 1, col. 1.

57. DeParle, "Trade Schools Near Success as They Lobby for Survival."

58. Quote appears in Melanie Hirsch, "What's in a Name? The Definition of an Institution of Higher Education and Its Effect on For-Profit Postsecondary Schools," *Legislation and Public Policy* 9 (2006): 827.

59. GAO, *Proprietary Schools: Poorer Student Outcomes at Schools That Rely More on Federal Student Aid,* GAO/HEHS-97-103, Proprietary Schools and Student Aid, June 1997, http://www.gao.gov/archive/1997/he97103.pdf.

60. "Higher Education Act Reduces Interest Rates, Increases Grants," in *CQ Almanac 1998*, 9–14.

61. In addition, lawmakers terminated the requirement that accrediting agencies make unannounced visits to the institutions they were evaluating, approved a distance learning demonstration project, and made other changes. Rebecca R. Skinner, "Institutional Eligibility for Participation in Title IV Student Aid Programs Under the Higher Education Act: Background and Reauthorization Issues,"

CRS Report for Congress, Congressional Research Service, March 9, 2007, http://assets.opencrs.com/rpts/RL33909_20070309.pdf.

62. Quote appears in Melanie Hirsch, "What's in a Name? The Definition of an Institution of Higher Education and Its Effect on For-Profit Postsecondary Schools," *Legislation and Public Policy* 9 (2006): 827.

63. Stephen Burd, "For-Profit Colleges Praise a Shift in Attitude at the Education Department," *Chronicle of Higher Education*, November 9, 2001, 24.

64. US Senate, Health, Education, Labor, and Pensions Committee, *Testimony of David Hawkins, Hearing on Marketing and Recruitment in For-Profit Education*, August 4, 2010, Washington, DC, http://www.help.senate.gov/imo/media/doc/Hawkins1.pdf.

65. Skinner, "Institutional Eligibility for Participation," 25. After an appointed panel failed to reach agreement and disbanded, the department issued regulations that effectively undermined existing law. Kelly Field, "Compensation in the Spotlight," *Chronicle of Higher Education*, June 29, 2009, http://chronicle.com/article/article-content/46958.

66. US Department of Education, Memorandum from William D. Hansen to Terri Shaw, "Enforcement Policy for Violations of Incentive Compensation Prohibition by Institutions Participating in Student Aid Programs," in author's possession.

67. *Testimony of David Hawkins*, 5.

68. *Frontline*, "College, Inc.," July 4, 2010, http://www.pbs.org/wgbh/pages/frontline/collegeinc; *60 Minutes*, "For-Profit Colleges Under Fire," September 5, 2010, http://www.cbsnews.com/video/watch/?id=6838088n; *60 Minutes*, "For-Profit College: Costly Lesson," April 12, 2005; Field, "Compensation in the Spotlight."

69. US Department of Education, Student Financial Assistance, San Francisco, CA, *Program Review Report PRCN 200340922254, University of Phoenix, OPEID 020988 00, Site Visit of 8/18/2003–8/22/2003*, quote on 15; 12–13, 15–17, 22–23.

70. US Department of Education, *Program Review Report PRCN 200340922254*, 6.

71. Mike Lillis, "GAO: Bush-era Rules Helped Schools Evade Banned Practices," *The Hill*, October 10, 2010, http://thehill.com/blogs/healthwatch/other/123551-gao-bush-era-rules-helped-for-profit-schools-evade-recruitment-lending-rules.

72. Chris Kirkham, "Deregulation of Online Learning, Leading to Explosive Growth at For-Profit Colleges," Huffington Post, July 29, 2011, http://www.huffingtonpost.com/2011/07/29/john-boehner-for-profit-colleges_n_909589.html.

73. Sam Dillon, "Online Colleges Receive a Boost from Congress," *New York Times*, sec. A, 1, col. 6. Meanwhile, during the previous two years, as part of the reauthorization of the Higher Education Act, the House had approved the softening of various other regulations, but the Senate failed to act on the legislation before the 2006 elections, when Democrats won control of both houses. Libby George, "2006 Legislative Summary: Higher Education Reauthorization," *CQ Weekly*, December 18, 2006, 3343.

74. Kirkham, "Deregulation of Online Learning."

75. Thomas B. Edsall, "Controversial Industries Have Backed Boehner," *Washington Post*, January 29, 2006.

76. Kirkham, "Deregulation of Online Learning."

77. Ibid.

78. Sam Dillon, "Online Colleges Receive a Boost from Congress," *New York Times*, sec. A, 1, col. 6.

79. Center for Responsive Politics, "Top National Donors: Based on Combined State and Federal Contributions, 2007–2008," http://www.opensecrets.org/orgs/list_stfed.php?order=A.

80. It included the PIRG groups, the United States Student Association (USSA), the National Education Association, American Federation of Teachers, American Association of Certified Registrars (AACRAO), and National Association of College Admissions Counseling (NACAC). The coalition took out ads and sought to publicize the issues. Confidential source, interview by author, Washington, DC, March 6–8, 2012.

CHAPTER FOUR

1. These figures, and much of the analysis in the section of this chapter called "Governing the Policyscape in the States," are drawn from statistical analysis of a dataset compiled by the author, using data from the US Census, US Bureau of Labor Statistics, National Center of Education Statistics, National Information Center for Higher Education Policymaking and Analysis, Grapevine reports (http://grapevine.illinoisstate.edu/historical/index.htm), and other sources. The dataset is available at http://government.arts.cornell.edu/faculty/mettler.

2. David Weerts, Thomas Sandford, and Leah Reinert, *College Funding in Context: Understanding the Difference in Higher Education Appropriations Across the States* (New York: Demos, 2012), 17–19, http://www.demos.org/sites/default/files/publications/HigherEducationReportDemos.pdf, 17–19.

3. Claudia Goldin and Lawrence F. Katz, "The Shaping of Higher Education: The Formative Years in the United States, 1890 to 1940,"*Journal of Economic Perspectives* 13, no. 1 (Winter 1999): 37–62; National Center of Education Statistics, *2007 Digest of Education Statistics*, Table 179.

4. Excellent sources on this trend include Donald E. Heller, ed., *The States and Public Higher Education Policy: Affordability, Access, and Accountability,* 2nd ed. (Baltimore: John Hopkins University Press, 2011); Ronald G. Ehrenberg, *What's Happening to the Public Higher Education? The Shifting Financial Burden* (Baltimore: John Hopkins University Press, 2006); Christopher Newfield, *Unmaking the Public University: The Forty-Year Assault on the Middle Class* (Cambridge: Harvard University Press, 2008); Douglas M. Priest and Edward P. St. John, *Privatization and Public Universities* (Bloomington: Indiana University Press, 2006).

5. Eric Kelderman, "Moody's Report Forecasts a Gloomy Future for Public Universities," *Chronicle of Higher Education,* August 14, 2013, http://chronicle .com/blogs/bottomline/moodys-report-forecasts-a-gloomy-future-for-public -universities/?cid=pm&utm_source=pm&utm_medium=en.

6. National Center of Education Statistics, *Digest of Education Statistics,* Table 349: Average Undergraduate Tuition and Fees and Room and Board Rates Charged for Full-Time Students in Degree-Granting Institutions, by Level and Control of Institution: 1964–1965 through 2010–2011, http://nces.ed.gov/programs /digest/d11/tables/dt11_349.asp.

7. Christopher J. Lucas, *American Higher Education: A History,* 2nd ed. (New York: Macmillan Palgrave, 2006), 104–105.

8. Alice Rivlin, *The Role of the Federal Government in Financing Higher Education* (Washington, DC: Brookings Institution, 1961), 9–13.

9. Northwest Ordinance, July 13, 1787, http://www.yale.edu/lawweb/avalon /nworder.htm.

10. Rivlin, *Role of the Federal Government in Financing Higher Education,* 9–13.

11. Lucas, *American Higher Education,* 117.

12. John R. Thelin, *A History of American Higher Education* (Baltimore, MD: Johns Hopkins University Press, 2004), 46–52.

13. Claudia Goldin and Lawrence F. Katz, *The Race Between Education and Technology* (Cambridge: Harvard University Press, 2008), 269.

14. For example, Robert C. Lieberman, *Shifting the Color Line: Race and the American Welfare State* (Cambridge: Harvard University Press, 1998); Suzanne Mettler, *Dividing Citizens: Gender and Federalism in New Deal Public Policy* (Ithaca, NY: Cornell University Press, 1998); Lee J. Alston and Joseph P. Ferrie, "Paternalism in Agricultural Labor Contracts in the U.S. South: Implications for the Growth of the Welfare State," *American Economic Review* 83, no. 4 (1993): 852–876; Ira Katznelson, *Fear Itself: The New Deal and the Origins of Our Time* (New York: Norton, 2013).

15. Rivlin, *Role of the Federal Government in Financing Higher Education,* 10.

16. Quoted in Lucas, *American Higher Education,* 118.

17. E. D. Eddy, *Colleges for Our Land and Time: The Land-Grant Idea in American Education* (New York: Harper, 1957), 27.

18. Richard Hofstadter and C. DeWitt Hardy, *The Development and Scope of Higher Education in the United States* (New York: Columbia University Press, 1952), 38–41.

19. Paul Wallace Gates, *The Wisconsin Pine Lands of Cornell University* (Ithaca, NY: Cornell University Press, 1943).

20. Willis Rudy, *Building America's Schools and Colleges: The Federal Contribution* (Cranbury, NJ: Cornwall, 2003), 23.

21. Several additional federal policies further encouraged the states to develop their own institutions. The Hatch Act of 1887 provided funding for agricultural

experiment stations at the land-grant colleges, and the Smith-Lever Act in 1914 provided federal funds for cooperative extension, through which land-grant colleges established a vast network of county-level agencies to work with farmers. Thelin, *History of American Higher Education*, 135–136.

22. Goldin and Katz, *Race Between Education and Technology*, 269–270, 274.

23. The south central region followed the South and Midwest in establishing both types at similar points.

24. Analysis of data compiled by author, see note 1 above.

25. Christopher Jencks and David Riesman, *The Academic Revolution* (Garden City, NY: Doubleday, 1968), 258.

26. Goldin and Katz, "Shaping of Higher Education," 42.

27. Ibid., 40–41, 49–50.

28. Ibid., 47–48.

29. Ibid., 50.

30. Arthur M. Cohen and Florence B. Brawer, *The American Community College,* 3rd ed. (San Francisco: Jossey-Bass, 1996), 15.

31. Lucas, *American Higher Education*, 230–233.

32. This can be thought of as belonging to the classic form of distributive policies described by Theodore J. Lowi, "American Business, Public Policy, Case Studies, and Political Theory," *World Politics* 16 (1964): 677–715; Theodore J. Lowi, "Four Systems of Policy, Politics, and Choice," *Public Administration Review*, July–August 1972, 298–310.

33. This dynamic process is a classic example of policy innovation of the sort described by Jack Walker, "The Diffusion of Innovations Among the American States," *American Political Science Review* 63, no. 3 (September 1969): 880–899.

34. For example, see Harry N. Scheiber, "Federalism and the American Economic Order, 1789–1910," *Law and Society Review* 10, no. 1 (Fall 1975): 57–118. Arguably, the development of universities and colleges is better understood as part of economic development, a function that Paul Peterson identifies as properly belonging to states because they are better poised to respond to distinct regional needs than national government. Paul Peterson, *Price of Federalism* (Washington, DC: Brookings Institution, 1995).

35. Clark Kerr, *The Great Transformation in Higher Education, 1960–1980* (Albany: State University of New York Press, 1991).

36. Kerr, *Great Transformation in Higher Education, 1960–1980,* xiv–xv.

37. Cohen and Brawer, *American Community College.*

38. Goldin and Katz, *Race Between Education and Technology*, 278.

39. Suzanne Mettler, *Soldiers to Citizens: The G.I. Bill and the Making of the Greatest Generation* (New York: Oxford University Press, 2005), 7, 66–69, 156.

40. During the postwar years, new forms of federal aid to institutions of higher education emerged as well, chiefly for scientific research. By the early 1960s, the amount of federal support received by universities had doubled from twenty

years prior. More than one-third of this aid was administered by the National Institutes of Health, but numerous federal agencies doled out dollars: the Department of Defense, National Science Foundation, the Atomic Energy Commission, the Department of Agriculture, and the National Aeronautics and Space Administration. Thelin, *History of American Higher Education*, 278.

41. Hugh Davis Graham, "Structure and Governance in American Higher Education: Historical and Comparative Analysis in State Policy," *Journal of Policy History* 1, no. 1 (1989): 80–107.

42. National Center for Public Policy and Higher Education, *Losing Ground: A National Status Report on the Affordability of American Higher Education* (San Jose, CA: National Center for Public Policy and Higher Education 2002), http://www.highereducation.org/reports/losing_ground/affordability_report_final_bw.pdf, 8–9, 12, 22–30; Donald E. Heller, "State Support of Higher Education: Past, Present, and Future," in *Privatization and Public Universities*, eds. Douglas M. Priest and Edward P. St. John (Bloomington: Indiana University Press, 2006), 11–37.

43. John Quinterno, *The Great Cost Shift: How Higher Education Cuts Undermine the Middle Class* (New York: Demos, 2012): 8–11, http://www.demos.org/sites/default/files/publications/TheGreatCostShift_Demos.pdf.

44. Analysis of dataset compiled by author; see note 1 above.

45. Quinterno, *Great Cost Shift*, 15.

46. These percentages were calculated using higher education appropriations data from Center for the Study of Education Policy, Grapevine Reports, 1980, 2010 and data on total expenditures by state from State and Local Government Finance Data Query System, http://www.taxpolicycenter.org/slf-dqs/pages.cfm; Urban Institute–Brookings Institution Tax Policy Center; data from US Census Bureau, *Annual Survey of State and Local Government Finances, Government Finances*, vol. 4, http://www.census.gov/govs/local, and Census of Governments (1980, 2010), http://www.census.gov/govs.

47. Roger L. Geiger and Donald E. Heller, "Financial Trends in Higher Education: The United States" (Working Paper no. 6, Center of the Study of Higher Education, College of Education, January 2011), 6–7, http://www.ed.psu.edu/educ/cshe/working-papers/WP%236.

48. Donald E. Heller, "Trends in the Affordability of Public Colleges and Universities," in *The States and Public Higher Education* (Baltimore: Johns Hopkins University Press, 2011), 21–22, updated with sources shown in Figure 4.1. Income quintiles pertain to the mean income family in each group.

49. Ibid., 23.

50. State Higher Education Executive Officers [SHEEO], "State Higher Education Finance FY 2012," 23–25, http://www.sheeo.org/news/state-higher-education-finance-shef-report-fy2012-released. Also see Michael J. Rizzo, "State Preferences

for Higher Education Spending: A Panel Data Analysis, 1977–2001," in *What's Happening to Public Higher Education? The Shifting Financial Burden,* ed. Ronald G. Ehrenberg (Baltimore: Johns Hopkins University Press, 2006), 6, 4–6; William Zumeta, "State Higher Education Financing: Demand Imperatives Meet Structural, Cyclical, and Political Constraints," in *Public Funding of Higher Education: Changing Contexts and New Rationales.,* eds. Edward P. St. John and Michael D. Parsons (Baltimore: Johns Hopkins University Press, 2004), 84–85.

51. Eric Kelderman, "As State Funds Dry Up, Many Community Colleges Rely More on Tuition Than on Taxes to Get By," *Chronicle of Higher Education,* February 6, 2011, http://chronicle.com/article/As-State-Funds-Dry-Up/126240.

52. Ronald G. Ehrenberg, "The Perfect Storm and the Privatization of Public Higher Education," *Change,* January–February 2006, 47–53.

53. Geiger and Heller, "Financial Trends in Higher Education," 8–9.

54. Here I am referring to spending per full-time equivalent student, or FTE. Original analysis in this section of the chapter used dataset compiled by author, described in note 1 above. Available at http://government.arts.cornell.edu/faculty /mettler.

55. SHEEO, "State Higher Education Finance FY 2012," 30.

56. The results of the OLS regression analyses underlying the discussion in this section of the chapter are available at the author's website, http://government.arts .cornell.edu/faculty/mettler.

57. Harold A. Hovey, *State Spending for Higher Education in the Next Decade: The Battle to Sustain Current Support* (San Jose, CA: National Center for Public Policy and Higher Education, State Policy Research, 1999), 19–20; Gary L. Shelley and David B. Wright, "Incremental State Higher Education Expenditures," *Atlantic Economic Journal* 37 (2009): 87–98; Jennifer A. Delaney and William R. Doyle, "State Spending on Higher Education: Testing the Balance Wheel Over Time," *Journal of Education Finance* 36 (2011): 343–368.

58. Michael K. McLendon, James C. Hearn, and Christine G. Mokher, "Partisans, Professionals, and Power: The Role of Political Factors in State Higher Education Funding," *Journal of Higher Education* 80 (2009): 686–713; David A. Tandberg and Erik C. Ness, "State Capital Expenditures for Higher Education: Where the Real Politics Happens," *Journal of Education Finance* 36 (Spring 2011): 394–423.

59. David A. Tandberg, "Politics, Interest Groups, and State Funding of Public Higher Education," *Research in Higher Education* 51 (2010): 416–450; quote on 434.

60. McLendon, Hearn, and Mokher, "Partisans, Professionals, and Power," 701.

61. Goldin and Katz, *Race Between Education and Technology,* 269–270, 274. The indicator I use to analyze this relationship is the date when the first private college or university was founded in the state. Analysis of descriptive statistics suggests that this is a reasonable proxy.

62. These kinds of resource effects are described in Paul Pierson, "When Effect Becomes Cause: Policy Feedback and Political Change," *World Politics* 45 (July 1993): 595–628.

63. Megan Thiele, Kristin Shorette, and Catherine Bolzendahl, "Returns to Education: Exploring the Link Between Legislators' Public School Degrees and State Spending on Higher Education," *Sociological Inquiry* 82 (2012): 305–328.

64. Andrea Louise Campbell, *How Policies Make Citizens: Senior Political Activism and the American Welfare State* (Princeton: Princeton University Press, 2003).

65. Rizzo finds that in states for which courts have declared the K-12 school system unsatisfactory, budgets for primary and secondary education subsequently crowd out spending on higher education. Rizzo, "State Preferences for Higher Education Spending," 17.

66. Zumeta, "State Higher Education Financing," 83–90; Thomas J. Kane, Peter R. Orszag, and David Gunter, "State Fiscal Constraints and Higher Education Spending" (Discussion Paper 12, Urban-Brookings Tax Policy Center, 2003), http://www.taxpolicycenter.org/UploadedPDF/310787_TPC_DP11.pdf; Michael Mumper, "The Paradox of College Prices: Five Stories with No Clear Lesson," in Donald E. Heller, ed., *The States and Public Higher Education Policy*, 48–51.

67. Thomas Kane et al., "Higher Education Appropriations and Public Universities: Role of Medicaid and the Business Cycle," *Brookings-Wharton Papers on Urban Affairs*, 2005, 124. My analysis found comparable results for Medicaid in 1990; David D. Weerts and Justin M. Ronca, "Understanding Differences in State Support for Higher Education," *Journal of Higher Education*, 83(2), 2012, 167.

68. Two economists, Robert Archibald and David Feldman, set up their analysis similarly, and it yielded similar results. Robert B. Archibald and David H. Feldman, "State Higher Education Spending and the Tax Revolt," *Journal of Higher Education* 77 (2006): 618–644; see pages 629 and 634 for discussion of this issue. Other studies, by contrast, treat the size of a state's budget as if it is a pie of a certain size, and thus they show that when other state priorities gain a larger slice, higher education gets a smaller slice. Such findings give us an accurate depiction of the *relative* share of state budgets reserved to public universities and colleges.

69. Analysis of dataset compiled by author, available at http://government .arts.cornell.edu/faculty/mettler/.

70. Archibald and Feldman, "State Higher Education Spending and the Tax Revolt," 641.

71. Ibid., 618–619.

72. Ibid., 640.

73. I conduct this analysis using polarization data from Boris Shor and Nolan McCarty, "The Ideological Mapping of American Legislatures," *American Political Science Review* 105 (2011): 530–551. Adding polarization to the same kind of analysis conducted earlier, I find that while it does not bear a significant relationship

to college funding in 2000, in 2008 it is associated with lower spending, indicating that higher polarization undermines support for increased funding.

74. Luciana Dar, "The Political Dynamics of Higher Education Policy," *Journal of Higher Education* 83 (2012): 769–794.

75. National Center for Education Statistics, Institute of Education Sciences, Table 377, http://nces.ed.gov/programs/digest/d11/tables/dt11_377.asp; Table 379, http://nces.ed.gov/programs/digest/d11/tables/dt11_379.asp.

76. Students per FTE Faculty 2009, Public: National Center for Education Statistics, *2010 Digest of Education Statistics,* Table 257; Students per FTE Faculty 2009, Private: National Center for Education Statistics, *2010 Digest of Education Statistics,* Table 258.

77. Paul Fain, "California Bill to Encourage MOOC Credit at Public Colleges," *Inside Higher Ed,* March 15, 2013, http://www.insidehighered.com/news/2013/03/13/california-bill-encourage-mooc-credit-public-colleges.

78. Di Xu and Shanna Smith Jaggars, "Adaptability to Online Learning: Differences Across Types of Students and Academic Subject Areas" (CCRC Working Paper no. 54, February 2013), http://ccrc.tc.columbia.edu/publications/adaptability-to-online-learning.html.

79. John Bound, Michael Lovenheim, and Sarah Turner, *Increasing Time to Baccalaureate Degree in the United States,* Population Studies Center, University of Michigan, Research Report 10-698, April 2010, http://www.psc.isr.umich.edu/pubs/pdf/rr10-698.pdf .

80. Ehrenberg, "Perfect Storm," 51.

81. F. King Alexander, "Private Institutions and Public Dollars: An Analysis of the Effects of Direct Student Aid on Public and Private Institutions of Higher Education," *Journal of Education Finance,* 1998.

82. College Board, *Trends in Student Aid 2012,* Trends in Higher Education Series (New York: College Board, 2012), Figure 17A, Excel spreadsheet, http://trends.collegeboard.org/student-aid.

83. Lora Cohen-Vogel et al., "The 'Spread' of Merit-Based College Aid: Politics, Policy Consortia, and Interstate Competition," *Educational Policy* 22 (May 2008): 339–362.

84. Susan Dynarski, "Hope for Whom? Financial Aid for the Middle Class and Its Impact on College Attendance," *National Tax Journal* 63, no. 3, pt. 2 (2000): 629–662.

85. Jennifer Steinhauer, "Schwarzenegger Seeks Shift from Prisons to Schools," *New York Times,* January 6, 2010, http://www.nytimes.com/2010/01/07/us/07calif .html.

Chapter Five

1. Nancy Pelosi, address to ASU, February 2007, http://www.youtube.com/watch?v=BmQgIvkOlM0.

2. Barack Obama, *The Audacity of Hope: Thoughts on Reclaiming the American Dream* (New York: Three Rivers), 159.

3. Barack Obama, Remarks of President Barack Obama: Address to Joint Session of Congress, February 24, 2009, http://www.whitehouse.gov/the_press_office/Remarks-of-President-Barack-Obama-Address-to-Joint-Session-of-Congress.

4. Confidential source, interview by author, Washington, DC, April 18, 2010.

5. Paul Pierson, "When Effect Becomes Cause: Policy Feedback and Political Change," *World Politics* 45 (July 1993): 608.

6. John W. Kingdon, *Agendas, Alternatives, and Public Policies,* 2nd ed. (New York: HarperCollins, 1995), 19–20, 87.

7. Suzanne Mettler, *The Submerged State: How Invisible Government Policies Undermine American Democracy* (Chicago: University of Chicago Press, 2011), 10–11.

8. Julie Bosman, "Colleges Relying on Lenders to Counsel Students,"*New York Times,* April 21, 2007; Sam Dillon, "Student Lender Discloses Ties to Colleges That Included Gifts to Officials," *New York Times,* April 21, 2007.

9. Confidential source, interview by author, Washington, DC, April 20, 2010.

10. Megan Barnett, Julian E. Barnes, and Danielle Knight, "Big Money on Campus," *U.S. News & World Report,* October 19, 2003.

11. Cliff Zukin et al., *A New Engagement? Political Participation, Civic Life, and the Changing American Citizen* (New York: Oxford University Press, 2006); Mark Hugo Lopez, Emily Kirby, and Jared Sagoff, "The Youth Vote 2004," Center for Information and Research on Civic Learning and Engagement, July 2005, http://www.civicyouth.org/PopUps/FactSheets/FS_Youth_Voting_72-04.pdf.

12. Karlo Barrios Marcelo et al., "Young Voter Registration and Turnout Trends," Center for Information and Research on Civic Learning and Engagement, February 2008, http://www.civicyouth.org/PopUps/CIRCLE_RtV_Young_Voter_Trends.pdf, 1–2.

13. For example, Stephen Burd, "Lenders Pay a Steep Price to be Noticed," *Chronicle of Higher Education,* July 30, 2004.

14. Barnett, Barnes, and Knight, "Big Money on Campus."

15. Diana Jean Schemo, "House Democrats Propose Cut in Student Loan Rates," *New York Times,* January 13, 2007.

16. Confidential source, interview by author, Washington, DC, May 4, 2010.

17. US General Accounting Office, *Federal Family Education Loan Program: Increased Department of Education Oversight of Lender and School Activities Needed to Help Ensure Compliance,* Report to Congressional Requestors, July 2007; Jonathan D. Glater, "Education Dept. Criticized for Loans Oversight," *New York Times,* August 2, 2007; US Department of Education, Office of Inspector General, *Review of Financial Partners' Monitoring and Oversight of Guaranty Agencies, Lenders, and Servicers,* Final Audit Report, September 2006.

18. Confidential source, interview by author, Washington, DC, May 4, 2010; Paul Basken, "As Student Loan Industry Hunkers Down, It Sees Friends in Education Department Disappearing," *Chronicle of Higher Education,* July 16, 2007.

19. Ian Shapira, "Bush Signs Sweeping Student Loan Bill Into Law, Adding an Asterisk," *Washington Post*, September 28, 2007.

20. Doug Lederman, "Democrats Set Education Budget Compromise," *Inside Higher Ed*, September 6, 2007, http://www.insidehighered.com/news/2007/09/06/budget.

21. Ibid.

22. Confidential source, interview by author, Washington, DC, March 7, 2012; confidential source, telephone interviews by author, April 5, 2013.

23. Confidential source, telephone interviews by author, April 5, 2013.

24. Iraq and Afghanistan War Veterans of America, "IAVA Successfully Shepherds New GI Bill to Victory," http://www.mpttt.org/portals/22/kim/IAVAGIBill Timeline.pdf.

25. Patrick Yoest, "New G.I. Bill Up Against Hill, White House Rebuffs," *CQ Weekly*, September 17, 2007, 2670–2671, http://library.cqpress.com.proxy.library .cornell.edu/cqweekly/weeklyreport110-000002585099; Daniel W. Reilly, "Iraq Vet Driven By Friend's Death," Politico, June 25, 2008.

26. Jim Webb, "Press Release: Webb, Hagel, Lautenberg Reintroduce '21st Century GI Bill' with Senator John Warner As Key Co-Sponsor," February 28, 2008, http://webb.senate.gov/newsroom/pressreleases/2008-02-28-01.cfm; Steven Lee Meyers, "Fear of Troop Exodus Fuels Debate on GI Bill," *New York Times*, May 22, 2008, http://www.nytimes.com/2008/05/22/washington/22soldiers.html ?_r=1&scp=16&sq=G.I.+Bill&st=nyt.

27. Confidential source, interview by author, Washington, DC, March 7, 2012; confidential source, telephone interviews by author, April 5, 2013.

28. Confidential source, telephone interviews by author, April 5, 2013.

29. Confidential source, interview by author, Washington, DC, March 7, 2012.

30. Confidential source, telephone interviews by author, April 5, 2013.

31. Martin Kady, "McConnell Move Causes Senate Meltdown," Politico Live, May 14, 2008, http://www.politico.com/blogs/thecrypt/0508/McConnell_move _causes_Senate_meltdown.html.

32. Confidential source, telephone interviews by author, April 5, 2013.

33. Confidential source, interview by author, Washington, DC, March 7, 2012.

34. David Rogers, "GI Bill Sparks Senate War," Politico, April 30, 2008, http:// www.politico.com/news/stories/0408/9966.html.

35. Confidential source, interview by author, Washington, DC, March 7, 2012.

36. Higher education benefited from several other smaller provisions of the stimulus bill, including research monies channeled through the National Science Foundation and National Institute of Health, $200 million for the work-study program, $53.6 billion for the state fiscal stabilization fund for modernizing college facilities and mitigating cuts to colleges; US Congress, H.R. 1, *An Act Making supplemental appropriations for job preservation and creation, infrastructure investment, energy efficiency and science, assistance to the unemployed, and State and local fiscal stabilization, for the fiscal year ending September 30,*

2009, and for other purposes, 111th Cong., 1st sess., http://www.gpo.gov/fdsys /pkg/CRPT-111hrpt16/html/CRPT-111hrpt16.htm; US Department of Education, "The American Recovery and Reinvestment Act of 2009: Education Jobs and Reform," February 18, 2009, http://www.ed.gov/policy/gen/leg/recovery /factsheet/overview.html; "Details of the Stimulus Plan," *CQ Weekly,* January 19, 2009, 127.

37. Confidential source, interviews by author, Washington, DC, April 18–20, 2010; May 24–25, 2010.

38. Susan Dynarski, "Hope for Whom? Financial Aid for the Middle Class and Its Impact on College Attendance," *National Tax Journal* 53, no. 3, pt. 2 (2000): 629–662; Bridget Terry Long, "The Impact of Federal Tax Credits for Higher Education Expenses" (NBER Working Paper no. w9553, JEL no. I2, H2 [2003]), 1–70.

39. Confidential source, interview by author, Washington, DC, April 20, 2010.

40. US Office of Management and Budget, "President Obama's Fiscal 2010 Budget: Opening the Doors of College and Opportunity," 2009, http://www.white house.gov/omb/fy2010_key_college.

41. Confidential source, interviews by author, Washington, DC, November 15, 2007 and May 3, 2010.

42. For example, Walter Alarkon, "Beneficiaries of Sallie Mae, Nelnet fight Obama's Student-Aid Proposal," The Hill.com, March 9, 2009, http://thehill.com /homenews/news/18654-beneficiaries-of-sallie-mae-nelnet-fight-obamas-student -aid-proposal.

43. Confidential source, interview by author, Washington, DC, May 3, 2010.

44. Doug Lederman, "Big Savings from Loan Proposal," *Inside Higher Ed,* March 23, 2009.

45. Josh Gerstein, "Dems Take Aim at W.H. on Student Loans," Politico, March 25, 2009.

46. Confidential source, interview by author, Washington, DC, April 18, 2010.

47. Barack Obama, "Remarks by the President on Higher Education," White House, Office of the Press Secretary, April 24, 2009, http://www.whitehouse.gov/the _press_office/Remarks-by-the-President-on-Higher-Education.

48. Ibid.

49. Ed Howard, "Nelson Cited as 'Emblematic' of Administration's Problems," *Nebraska State Paper,* April 1, 2009, http://nebraska.statepaper.com/vnews/display .v/ART/2009/04/01/49d355604df9c; "Ben Nelson: Summary Data," OpenSecrets .org, http://www.opensecrets.org/politicians/summary.php?cycle=2010&type=I& cid=N00005329&newMem=N.

50. Gerstein, "Dems Take Aim at W.H. on Student Loans."

51. Confidential source, interview by author, Washington, DC, May 4, 2010.

52. Kelly Field, "Congress Is Poised to Ease Passage of Obama's Plan to End Bank-Based Lending," *Chronicle of Higher Education,* April 27, 2009.

53. Gerstein, "Dems Take Aim at W.H. on Student Loans."

54. Confidential source, interviews by author, Washington, DC, April and May, 2010.

55. Kelly Field, "Lenders and Guarantors Offer Alternatives to President's Loan-Overhaul Plan," *Chronicle of Higher Education*, July 1, 2009.

56. Confidential source, interviews by author, Washington, DC, May 4, 2010 and May 20, 2010.

57. Ibid.

58. David M. Herszenhorn, "Obama Student Loan Plan Wins Support in House," *New York Times,* September 10, 2009.

59. Two Republicans who also voted in favor were Tom Petri (WI) and Todd R. Platts (PA). Stephen Burd, "Sallie Mae's Influence Peddling," *Higher Ed Watch*, August 6, 2009, http://www.newamerica.net/blog/higher-ed-watch/2009/sallie-maes-influence-peddling-13759; Molly Peterson, "Obama's Student-Loan Overhaul Passes House Committee," Bloomberg.com, July 21, 2009, http://www.bloomberg.com/apps/news?pid=20601213&sid=ai0WwIo6jyAg.

60. The only substitute amendment, offered by Republican Brett Guthrie (KY), essentially asked Congress to proceed more slowly, retaining the existing student loan system while conducting a study intended to find "a new model for maintaining a strong public-private partnership for student lending." It was rejected by the same group of twenty-eight Democrats and two Republicans who approved the legislation. US Congress, House Education and Labor Committee Markup, *Roll Call 1 H.R. 3221,* 2009, http://edlabor.house.gov/documents/111/pdf/markup/FC/HR3221TheStudentAidandFiscalResponsibilityAct/rcv1_guthrie.pdf.

61. Confidential source, interviews by author, Washington, DC, April and May 2010.

62. Republican supporters included Buchanan, Cao, Johnson (IL), Petri, Platts, and Ros-Lehtinen. Democratic opponents included Kanjorski, Herset Sandlin, McMahon, and Boyd; US Congress, "Student Aid and Fiscal Responsibility Act of 2009: Roll Call Votes 710–719," *Congressional Record*, September 17, 2009, H9675-9702.

63. Tamar Lewin, "House Passes Bill to Expand College Aid," *New York Times*, September 18, 2009; Kelly Field, "Houses Passes Bill to End Bank-Based Lending," *Chronicle of Higher Education,* September 17, 2009; Doug Lederman, "House Passes Student Aid Bill," *Inside Higher Ed*, September 18, 2009; US Congress, "Student Aid and Fiscal Responsibility Act of 2009," *Congressional Record*, September 16, 2009, H9594-9637.

64. Libby Nelson, "Sallie Mae Fights for Student-Loan Role in a Campaign That's All About Jobs," *Chronicle of Higher Education*, November 22, 2009, http://chronicle.com/article/Sallie-Mae-Fights-for-Stude/49224; Eric Lichtblau, "Lobbying Imperils Overhaul of Student Loans," *New York Times*, February 5, 2010, http://www.nytimes.com/2010/02/05/us/politics/05loans.html?pagewanted=all&_r=0.

65. Walter Alarkon, "Beneficiaries of Sallie Mae, Nelnet fight Obama's Student-Aid Proposal"; David M. Herzenhorn, "Obama Student Loan Plan Wins Support in House," *New York Times,* September 10, 2009; Danielle Knight, "Lobbying Showdown over the Future of Student Loans," Huffington Post Investigative Fund, July 30, 2009, http://www.huffingtonpost.com/2009/07/29/lobbying-show down-over-th_n_247506.html; Maryann Dreas, "Private Lenders Focus on Jobs in Student Loan Fight," The Hill, November 30, 2009, http://thehill.com/business -a-lobbying/69873-private-lenders-focus-on-jobs-in-student-loan-fight.

66. Dreas, "Private Lenders Focus on Jobs in Student Loan Fight."

67. Corey Boles, "Alternate Senate Student Loan Plan Would Retain Role for Banks," *Dow Jones News Wire,* December 2, 2009.

68. Confidential source, telephone interview by author, January 18, 2011.

69. Confidential source, interviews by author, Washington, DC, May 4, 2010; confidential source, telephone interview by author, January 18, 2011.

70. Ibid.

71. Doug Lederman, "What Now for Student Aid Bill?" *Inside Higher Ed,* March 8, 2010; Daniel De Vise, "House Approves Huge Changes to Student Loan Program," *Washington Post,* March 22, 2010.

72. Confidential source, interview by author, May 4, 2010.

73. Jason Delisle, "Senator Conrad's Choice on Student Loan Bill," New America Foundation, 2010, http://higheredwatch.newamerica.net/blogposts/2010/senator _conrads_choice_on_student_loan_bill-26445.

74. Lori Montgomery and Shailagh Murray, "Key Senators Balk at Adding Student Loan Overhaul to Health Care Legislation," *Washington Post,* March 11, 2010.

75. The letter was signed by senators Thomas Carper (DE), Blanche Lincoln (AR), Ben Nelson (NE), Bill Nelson (FL), Mark Warner (VA), and Jim Webb (VA). David M. Herzenhorn, "Obama's Student Loan Overhaul Endangered," *New York Times,* March 10, 2010; Manu Raju and Glenn Thrush, "Conrad, Dems Split in Loan Spat," Politico, March 19, 2010.

76. Vicki Needham, "Conrad asks for Removal of Bank Exemption," The Hill, March 18, 2010, http://thehill.com/homenews/senate/87767-conrad-drops -support-for-north-dakota-provision-to-avoid-healthcare-controversy.

77. Confidential source, interview by author, Washington, DC, May 4, 2010.

78. Paul Basken, "Student-Loan Bill Begins Showdown Week," *Chronicle of Higher Education,* March 15, 2010.

79. Paul Basken, "Historic Victory for Student Aid is Tinged by Lost Possibilities," *Chronicle of Higher Education,* March 25, 2010; confidential source, interview by author, Washington, DC, May 4, 2010.

80. In the end, the bill included $2 billion for awards somewhat consistent with AGI's rationale by providing funds for a program already approved by Congress in the stimulus bill—the Community College and Career Training Grant Program. Meanwhile, the College Access Challenge grants, for which the House had set aside $3 billion in SAFRA, were pared down to $750 million.

81. In addition, $1.5 billion was added to increase income-based repayment benefits for student loan borrowers. This program, which began with the College Cost Reduction and Access Act of 2007, enables those who work in low-paying jobs to have their payments reduced and stretched out over a longer period than the normal ten-year window; also, those employed in public service may have their debt forgiven after ten years of making payments. Amanda Becker, "Graduates Can Find Help Scaling Mountains of Debt," *Washington Post*, July 5, 2009; interviews by author, 2010.

82. Confidential source, interview by author, Washington, DC, May 4, 2010.

83. National Student Clearinghouse Research Center, "National Postsecondary Enrollment Trends: Before, During, and After the Great Recession," Table 1, http://www.studentclearinghouse.info/signature/1/NSC_Signature_Report_1.pdf.

84. College Board, "Pell Grants: Total Expenditures, Maximum and Average Grants, and Number of Recipients over Time," http://trends.collegeboard.org /student-aid/figures-tables/fed-aid-pell-grants-total-expenditures-maximum-and -average-grants-and-number-recipients-over-time#KeyPoints.

85. Veterans Benefits Administration, "Post 9-11 GI Bill Update," http://www .detc.org/85thannualconference/downloads/040511_BBouge_handouts.pdf.

86. Table 3.3, All Returns: Tax Liability, Tax Credits, and Tax Payments by Size of Adjusted Gross Income, Tax Year 2010, http://www.irs.gov/uac/SOI-Tax-Stats —Individual-Statistical-Tables.

87. For example, Megan Eckstein, "Colleges Cite Inequities in New Benefits for Veterans," *Chronicle of Higher Education*, April 17, 2009, A1; Rick Maze, "'GI Bill 2.0' Passes Senate Committee, Gains Support," *Navy Times*, August 16, 2010.

CHAPTER SIX

1. US Senate, Health, Education, Labor and Pensions [HELP] Committee, *For-Profit Higher Education: The Failure to Safeguard the Federal Investment and Ensure Student Success*, Majority Committee Staff Report and Accompanying Minority Committee Staff Views, July 30, 2012, 69–70, http://www.help.senate.gov /imo/media/for_profit_report/PartI.pdf.

2. US Senate, HELP Committee, *Benefiting Whom? For-Profit Education Companies and the Growth of Military Educational Benefits*, December 8, 2010, 9, http://www.harkin.senate.gov/documents/pdf/4eb02b5a4610f.pdf.

3. US Senate, HELP Committee, *Where Are Federal GI Bill Dollars Going?* http://www.harkin.senate.gov/documents/pdf/4ecbffe07af8e.pdf.

4. Hollister K. Petraeus, "For-Profit Colleges, Vulnerable G.I.'s," *New York Times*, September 21, 2011, http://www.nytimes.com/2011/09/22/opinion/for -profit-colleges-vulnerable-gis.html.

5. US Senate, HELP Committee, *For-Profit Higher Education*, 69–70.

6. The data came from the US Departments of Veterans Affairs and of Education. US Senate, HELP Committee, *For-Profit Higher Education*, 55.

7. US Senate, HELP Committee, *Where Are Federal GI Bill Dollars Going?*

8. US Senate, HELP Committee, *For-Profit Higher Education*, 56, 110–111, 120–122.

9. David Zucchino and Carla Rivera, "Anger Grows over GI Bill Profiteers," *Los Angeles Times*, July 16, 2012, http://articles.latimes.com/2012/jul/16/nation /la-na-vets-colleges-20120716.

10. Sandy Baum and Kathleen Payea, *Trends in For-Profit Postsecondary Education: Enrollment, Prices, Student Aid, and Outcomes*, Trends in Higher Education Series (Washington, DC: College Board, Advocacy and Policy Center, 2011), http:// advocacy.collegeboard.org/sites/default/files/11b_3376_Trends_Brief_4Pass _110414.pdf.

11. Author's calculations using data from National Center for Education Statistics, *2010 Digest of Education Statistics*, Tables 197, 198, 201, http://nces.ed.gov /programs/digest/d10/tables/dt10_197.asp; http://nces.ed.gov/programs/digest/d10 /tables/dt10_198.asp; http://nces.ed.gov/programs/digest/d10/tables/dt10_201.asp.

12. US Senate, HELP Committee, *For-Profit Higher Education*, 26.

13. Confidential source, interview by author, Washington, DC, March 6, 2012.

14. Confidential sources, interviews by author, Washington, DC, March 5–8 and July 13–14, 2012.

15. Richard L. Hall and Frank W. Wayman, "Buying Time: Moneyed Interests and the Mobilization of Bias in Congressional Committees," *American Political Science Review* 84, no. 3 (1990): 797–820.

16. Stephen Ansolabehere, John M. de Figueiredo, and James M. Snyder Jr., "Why Is There So Little Money in U.S. Politics?" *Journal of Economic Perspectives* 17, no. 1 (Winter 2003): 105–130.

17. Goldie Blumenstyk, "Economic Downturn Brings Prosperity and Opportunities to For-Profit Colleges," *Chronicle of Higher Education*, December 19, 2008, 13.

18. Author's analysis based on annual reports, company filings (Form 10-K), US Securities and Exchange Commission, Washington, DC, http://www.sec.gov/edgar /searchedgar/companysearch.html. For example, see Apollo Group, Inc., 10-K Annual Report 2011, http://www.sec.gov/Archives/edgar/data/929887/000144 530511003026/apol-aug312011x10xk.htm.

19. Shelly K. Schwartz, "Pay for CEOs of For-Profit Colleges Top of the Class," CNBC.com, December 21, 2010, http://soa.li/ClSTVMj; Sandy Baum, "Drowning in Debt: Financial Outcomes of Students at For-Profit Colleges," Testimony to the Senate Health, Education, Labor and Pension Committee, June 7, 2011, http://www.help.senate.gov/imo/media/doc/Baum.pdf.

20. John Hechinger and John Lauerman, "Executives Collect $2 Billion Running U.S. For Profit Colleges," http://www.bloomberg.com/news/2010-11-10 /executives-collect-2-billion-running-for-profit-colleges-on-taxpayer-dime.html.

21. Jennifer Gonzalez, "For-Profit Colleges, Growing Fast, Say They Are Key to Obama's Degree Goals," *Chronicle*, November 8, 2009, http://chronicle.com/ article/For-Profit-Colleges-Say-They/49068.

22. Confidential sources, interviews by author, Washington, DC, March 6, 2012; July 13, 2012; July 16, 2012.

23. Doug Lederman, "Ferment over For-Profit Colleges," *Inside Higher Ed*, June 16, 2009, http://www.insidehighered.com/news/2009/06/16/cca.

24. "Department of Education Establishes New Student Aid Rules to Protect Borrowers and Taxpayers," October 28, 2010, http://www.ed.gov/news/press-releases /department-education-establishes-new-student-aid-rules-protect-borrowers-and-tax.

25. US Federal Register, Department of Education, "34 CFR Chapter VI, Negotiated Rulemaking Committees, Establishment," 74, no. 99, May 26, 2009, http:// www.gpo.gov/fdsys/pkg/FR-2009-05-26/pdf/E9-12092.pdf; Jennifer Gonzalez, "Panel That Will Re-Examine Federal Rules for For-Profit Institutions Starts Its Work," *Chronicle of Higher Education*, November 2, 2009, http://chronicle.com /article/Re-Examination-of-Federal/49027.

26. Lederman, "Ferment over For-Profit Colleges."

27. US Department of Education, Conference Call with Deputy Undersecretary Robert Shireman of the US Department of Education, May 29, 2009, 12:30 PM ET, http://www2.ed.gov/policy/highered/reg/hearulemaking/2009/call-analysts.pdf; Field, "Compensation in the Spotlight."

28. Lederman, "Ferment over For-Profit Colleges."

29. Libby A. Nelson, "Your Guide to Gainful Employment," June 3, 2011, *Inside Higher Ed*, June 3, 2011, http://www.insidehighered.com/news/2011/06/03/list _looking_at_gainful_employment_changes.

30. Kelly Field, "For-Profits Spend Heavily to Fend Off New Rule," *Chronicle of Higher Education*, September 5, 2010, http://chronicle.com/article/For-Profit -Colleges-Wage/124303.

31. US Government Accountability Office, "For-Profits Colleges: Experiences of Undercover Students Enrolled in Online Classes at Selected Colleges," October 31, 2011, http://gao.gov/products/GAO-12-150.

32. Confidential source, interview by author, Washington, DC, March 6, 2012.

33. Ibid.

34. Confidential source, interview by author, Washington, DC, July 16, 2012.

35. Jennifer Gonzalez, "Officials of For-Profit Colleges See Department's Proposed Rule Changes as 'Aggressive,'" *Chronicle of Higher Education*, December 1, 2009, http://chronicle.com/article/For-Profit-Colleges-See-Dep/49305.

36. Jennifer Gonzalez, "Proposed Rules on Measuring 'Gainful Employment' of Graduates Please For-Profit Colleges," *Chronicle of Higher Education*, April 13, 2010, http://chronicle.com/article/Proposed-Rules-on-Measuring/65048.

37. Mike Lillis, "White House Clarifies: No Effective Change to For-Profit College Rules," The Hill, September 26, 2010, http://thehill.com/blogs/blog-briefing-room/ news/120983-white-house-clarifies-no-effective-change-to-for-profit-college-rules.

38. Kelly Field, "In Final Rules, Education Department Makes Several Concessions to Colleges," *Chronicle of Higher Education*, October 28, 2010, http://chronicle .com/article/In-Final-Rules-Education/125134.

39. The higher standards included at least a 45 percent repayment rate, a debt-to-income ratio lower than 8 percent, and debt-to-discretionary income ratio lower than 10 percent. Libby Nelson, "Your Guide to 'Gainful Employment,'" *Inside Higher Ed*, June 3, 2011, http://www.insidehighered.com/news/2011/06/03/list _looking_at_gainful_employment_changes.

40. Eric Lichtblau, "With Lobbying Blitz, Profit-Making Colleges Diluted New Rules," *New York Times*, December 10, 2011, sec. A, 1.

41. Chris Kirkham, "For-Profit Colleges Mount Unprecedented Battle for Influence in Washington," http://www.huffingtonpost.com/2011/04/25/for-profit -colleges_n_853363.html.

42. Field, "For-Profits Spend Heavily to Fend Off New Rule."

43. "Top For-Profit College Spenders," *New York Times*, December 9, 2011, http://www.nytimes.com/interactive/2011/12/10/us/top-for-profit-college -spenders.html.

44. Center for Responsive Politics, "PACs, Education, PAC Contributions to Federal Candidates, 2006," http://www.opensecrets.org/pacs/industry.php?txt =W04&cycle=2006; Center for Responsive Politics, "PACs, Education, PAC Contributions to Federal Candidates, 2010," http://www.opensecrets.org/pacs /industry.php?txt=W04&cycle=2010. Figures for 2006 and 2010 were compared with author's calculations.

45. Kirkham, "For-Profit Colleges Mount Unprecedented Battle for Influence," 3.

46. Center for Responsive Politics, "Election Stats: 2010," http://www.opensecrets .org/bigpicture/elec_stats.php?cycle-2010.

47. Center for Responsive Politics, "PACS, Association of Private Sector Colleges and Universities Contributions to Federal Candidates, 2010," http://www.open secrets.org/pacs/pacgot.php?cmte=C00213066&cycle=2012.

48. Kirkham, "For-Profit Colleges Mount Unprecedented Battle for Influence," 12.

49. Ibid., 13.

50. Sean D. Ehrlich, *Access Points: An Institutional Theory of Policy Bias and Policy Complexity* (New York: Oxford University Press, 2011), 28–31.

51. Tamar Lewin, "Rifts Show at Hearings on For-Profit Colleges," *New York Times*, September 30, 2010, http://www.nytimes.com/2010/10/01/education/01 education.html?_r=0.

52. US Senate, Letter from Michael B. Enzi and Nine other Senators to Tom Harkin, Chair, Senate Committee on Health, Education, Labor and Pensions, April 13, 2011, http://www.help.senate.gov/imo/media/doc/HELPCommitteeGOP LettertoHarkin.pdf; US Senate, Letter from Michael B. Enzi to Tom Harkin, Chair, Senate Committee on Health, Education, and Pensions, May 31, 2011, http://dailycaller.com/wp-content/uploads/2011/05/enzi-boycott-letter.pdf. Republicans were not the only observers to object to the hearings. Citizens for Responsibility and Ethics in Washington (CREW) also objected to including Steven

Eisman, an investor for FrontPoint Partners, a hedge fund unit of Morgan Stanley, as a witness. As a short-seller, Eisman had made his reputation by predicting the real estate bubble would burst before it did, and he believed that the for-profit sector bore several similarities to it. CREW criticized the HELP Committee and filed a complaint with it, criticizing Eisman's testimony on the grounds that he had no expertise on for-profit colleges and had a conflict of interest as a party that could benefit from new regulations that might cause the value of their stock to decline. CREW also made a Freedom of Information Act request of the Department of Education to release emails, suspecting that Eisman influenced the pursuit of regulations of the for-profits. Mike Elk, "Why Are Progressives Fighting Student-Loan Reform?" *American Prospect,* October 5, 2010, http://prospect.org /article/why-are-progressives-fighting-student-loan-reform-0. Meanwhile, advocates of reform suspected that CREW had been influenced by those with an interest in the for-profits. Confidential sources, interviews by author, Washington, DC, March 7, 2012; March 8, 2012; July 13, 2012.

53. US Senate, HELP Committee, *For-Profit Higher Education.*

54. Mike Lillis, "Senate Dems, For-Profit Educators Joust Over Proposed Restrictions," The Hill, September 11, 2010, http://thehill.com/homenews/senate /118185-senate-dems-for-profit-educators-joust-over-proposed-restrictions; Goldie Blumenstyk, "Senators Want 'GI Bill' Trademarked to Curb Abusive Marketing to Veterans," *Chronicle of Higher Education,* March 2, 2012, http://chronicle .com/article/Senators-Want-GI-Bill/131062; Paul Fain, "Breaking Gridlock for Veterans," *Inside Higher Ed,* November 2, 2012, http://www.insidehighered.com /news/2012/11/02/washington-pushes-protections-veterans; Stephen Burd, "New Senate Bill Seeks to Crack Down on One of For-Profit Colleges' Worst Abuses," New America Foundation, August 7, 2012, http://higheredwatch.newamerica.net /blogposts/2012/new_senate_bill_seeks_to_crack_down_on_one_of_for_profit _colleges_worst_abuses-70262.

55. US Congress, Letter from John Kline and 11 others, House Education and Workforce Committee, to Harold Rodgers, Chairman, Committee on Appropriations, and 3 others, April 4, 2011; http://edworkforce.house.gov/uploadedfiles /4_4_11_kline_ge.pdf.

56. Derek Wallbank, "U.S. House Votes to Ease Restrictions on For-Profit Colleges," Bloomberg.com, February 28, 2012, http://www.bloomberg.com/news/2012-02-28 /u-s-house-votes-to-ease-restrictions-on-for-profit-colleges.html.

57. Andrew Kreighbaum, "Congress Shines Light on For-Profit Education Sector as Industry Makes Lobbying Surge," OpenSecretsblog, June 23, 2010, http:// www.opensecrets.org/news/2010/06/congress-shines-light-on-for-profit.html; Kirkham, "For-Profit Colleges Mount Unprecedented Battle for Influence."

58. "Education: Glakas," *CQ Weekly,* February 21, 2011, 377.

59. Field, "For-Profits Spend Heavily to Fend Off New Rules."

60. Confidential source, interview by author, Washington, DC, March 6, 2012.

61. "Minority Groups Call for Sen. Duncan to Stop Gainful Employment Rule until 'Minority Student Impact Assessment' is Conducted," May 9, 2011, http://education.verticalnews.com/articles/5330231.html.

62. Field, "For-Profits Spend Heavily to Fend Off New Rules."

63. Jennifer Epstein, "In Whose Interest?" *Inside Higher Ed*, July 30, 2010, http://www.insidehighered.com/news/2010/07/30/lobby.

64. Nick Anderson, "Democrats Join GOP in Voting to Block Tighter Regulation of For-Profit Schools," *Washington Post*, February 19, 2011, http://www.washingtonpost.com/wp-dyn/content/article/2011/02/18/AR2011021807474.html.

65. Goldie Blumenstyk and Kelly Field, "In a Fight to Preserve their Market, For-Profit Colleges Lobby Hard Against a Proposed Rule," *Chronicle of Higher Education*, May 19, 2010, http://chronicle.com/article/To-Battle-a-Proposed-Rule/65616.

66. Daniel Golden, "Apollo Suffers New York Snub as SEC Probes Phoenix (Update 3)," Bloomberg.com, January 19, 2010, http://www.bloomberg.com/apps/news?pid=newsarchive&sid=a8KowaDIl9Os.

67. Shawn Zeller, "Tuition Rule's Unusual Foes," *CQ Weekly*, May 23, 2011, 1108.

68. Mancur Olson Jr., *The Logic of Collective Action: Public Goods and the Theory of Groups*, 2nd ed. (Cambridge: Harvard University Press, 1971).

69. Kay Lehman Schlozman, Sidney Verba, and Henry E. Brady, *The Unheavenly Chorus: Unequal Political Voice and the Broken Promise of American Democracy* (Princeton: Princeton University Press, 2012), 440.

70. Kelly Field, "Education Dept. Gets Record Number of Comments on 'Gainful Employment' Rule," *Chronicle of Higher Education*, September 10, 2010, http://chronicle.com/article/Education-Dept-Gets-Record/124390.

71. Stephen Burd, "Higher Ed Watch Investigation into Astro-Turf Lobbying by For-Profit Colleges Cited in USA Today," Higher Ed Watch, New America Foundation, May 25, 2011, http://higheredwatch.newamerica.net/blogposts/2011/higher_ed_watch_investigation_into_astroturf_lobbying_by_for_profit_colleges_cited_in.

72. Blumenstyk and Field, "In a Fight to Preserve"; Field, "For-Profits Spend Heavily."

73. See ads created by the main campaign site established by the industry at http://mycareercounts.org.

74. Mike Lillis, "Business Lobby Blasts New 'Gainful Employment' Proposal for Career Colleges," *The Hill*, August 19, 2010, http://thehill.com/blogs/healthwatch/corporate-news/115065-business-lobby-blasts-new-gainful-employment-proposal-for-career-colleges.

75. Lichtblau, "With Lobbying Blitz, Profit-Making Colleges Diluted New Rules," sec. A, p. 1.

76. Kevin Bogardus, "'For-Profit' School Lobbyists Flock to OMB," *The Hill*, June 9, 2011, http://thehill.com/business-a-lobbying/165515-lobbyists-flock-to-omb-on-for-profit-schools; confidential sources, interviews by author, March 6–8, 2012.

77. US Department of Education, press release, "Obama Administration Announces New Steps to Protect Students from Ineffective Career College Programs," June 2, 2011.

78. Nelson, "Your Guide to 'Gainful Employment.'" Some of the other major differences between the original plan and the final version include: the requirement that schools which fell in between the minimal and acceptable levels—in a so-called yellow zone—would have been required to inform their students if their status was omitted; data collection was delayed until 2012; and the earliest a school could lose its eligibility was 2015, rather than immediately. US Department of Education, "Obama Administration Announces New Steps."

79. Stephen Burd, "The Gainful Employment Rule's Potentially Fatal Flaw," Higher Ed Watch New America Foundation, June 3, 2011, http://higheredwatch .newamerica.net/blogposts/2011/the_gainful_employment_rules_potentially _fatal_flaw-52382.

80. Confidential source, interview by author, March 7, 2012.

81. Kevin Carey, "Sorry, Obama Didn't Sell Out to the For-Profit College Lobby," Ten Miles Square (blog), *Washington Monthly*, June 7, 2011, http://www .washingtonmonthly.com/ten-miles-square/2011/06/sorry_obama_didnt_sell _out_to030089.php.

82. Confidential source, interview by author, March 6, 2012.

83. Kelly Field, "For-Profit Colleges Win Major Concessions in Final 'Gainful Employment' Rule," *Chronicle of Higher Education*, June 2, 2011, http://chronicle .com/article/For-Profit-Colleges-Win-Major/127744.

84. John Lauerman and John Hechinger, "For–Profit Colleges Get More Time to Comply with Aid Rules," Bloomberg.com, June 2, 2011, http://www.bloomberg .com/news/2011-06-02/for-profit-colleges-get-more-time-to-comply-with-aid -rules-2-.html.

85. Chris Kirkham, "For-Profit College Stocks Soar, Indicating New Regulations Won't Hinder Industry Growth," Huff Post Business, June 2, 2011, http://www .huffingtonpost.com/2011/06/02/for-profit-college-stocks-weak-regulations_n _870604.html.

86. Charles Huckabee, "Judge Strikes Down Several Provisions of 'Gainful Employment' Rule," The Ticker, *Chronicle of Higher Education*, July 2, 2012, http:// chronicle.com/blogs/ticker/judge-strikes-down-several-provisions-of-gainful -employment-rule/45125.

87. Goldie Blumenstyk, "Education Dept. Releases Draft Language for New Gainful-Employment Rule," *Chronicle of Higher Education*, August 30, 2012, http:// chronicle.com/article/Education-Dept-Releases-Draft/141347.

88. Stephanie Riegg Cellini and Claudia Goldin, "Does Federal Student Aid Raise Tuition? New Evidence on For-Profit Colleges" (Working Paper no. 17827, National Bureau of Economic Research, February 2012), http://www.nber.org/ papers/w17827.

CHAPTER SEVEN

1. Benjamin Franklin, "Proposals Relating to the Education of Youth in Pensilvania [sic] 1747," National Humanities Center Resource Toolbox, Becoming American: The British Atlantic Colonies, 1690–1763, http://nationalhumanities center.org/pds/becomingamer/ideas/text4/franklinproposals.pdf.

2. US President's Commission on Higher Education, *Higher Education for Democracy* (New York: Harper & Brothers, 1949), 35–36.

3. For example, Claudia Goldin and Lawrence F. Katz, *The Race Between Education and Technology* (Cambridge: Harvard University Press, 2008).

4. Business Higher Education Forum, *The National Higher Education and Workforce Initiative: Forging Strategic Partnerships for Undergraduate Education and Workforce Development* (Washington, DC: Business-Higher Education Forum, 2013), http://www.bhef.com/sites/bhef.drupalgardens.com/files/201308/2013 _report_playbook.PDF.

5. US National Archives, "Thomas Jefferson to the Trustees of the Lottery for East Tennessee College, 6 May 1810," Founders Online, http://founders.archives .gov/documents/Jefferson/03-02-02-0322.

6. Ibid.

7. Anthony P. Carnevale and Stephen J. Rose, *The Undereducated America* (Washington, DC: Georgetown University, Center on Education and the Workforce, June 2011), http://cew.georgetown.edu/undereducated.

8. For example, Larry M. Bartels, *Unequal Democracy: The Political Economy of the New Gilded Age* (New York: Russell Sage, 2008); Martin Gilens, *Affluence and Influence: Economic Inequality and Political Power in America* (New York: Russell Sage, 2012); Jacob S. Hacker and Paul Pierson, *Winner-Take-All Politics: How Washington Made the Rich Richer—and Turned Its Back on the Middle Class* (New York: Simon & Schuster, 2010); Lawrence R. Jacobs and Theda Skocpol, eds., *Inequality and American Democracy: What We Know and What We Need to Learn* (New York: Russell Sage, 2005).

9. Century Foundation Task Force on Preventing Community Colleges from Becoming Separate and Unequal, *Bridging the Higher Education Divide* (New York: Century Foundation Press, 2013), 42–52.

10. F. King Alexander et al., *"Maintenance of Effort": An Evolving Federal-State Policy Approach to College Affordability, Higher Education Policy Brief* (Washington, DC: American Association of State Colleges and Universities, April 2010), http://www.aascu.org/policy/publications/policy-matters/April2010.

11. Richard D. Kahlenberg, "Anthony Marx's Legacy at Amherst," *Chronicle of Higher Education,* October 14, 2012, http://chronicle.com/blogs/innovations /anthony-marx%E2%80%99s-legacy-at-amherst/27585; Stephen Burd, *Undermining Pell: How Colleges Compete for Wealthy Students and Leave the Low-Income Behind* (Washington, DC: New America Foundation, 2013), 9.

12. Burd, *Undermining Pell*; Richard Perez-Pena, "Efforts to Recruit Poor Students Lag at Some Elite Colleges," *New York Times,* July 30, 2013, http://www.nytimes.com/2013/07/31/education/elite-colleges-differ-on-how-they-aid-poor.html?pagewanted=all.

13. Burd, *Undermining Pell,* 29.

14. Stephen Burd, "Moving On Up: How Tuition Tax Breaks Increasingly Favor the Upper-Middle Class," *Education Sector,* April 2012, http://www.educationsector.org/sites/default/files/publications/TaxCredit_CYCT_RELEASED.pdf.

15. College Board, "Distribution of Total Undergraduate Debt by Sector and Type of Degree or Certificate, 2007–2008," Trends in Higher Education, Trends in Student Aid, http://trends.collegeboard.org/student-aid/figures-tables/distribution-total-undergraduate-debt-sector-and-type-degree-or-certificate-2007-08.

16. College Board, "Distribution of Graduate School Debt Levels for Graduate Degree Recipients, 2007–2008," Trends in Higher Education, Trends in Student Aid http://trends.collegeboard.org/student-aid/figures-tables/distribution-graduate-school-debt-levels-2007-08-graduate-degree-recipients-2007-08.

17. Libby A. Nelson, "An Underused Lifeline," *Inside Higher Ed,* October 23, 2012, http://www.insidehighered.com/news/2012/10/23/despite-student-debt-concern-income-based-repayment-lags; Ann Carrns, "Relief from Student Loan Debt for Public Service Workers," *New York Times,* September 10, 2013, http://www.nytimes.com/2013/09/10/your-money/relief-from-student-loan-debt-for-public-service-workers.html?smid=pl-share.

18. Thomas E. Mann and Norman J. Ornstein, *It's Even Worse Than It Looks: How the American Constitutional System Collided with the New Politics of Extremism* (New York: Basic Books, 2012), 164–170.

19. Mann and Ornstein, *It's Even Worse Than It Looks,* 159–160.

20. Steven J. Rosenstone and John Mark Hansen, *Mobilization, Participation, and Democracy in America* (New York: Macmillan, 1993); Mann and Ornstein, *It's Even Worse Than It Looks,* 131–143.

21. Theda Skocpol, *Diminished Democracy: From Membership to Management in American Civic Life* (Norman: University of Oklahoma Press, 1993).

22. US President's Commission on Higher Education, 36.

INDEX